The Invention of the Self

THE HINGE OF CONSCIOUSNESS
IN THE EIGHTEENTH CENTURY

John O. Lyons

Southern Illinois University Press • *Carbondale and Edwardsville*

Feffer & Simons, Inc. • *London and Amsterdam*

Grateful acknowledgment is made to Hacettepe University Press for permission to use
material in chapter 1, "Out of the Void," from the author's article "The Invention of the
Self," *Hacettepe Bulletin of Social Sciences and Humanities,* Vol.5, No. 1 (June 1973).

Library of Congress Cataloging in Publication Data

Lyons, John O.
  The invention of the self.

  Bibliography: p.
  Includes index.
  1. Civilization, Modern—18th century.
2. Literature, Modern—18th century—History
and criticism. 3. Self. I. Title.
CB411.L9   909.7   77–27103
ISBN 0–8093–0815–0

"For Mimi"

Contents

The Invention of the Self

1

Out of the Void

> Now, as everyone knows, it has only been in the last
> two centuries that the majority of people in civilized
> countries have claimed the privilege of being individu-
> als. Formerly they were slave, peasant, laborer, even ar-
> tisan, but not person.
> —Saul Bellow, *Mr. Sammler's Planet*

It is a common assumption that man has always been essentially what he is. Physiologically this is true, for ever since man has dropped from the trees or emerged from the caves the differences in cranial capacity, or race, or height and weight have not made significant differences in his basic social organization or his ability to adapt himself to his environment. His use of the wheel, fire, and language has marked significant steps in his history, but nothing has altered his basic physical need for food, shelter, and clothing. The variety of the solutions to these needs—both through history and at any point in history—is astonishing. This variety may even be thought to set man off from the other species, but the needs remain the same, and his choice of a thatched hut or a prestressed concrete skyscraper is in a sense incidental. The strangeness that we find in cultures other than our own is always fascinating, but beyond the shock or amusement is the rediscovery of the arbitrariness of our customs and gestures, and we nod in agreement that beneath the others' oddity man is universally the same. The audience is expected to laugh when one stage Englishman warns another who is going to France that all the people there speak French.

This sense of the essential sameness of mankind is reenforced by technology and science. Culture, no matter how "primitive," is no barrier to the mastery of modern gadgets—even the most destructive ones. The emphasis in the study of ritual and myth has been for half a century on the curious sameness under the variety of practices and beliefs, even in the case of completely isolated societies. Three centuries ago Milton found confirmation of the Biblical story of Noah in the Greek tale of Deucalion and in the Flood of Nordic sagas.[1] His theory was unitary and based upon the analogy of a single and linear descent, as in a single family. Now we may be more sophisticated, but the implications

1

of Frazer's *The Golden Bough*, Jessie Weston's *From Ritual to Romance*, or Jung's theory of the collective unconscious are just as unitary.[2] If it can be shown that children from disparate cultures draw a square or "mandala" to represent what they see when their eyes are closed, the arbitrariness of such alternatives as stairs, circles, crescents, or triangles is suggested, and the mechanism behind the universality of the swastika and its variants is made physiological.[3] In such a world there is little room for a "Chosen People" or an "Elect," and the shakers of the world must convince themselves and us of their uniqueness in the teeth of modern historiography, psychology, and biology.

This overriding sense of the sameness of mankind has another face. For the thought occurs to all that if man is everywhere essentially the same, that we are one world and all men are brothers, it tends to diminish each of us individually. Confronted with this sense of diminishment we lovingly caress our memories, moods, and prejudices, for we feel that they are our own and give us authenticity and meaning—even if of a slightly unsettling kind. The demands of all those forces that presume to hold our precarious world together, the tax and opinion gatherers, hammer on our sameness—always, they tell us, for our own good. And we respond with sullen despair or resist with dumb fury. The minorities of the world grow more shrill, and the majorities sulk. Every public issue might be reduced to the terms of this battle between the privacy of the self and the duty to the commonwealth.

The terms of this battle seem to have grown more raucous in this generation, so we often have the impression that it is a new struggle. It is not; there is a cultural lag here in this largest of matters as there is in small, like nudity on the stage which has propagated from Off-Broadway to 42nd Street, the Metropolitan, then to Midwest marquees and living rooms. The seige laid upon our sense of self was inherent in the revolutions in the West two centuries ago. Those, particularly the French, did much to create the modern sense of the self, for they proposed to free men from the authority of the church and state, and this unfettering was intended to allow the individual to define himself by making choices. This sense of the self as that which chooses is the implied definition in the work of the liberal revolutionists of the late eighteenth century. It rises with the American, as in *The Federalist Papers*, in which the self appears as a rational and legal entity which chooses its governance in an open market.[4] What is revolutionary about this is not the complex machinery by which the rights of minorities are protected, but the idea that the reason which is to guide us in our choices is the property of individual men and not something eternal and unchanging that exists independently. The self is here compounded of choices made through consultation with our reason, self-interest, and often appetite. In such a world man is freed to discover the uniqueness of his own self, to pursue his own happiness in nature, God, or the marketplace in his own way. But there is a rub, for his reasoned choice is effectual only if it coincides in some helter-skelter way with that of an unseen mass of franchised humanity, and this degrades and dirties at least the vestments of this new self. Let Truth, says Milton, and "Falsehood grapple; who ever knew Truth put to the worse, in a free and open encounter."[5] All well and good, but the race is not always equal, the battle not always free and open, and appetite is usually disguised as reason. These are Hamilton's reservations, and for the cannier Victorians like Carlyle and Mill it was their despair. Surely it was bliss in that Romantic dawn to be alive, for many made the self sing and some made it fly, but to do so they had to tear the increasingly complex fabric of society woven by post-revolutionary Liberalism. There is a gamut in Liberty, Equality, Fraternity. The first frees the self to discover what it is, to find Truth in its own memories, experiences, and reason. The second suggests a reservation, for to be equal with others is to imply that our Truth is conditional—it is only ours, or it is only true, as it conforms to that of others. And Fraternity insists that we merge our unique self with that of others, and deny ourselves uniqueness—perhaps the self itself.

The gloom that hangs over much of the nineteenth century may be traced to the betrayal of the unfettered Romantic and Revolutionary self. The period has its philosophers of uplift, but they were invariably victims of what C. S. Lewis called "the fatal serialism of the modern imagination" which simply sees more as better.[6] It took many forms. For Bishop Wilberforce it was numbers of souls saved, for Robert Owen it was efficiency applied, for Roebuck it was goods manufactured. For others it could be soldiers armed, votes cast, acres tilled, or miles of rail laid. A few, like Emerson who found little solace in the cornucopia as progress, could still dismiss tragedy as a quirk of the eye of the beholder and place their hopes on a beneficent unseen. Now, however, late in the next century we sense a truer vision in those who suffered the nil and vacuum in the self. The names that have gained respect are those of Carlyle, Schopenhauer, Dostoyevsky, Kierkegaard, Melville, Baudelaire, Nietzsche, Henry Adams—to weave a dour trans-Atlantic fraternity of soothsayers. In all of these writers there is a sense that the times have decayed, that the touted Progress of their age is a delusion. Their diagnosis pins the blame on the railroad, the factory system, the extension of suffrage, the sheer press of numbers, the loss of faith, or the increase of zeal, in godless science or scientific religion. The body politic is treated as a corpse, and Henry Adams sweeps away the idea of progress through Darwinian natural selection simply by contrasting Washington with Grant. What was felt to be lost is as much a mishmash as the diagnosis. It is a sense that in earlier ages people felt more deeply, but were also more rational; that they were simpler, and yet bore a dignity that was the foundation of greatness; that their lives had a rhythm defined by their faith and determined by their tillage and harvesting that they understood and to which they were reconciled. These Jeremiahs saw that the mass of men lived their lives seeing no farther than the horizon, and seeing further themselves they wished to be blinded.

What mainly was lost was the feeling that the self had no stage on which to play out its drama. In the beginning of the century—or even earlier, during the last four decades of the eighteenth century—promises had been made that could not be kept. These promises were based on the replacement of the soul with the self. The soul was seen as an unscientific instrument of Church and State to demean men. It might be identified with the mind or heart or pituitary to sway the credulous, but its function was to keep men content with the treadmill of their lives, to force them to accept the caste or castle into which they were born, the prince who protected their worldly goods, and the priest who mediated with God for their salvation. For this soul was not truly theirs, but a gift from out of the bag of eternity placed in their incompetent keeping. What was theirs was the body which weighed upon the soul with its animal flesh. Man in such a view is little more than rotting meat. No wonder he needs assistance from his betters to see the Truth, for it must be beaten into him with the fear of punishment now and hereafter. Even Locke, that father of reason and liberty, recommended that the schoolboy wear leaky shoes so to keep his own mortality in constant memory. With such a view Man may be a child of God, but he is also and most significantly a wayward lad.

So the Romantic's view of the past was a contradictory one. For some it was a dark age haunted by priests and kings; a time when Reason and Tradition were used to hammer men into a hated uniformity. For such writers the victims of the old ways were figures of pathos—the orphaned beggar child, the wounded soldier sacrificed by the great to a war of religion or succession or aggrandizement, the old crone bent by neglect and penury. This is the view of such different writers as Crabbe and Byron, whereas a few decades before their time the same figures were the objects of ridicule and raillery. For other Romantics (or for the same in other moods) the past could be a bucolic tapestry on which noblemen nobly hunted the hart and happy rural types frolicked on the green. This is the view of Goldsmith in "The Deserted Village," and there are elements of this attitude in

Wordsworth and Keats. Burns (who may have known best what he was talking about) is one who famously plays it both ways, as in the contrast between "The Cotter's Saturday Night" and "Wee Willie's Prayer."

But whether the past is seen as a golden age or a slough of despair it is important that it was seen. Before the end of the eighteenth century the past was generally treated as a seamless whole, marvelously uniform and almost indistinguishable from the present. The poet lamented the passing of friends, the heroes of yore, or the snows of yesteryear, but there is little sense of change or the possibility of change. For if Truth is eternal and immutable it is also external to man and there can be no change—much less progress. But when Truth is a product and possession of the slowly maturing self the past is a model or a warning for the imagination. This is the impetus behind the phenomenal growth of an interest in history and the refinement of a sense of time two centuries ago. J. H. Plumb has argued that history in the modern sense begins only a century ago, that all before is "the past" retold to support some political, theological, or whimsical predisposition. He argues that we are cut off from what went before by the press of numbers and technology—that only the last hundred years are relevant to us.[7] The thesis is depressingly persuasive, but an earlier birth of history was overseen by Gibbon, Hume, and nurtured by Michelet, Macaulay, von Ranke, Prescott, and Motley—for in spite of their prejudices their methods were essentially the modern "scientific" ones. For them, and this was the mark of their time, a mind could encompass a portion of the past and arrive at a truth that was not eternal, but was a portion of their selves.

The same flowering and metamorphosis is more clearly seen in biography—that poor sister of history. We know a great deal about the great of ancient times, the Alexanders and Caesars. Their comings and goings were the gossip of the historians. And they themselves (Caesar, Claudius, Marcus Aurelius) were historians. Yet we know little of them compared to our knowledge of a Washington or a Napoleon. We sense that those conquerors and emperors knew a force of ego that was necessary to sustain an empire, and that they knew very well who they were. Yet the very imperiousness of those about whom we do know a great deal sets them off from humanity and in a subtle way makes them less rather than more human. They are the sons of gods, and sometimes like Augustus even became deified before their deaths. It could be argued that before printing it would have been thought an extravagance to record the kind of personal minutia that has bobbed in the flood of books printed in the last two centuries. Perhaps, yet the ancient historians and biographers were not short-winded and we have much of what they wrote. What we have are public speeches (real and imagined), duty and business letters, documents of state, king lists and chronicles. Hence our view of a man, as we have come to conceive of a man, must be pieced together from this gossip and intractable fact. Even Plutarch, the best of the ancient biographers, thought of his *Parallel Lives* as a kind of popular didacticism, and considered his abstract *Moralia* as the true work of his life. His tales are fascinating, but they are obviously written so that he can beat the Romans with his favored Greeks. If printing had made the difference we would know more about Shakespeare than we do. But as it is, in spite of the shelves stuffed with the subject, all we know of him is based on legal, business, and church documents—and an occasional sprinkling of accidentally recorded tavern bonhomie. There is just enough so that the eccentric can amuse themselves to the despair of the scholars that Bacon, Oxford, the queen, or a man named Shakespeare (but not *the* Shakespeare) wrote Shakespeare. I have no knowledge that it has ever been suggested that someone other than Goethe, Wordsworth, or Dickens wrote the works commonly attributed to them. Even the Baconians have carried his authorship no further than the works of Defoe.[8]

The thought occurs that perhaps those ancients, as well as our fourfold great grandfathers, not only neglected to write about themselves as we would have them, but that they thought about themselves (when they bothered to) in quite a different way. As I have suggested in other areas, the turn in this appears to come toward the end of the eighteenth century. An enormous difference exists between Dr. Johnson's *Lives of the Poets* and Boswell's *Life of Samuel Johnson*. It takes little imagination to guess what Johnson's reaction to Boswell's version of his life would have been had he lived to see it. He would have been confused, ashamed, aghast, astonished. Not at the details—although he would surely have emendations and corrections for every page—but at the motive behind such an undertaking.[9] Boswell was Johnson's junior by thirty-one years, and may have been in that very generation that the change took place. For Johnson a man was the leaky vessel of his soul; for Boswell he was an organic complex of the self. Johnson thought that his own meaning and that of the poets whose lives he wrote consisted in the products of the pen. For him style was almost a distraction from the proper anonymity of the writer. Even his own private prayers tend to formalize his anguish of spirit. Not so for Boswell. Now we know from the *Journals* that from the very beginning he was a recorder of the minutiae of fact and feeling—as though the sum of every minute of his life was his true self. The theory is publicly displayed in the *Life of Johnson*. Boswell plays a large role in that work, but he can efface himself by making another his subject.

This reticence about the kind of confessions Boswell indulged himself with (and which were finally hidden with an old croquet set in Ireland) hung on for a century or more in spite of the giants who fondled their egos and feelings in the next decades. They told their stories, but they invariably found some extenuating excuse for doing so. Now athletes, politicians, and callow folk heroes of every stripe sell what they claim are their inmost secrets without pause or blush. But even Rousseau excused his *Confessions* on the grounds that they justified him before his enemies, real or imagined—and they were published posthumously. Casanova didn't think deeply about such matters as modesty, but he still excused his *Memoirs* on the grounds that they would pleasantly help to pass the hours of ladies and gentlemen.[10] Goethe prefaces his *Dichtung und Wahrheit* with a letter from an anonymous admirer asking for some information on the poet's life, and is obviously delighted to furnish seven hundred pages of reminiscence. Wordsworth had the unintentionally comic audacity to turn such private material into an epic—that most anonymous of poetic forms—protesting that he was incompetent to treat one of the more usual epical subjects.[11] No critic has suggested that Wordsworth writes of anyone but himself in *The Prelude*, in spite of the widow's attempt to imply universality with the subtitle, *Or, The Growth of a Poet's Mind*.[12] In a century things had become topsy-turvy. It began with the proper study of man being Man; it ended with the proper study of man being himself.

In one sense this change, this turn, this invention of the self occurred suddenly; in another it was a long time coming, and the discovery is still to come to remote parts of the world and mind. The historian R. R. Palmer has called the 1760s the "Age of Democratic Revolution," and all this phrase implies has something to do with the change.[13] Northrop Frye, in an objection to the term preromantic, makes a case for calling the period the "Age of Sensibility," and suggests it begins about the seventh decade of the eighteenth century.[14] Epochs begin with symbolic rather than real thunderclaps. These can be found if one is willing to look in any decade of the eighteenth century. Yet they might be found most easily in the sixties. In 1760 George III came to the throne of England and the handsome young king brought with him promises of great liberality. The next year Hume completed his *History of Great Britain*, and in 1764 Edward Gibbon was given the inspiration for *The Decline and Fall of the Roman Empire* while brooding in the Forum in Rome. In 1761 Rousseau published *La Nouvelle Héloïse*, and the next year *Le Contrat Social*. In 1762

Macpherson's *Fingal* was published, and Goldsmith finished *The Vicar of Wakefield*. In 1763 Boswell came to London and his famous meeting with Johnson took place in Davies's bookshop. And from 1760 to 1767 Sterne brought out *The Life and Opinions of Tristram Shandy*. Horace Walpole published *The Castle of Otranto* in 1764, and Bishop Percy the *Reliques of Ancient English Poetry* in 1765. In these events there are significant turns of form and mind in history, politics, education, and biography. The man of feeling is encouraged to keep his emotions in condition with the Gothic novel, the novel of sentiment, and the heady passions of the ballad and saga. All of these events contribute to the unheard clarion or claxon announcing the discovery of the invention of the self.

Not that there were not points of discovery in earlier years, but those discoveries were often like Eric the Red's, and the claim is beside the point because of the gaps of darkness that followed in later years. There is Montaigne in his tower meditating on himself, but (as Donald Frame puts it) "unlike the Romantics later, he considered himself typical and sought mankind in himself."[15] There is Hamlet's doubt and introspection which might have frightened his creator, but which might also have been intended to amuse with its sickly pusillanimity.[16] Further, we have Bacon and Locke and Descartes whittling away at the old sources of truth and finally looking blankly at the flux of experience. There are also Dürer and Rembrandt painting themselves in a mirror. Or Milton turning in upon himself when his blind orbs roll in vain the see the Book of Nature, and also Pope manipulating the Augustan machinery of anonymity so that he can publish his own corrected correspondence before his death. Or the English poets from the 1730s onward seeking to heighten their passions in graveyards, or in the contemplation of ancient barbarisms, and the exoticism of the Orient. But these were all rivulets—or sometimes trickles, or even pools—distantly related to the full tide of the Romantic self. It also took later decades to articulate fully in debate and blood the poltiical freedom implicit in the unchained self. It wasn't until the 1780s that Kant propounded the idea that all knowledge begins with the sensations, although others (Descartes, Locke, Berkeley, David Hartley, Hume) had been pushing epistemology in that direction. No, the invention of the self cannot be dated from a cry of excelsior from a bathtub, for it was made up of parts and accretions—like the automobile. But the assembly of those parts (and the destruction of old ways of thinking) becomes most evident in the 1760s.

What strange forms this anatomizing of the self could take. If it is doubted that Truth is not eternal and external the Holy Ghost becomes almost useless to the devout and they must be moved by enthusiasm and zeal to confirm—even earn—their salvation. Because of this the period was one that saw the old prescriptions thrown out, and the creeds and prayers had to come spontaneously from the heart and experience of the worshiper. This democracy of religion, as shown in such different groups as the Hasidim, Moravian Brethren, and Methodists, was offensive to both established church and state. This was also the great age of pornography, for if the senses could be struck from above with such force that one could validate God's immanence, they could also be struck from below with ecstasy. Many have noted the sexual nature of the revival meeting, and others have pointed out that the language of seduction often borrows from that of devotion. Both exercises bred personal narratives—called witnesses if one believed in damnation, or confessions if one did not and harlotry was the subject.

The Methodists abhorred dancing because it blinded the windows of the senses so that they were of no use in perceiving God's presence. Their contemporary pornographers sought to discover a related ecstasy through the exercise of the senses. But when these two approaches to a superior private knowledge were elaborated in confessions, although one is sacred and the other profane, there is a similar attention to detail, an attention that assumes the importance of the experience and feeling of the moment. There is a long history of pious personal narratives, but before the eighteenth century they tended to be formulaic, and specific experience was invariably seen as glozed with a thick coat of allegory and interpreted through the doctrine of God's universal signature on the world. A similar shift occurs in pornography, for before the eighteenth century the performers are seen from the outside, in the third person. They are faceless and interchangeable in all their parts, as with the sexual gymnasts in Boccaccio, Bandello, or Aretino. The interest is here in sexual machinery which was a mere aspect of that rotting flesh, and could be divorced from the eternal soul for purposes of titillation. Such is the attitude of Friar Lawrence and Mercutio on the quivering thigh beside, or the Countess of Pembroke who, according to Aubrey, had a vedette through which she and her guests could view the horses mating in a handy field. But in the eighteenth century, although technique is not neglected, the main concern is with the rapture which gives the confessor a heightened sense of his own existence because his existence is rooted in feeling. When Fanny Hill is reunited with her beloved Charles after three years of delightful bawdry there are no recriminations and few regrets. There is a sense that the essential Fanny, her capacity to love, is untouched by those three years. In fact her self seems to have been defined and amplified by her experience so that she can love her Charles all the more deeply as well as expertly. These are truly memoirs—confession has little to do with it for the concept of the soul has flown. In spite of their many differences, the same can be said of Rousseau and Casanova, for they too have few regrets for the passions in which they have indulged.

There are many ways in which to look at the shifts wrought by the invention of the self, for it left no human activity untouched. It altered the very way in which men looked at themselves, what they thought, and how they thought. It might be impossible to say exactly why this alteration came about, but by looking at the ways this change was expressed we might be able to understand its nature, to see just how history was cleaved, and perhaps thereby to understand ourselves. This is a large order and I don't expect to fill in the entire canvas, but I do hope to look at some central figures and themes. I wish also to glance into some forgotten corners where the case I am putting is put all the more strikingly because a figure is not posturing, for he is unconscious of being watched.

In one of these corners there are the writers of travel literature. The new interest in sensation, passion, and uniqueness of the self led many to an interest in far places as well as faraway times. The splash made by George Psalmanazar, the false Formosan, is evidence of this;[17] another is Chateaubriand's *Lettres Persians* and Goldsmith's imitative "Chinese Letters" from *The Citizen of the World.*[18] The goal of all this was for people to define themselves by seeing how they looked in the eyes of others. Of course the device lends itself to satire of a social sort—on fashions and the hypocrisies of the beau monde—but the main drive in Chateaubriand and Goldsmith is to define how manners make a man what he is. How differently Swift uses the device of contrasting manners in *Gulliver's Travels*. There the concern is moral, if not theological. He wishes to place Man on the proper rung of a scale running from the angelic to the animal. His concern is with pride, in a theological sense, whereas later in the century the concern was with social pride, or what Fielding called affectation. But it is the writers of true travels with which I am concerned.

In this nook of literature the writer's attitude toward himself is most clearly revealed simply because his presumed subject is not himself. Chaucer's Wife of Bath walked to the Holy Land three times, or about twelve thousand miles as the crow flies.[19] But as garrulous as she is we hear nothing of this, and if we were to hear of her journeys we would probably get a confused itinerary. That is what we have in the Palestine Pilgrims' Text Society accounts.[20] Possibly these pilgrims were dulled from putting one foot in front of the other, yet what adventures they must have had—now all lost through their reticence. For them a journey had a specific purpose—business, piety, discovery, battle—and to get to where they were going they passed through a vacuum in which there were no trees, deserts, mountains, rapacious or jolly innkeepers; only an occasionally memorable brigand. We can reconstruct the journeys of Saint Paul, but he doesn't help us much and certainly doesn't reflect on the topography along the way. There is speculation that Plato traveled in the East, perhaps to India, but he doesn't seem to remember it. Herodotus might have known the whole of the Middle East, but as chatty as he is we cannot be sure.

Travel, in spite of the boredom and languor of conveyance, is a manner of intensifying experience. But the ancients, and all travelers before the eighteenth century, apparently did not look upon it this way. For experience, personal experience, was largely beside the point and they saw with eyes that they assumed to be no different from any others. Some travelers, when they bothered to, wrote well and others not so well, but they all saw what they expected to see, for the Truth was "out there" and unrelated to themselves. Marco Polo left a re-markable account of his journeys to China (gracious hosts who offered the traveler their wives, the garden and palace of the great Khans, flying dishes at the dinner table, etc.), but he doesn't tell us what he thought of all this. When there is a passage of reflection it is given such a literary flair that we suspect it comes from his poet-secretary to whom he dictated his account in a Genoese prison. He was essentially a merchant, so when he does describe something he does so as though he were trying to sell it—a hawk is jet black and the swiftest he has seen, a horse is the largest and strongest there is. Marco Polo in all this remains a faceless and anonymous middleman, and we see through him to his experiences, for his feelings and impressions never stand in the way. How different this is from Rousseau's ecstasy at the dizziness deliberately courted by peering over a gorge in the Alps. For Marco Polo, who walked over more mountains than Rousseau could have named, nature was simply there to be traversed, and hardly worth mention. For Rousseau mountains were a challenge and offered occa-sion to stimulate his passions, in which he felt his true self lay. Perhaps he wrote just late enough that he felt he had to reach across the trinkets and gadgets of a fledgling technology to touch some older truth in nature. But in doing so he presents it in a very different way from older writers whom we must believe knew it very well.

Howard Mumford Jones proposes that the early explorers of the New World saw what they expected to see and what their patrons expected them to see.[21] They had to justify the bravery and expense of their ventures, so the storms are fierce and the crews mutinous (we have no reason to believe that this was not the case), but the Indians are all naked and well-formed and the climate salubrious in accord-

ance with ideas of the innocent Golden Age. Raleigh's rivers of
Guinea even run with gold, in satisfaction of simple avarice. All this
reportage is curiously impersonal and clouded with rhetorical formulae. It is in its way less informative about the feelings of the viewer
than the "Wow!" "Golly!" and recorded pieties of modern astronauts.
The shift, once more, comes in the eighteenth century. A trip to France did not appeal to Dr. Johnson, for, as he put it, the grass there
was the same as it was in England.[22] Not so Boswell, whose *Journals*
record the changing flora and fauna along the way during his extensive tours. When they both went to the Hebrides Johnson records the
itinerary and comments on the manners and customs of the people,
whereas Boswell is attracted to the picturesque and tells us when and
how he is moved. They saw the same things with different eyes;
Johnson's were eyes that he assumed were no different from his
readers', but Boswell's were his own. It was in the late eighteenth
century when people began to take a walk to take a walk—not especially to get somewhere; the Reverend William Gilpin through Wales,
Goethe among the castles on the Rhine, the young Wordsworth and
Coleridge in the Scottish Highlands. Seeing became a confirmation of
the self rather than a process by which the outer world of nature was
understood.

The explorers of the period often show a steely and unimpassioned
eye for the fact observed. They mapped, measured, and recorded the
temperature, but they could also record how they were moved or
amazed by a sunset or view around a bend in the river. No matter
how "scientific" they tended to be, and even though they were often
driven by the practical considerations of trade, they come through to
us clearly as individuals. In confronting foreign places and peoples
they were forced to question what they themselves were. The first
reaction was to find assurance of their technique and culture. After all,
they were the discoverers of strange places, not the strange places of
them. So they wrote to the stay-at-homes as though they were their
readers' surrogates, but the process included their own reflections and
emotions, which made them visible in a way that Marco Polo, for
example, never is. There are moments in these accounts that grow
from the intensity of the feeling of the viewer; Mungo Park's first encounter with the Niger, Meriweather Lewis's amazement in the valley
of the Yellowstone, Henry Layard brooding upon eternity in the
trench before the portal statues of men-beasts at Nineveh. All three
were hard-boiled sons of the new objective science in an age of
technology, but they had also been touched by the idea of the rele-
vance of the self.

Alexander Laing was one of the first of these travelers to put off the identifying garments of the European in order to travel among the uncivilized.²³ He wore the dress of a Berber to cross the Sahara. He did so for reason of safety, but the objectors to his choice insisted that he was deserting his responsibility as an Englishman to display the flag. He was a man of talent, fortitude, and will, and probably felt to be more truly himself hidden in a dishdasha than if he were to carry on his person the more anonymous identity of an Englishman. He was ill, he was newly married, and during his trip to Timbuctoo he was robbed, mutilated, and left for dead by thieves. He did not survive, but his disguise and the falling away of what was his (his money, his camel, his ear and fingers) must have thrown him back onto what was essentially himself as in few other cases.

The sense that the physical self is part of the essential being is behind much of the humanitarian agitation of the eighteenth century. Physical suffering leads to pathos if the flesh of man (and by extension animals) is no longer considered as merely a temporary husk of the soul. The victims of the Inquisition could praise their torturers and cheer them on in their work, for they had been convinced that the devil had perversely chosen their flesh for a residence and that he could be routed only by fire and twisting. But this had little to do with them—as though they watched the process from afar. The same idea lies behind the sadistic slapstick of Renaissance drama in which the fools, villains, and spoilsports are treated to punishment and indignity that is painful to later audiences. Shakespeare was probably running after an easy laugh in his treatment of Malvolio and wouldn't have understood later critics who wondered if he was subtly criticizing the frivolity of the society that humiliated him. The change in these attitudes comes again in the 1760s. Dr. Johnson contended that a hanging did not prevent him from eating a full meal afterward, but the report comes from Boswell, and he implies that he and the other auditors—men of the new sensibility—are shocked by such an assertion.²⁴ They were the ones whose opinions led to the suppression of the slave trade, and it was those countries like England and Holland, where the line of thought running from the Reformation to empirical science to the new sensibility was most evident, that took the lead in the suppression. Of course convenience and profit had much to do with the continuation of the trade by Spain, Portugal, and the Ottoman Empire, but those were also places largely untouched by the new sensibility. Such different people as Hogarth and William Cowper find common ground in opposition to those "evils" that cloud the senses. Slavery and the mistreatment of animals dulls the moral sensibilities of the master, but gambling, drunkenness, and noise also dull his senses. In the view of the new sensibility the body was the altar of the self.[25]

The sufferer in the dungeons of the Inquisition might have been able to sense that he could stand aloof from himself and watch his own suffering, but that feeling of separateness was not intended to allow him to understand himself. All the understanding he needed he had, and that was what permitted him his sense of otherness. In a later age this standing apart is a device of desperation through which the individual attempts to understand himself. When Defoe calls *Robinson Crusoe* his spiritual biography, he suggests that through the examination of another's human condition (for the ghost of Alexander Selkirk on whose experience Defoe depended walks through the events of the work) he tries better to understand his own. It is hard to take Defoe seriously in matters of the spirit, for he wrote in an age of comic ventriloquists—Swift falsettoing Gulliver and his Cousin Sympson, Pope wearing the straight pedantic mask to write the learned notes to his own poems, or Addison and Steele creating the eidola of the *Spectator* and *Tatler* papers. Here the trick demanded that the author maintain a distance between himself and his comic creation. The elaborate machinery of anonymity during the Augustan period was often intended to hide the true author completely, and canny readers understood this. When later ages thought that Swift was Gulliver, for example, they were seduced by intervening literary attitudes. Swift would undoubtedly have been astonished at such an identification, if he did not believe that the folly of men was infinite, for he would never have said that he was Gulliver—as Flaubert claimed that he was Madame Bovary. But just such identification became increasingly fashionable as the eighteenth century progressed.

What is deceptive in all this is that the techniques of handling the distance between the author and his creation often appear to be the same as those used by writers in earlier centuries, and in many ways—especially the rhetorical ones—they are. But the purpose of the distance is quite different. For the neoclassical mind the distance allowed the writer and his reader to examine a type objectively; to present an abstract and eternal Truth in a form that appetizingly looked like literature. Later writers preferred to pretend that what they created was life, and only accidentally looked like fiction. Fielding contends that everything he writes in *Tom Jones* is drawn from life, and (like his revered Cervantes) makes sport of those who confuse life and art. Such a commitment to reality is a step on the way to Goethe saying that everything he wrote was autobiographical, so that Werther is Goethe without a gun and Wilhelm Meister is Goethe without the genius. It is astonishing how rapidly writers and their readers came to assume such identifications as the norm, so Sterne becomes Tristram Shandy, Byron, Childe Harold (who was originally Childe Byron), and an inversion of initials makes Charles Dickens David Copperfield. The difference is at times razor thin, and the names are changed only to maintain the domain of fiction and to protect the creator's innermost privacy of self.

Yet there is still this standing aside. It is as though the author's contemplation of his self is a fearful process; his gaze paradoxically becomes deflected, and there is a tacit assumption that he and we best understand him when his self is reflected in mirrors, sensed in shadows, haunted by the doppelgänger, or glimpsed through the slits of a mask. The traditional use of disguise is to deceive so that the disguised can escape danger or pretend he is something he is not in order to obtain an inheritance or bed a lady. Masks can also be used at times of revelry in which the wearer traditionally acknowledges his spiritual link to the lower beasts. Edgar in *King Lear* knows very well who he is and what his purposes are when he wears the disguise of a lunatic and beggar; Horner in *A Country Wife* knows very well what he is about when he pretends to be impotent. In neither case does the wearer of the disguise gain illumination of himself through the disguise. Such characters are pawns in a plot and what we know them to be they are, and they know who they are. When they turn out to be different from what we assumed (as in the case of Bridget Allworthy who is not only an ugly prude but the mother of the illegitimate Tom Jones, or Humphrey Clinker who is not only the ill-clothed postilion but the foundling son of Matthew Bramble), it is simply a matter of our being deceived in the first place. The later Romantic hero wears disguise not to escape trouble or to deceive, but to understand himself by playing a role just to see if it fits. The first clear instance of this occurs in *Wilhelm Meister's Apprenticeship*. When Wilhelm is sent about the country on his father business he enjoys wearing the apparel of a fop. We are invited to be amused at him because he *is* a fop and his lace ruffs and slashed sleeves are prtentious. Later when he falls in with a troop of wandering players he wears an outlandish antiquated costume which he tells himself is appropriate for a pedestrian. Goethe calls this a "self-deception" and the result a "mask." In such a case he does not know who he is and is only trying on the role of actor and godson of Shakespeare. The spritely women of the company "all asserted that this garb became him very well," and we guess were much amused. They might not know truly who he is, but they know he is not what his mask suggests. And Wilhelm does not intend to deceive, but in this way to discover something about himself. There is a similar motive behind Byron dressing up as an Albanian corsair to have his portrait painted.

The self is defined by the philosopher H. J. Paton as "simply that which knows and wills and feels." This is a very modest claim for something which is in large part the cornerstone of modern social and psychological thought. Paton makes the matter even more scary by saying that knowing and willing and feeling cannot be observed. "In all cases of attempted introspection I seem to find myself observing not a mental activity but the object to which it is directed or by which it is accompanied." Three pages later Paton concludes that "we have no direct or relatively immediate acquaintance with a special object or fact called the self which is capable of being observed in isolation from other objects as sound or color can be said to be observed in isolation from other objects."[26] The implication of this is that those Romantic breast-beatings on the mountaintops and fallings on the thorns of life were attempts to understand and reveal something that might not have been there. But the Romantics revered the self as an alternative to the dead soul, and so they had to have a pious faith in it—in the same way that they had a pious faith in the imagination which they set against the mind-forged manacles of reason. Yet it may have been less than a bubble, and no more demonstrable than the theologian's soul or the philosopher's stone. Such a view casts a suspicious light on Feuerbach's concept of alienation, for if there is really no self it cannot be alienated. This does not mean that the misery that Feuerbach is concerned with is no less miserable, but rather that he and Marx after him took an odd turn to get to where they were going. This view also suggests that the psychoanalytic version of man may often end in fictions because it begins with a fiction.

Whether the self exists or not or in what manner it exists may be beside the point, because for two centuries men have acted as though it did exist and each has fondled it in his own way. This is a modern phenomenon, and like other things modern, it has run a rapid course. Under the sails of philosophy, religion, politics, and the arts the self was invented shortly after the middle of the eighteenth century. It first was treated as the whole organic complex of the perceiving being in sympathetic relation to the world around it. Such a concept of the self was expressed in the concern with the passions, the minute perception of human motive, and the reality of nature, for it assumed the efficacy of inductive science. Such a concept of the self is found in biography, libertarian economics and politics, the literature of travel, and pornography. The second concept was of the self as the ineffable something in a human being that was an abstract of the pure and intuited natural laws without. This concept of the self is expressed in the revivalistic zeal of the period, the Romantic egomanias, visionary millenarianism, Transcendental metaphysics, and pantheism. In the first concept the mind is directed outward to the world where it finds the self reflected. In the second the mind is directed inward where the world of things is mystically erased in the self. Paradoxically the first is the child of French rationalism and is microscopic in its operation; the second of German pietism and is macroscopic.

2

Dancing on the Head
of a Pin

The whole dear notion of one's own Self—marvelous old
free-willed, free-enterprising, autonomous, independent, isolated island of the Self—is a myth.
                    —Lewis Thomas, *The Lives of a Cell*

Although I will be forced to use the term *self* in this essay it will often
be with an archness that may not be apparent in cold type. It is one of
those words—like *nature* and *reality* (Vladimir Nabokov has suggested
that the second should never be used without quotation marks)—
which have a slipperiness about them that allow a writer to disguise
his failure of reflection. Of the three terms *self* may be the most popular among cultural and literary pundits. Along with terms like *alienation, phenomenological, existential,* and *authentic* (as in, "modern man
has failed to make his existence authentic"), *self* has recruited an army
of admirers among book reviewers and commencement day speakers.
Among them the self has a difficult time (much as did God within
recent memory), for they rebuke it for being invisible and to it attribute our collective schmerz because it is divided or fragmented or in
hiding, and the advice is often to the effect that we must beat the
bushes of our beings to bring it out into the open like a snipe. I wish
to offer a medicinal argument, although the dose might be considered
harsh by many. My message is, put baldly, that the self, which modern doomsayers accuse of being invisible, was a fiction in the first
place. This may not ease the pain and feeling of loss, for a hypochon-
driac suffers just as grieviously as the truly sick, but it may help us
understand the illness.

The self is not only that upon which we presently brood, but this
brooding tends to make it proliferate and breed more confusion. The
term is a member of a group of terms which would be nice to keep
distinct, but which in practice inevitably become muddled. This family includes *individual, person, ego,* the "I," *mind, will, soul, being,* and a

18

litter of hyphenated combinations. In one issue of the *New York Reivew of Books* I find Benjamin DeMott referring to "personhood" and a book by Robert M. Adams described as dealing with "self-ideal."[1] No doubt such terms are used partly so that writers can avoid awkward tautology, but they also tend to confuse an already confusing subject. It is a subject on which heavy hands have been laid by cultural historians, anthropologists, philosophers, and psychologists, and each has his own notion of the truth which is slightly and sometimes radically different from that of his neighbor. What is rarely acknowledged is that the central term—the self—is of recent vintage in its meaning of "the realization or embodiment of an abstraction"—as it is put in *Webster's Collegiate*. In this sense the term is an attempt to secularize the traditional dichotomy—both Platonic and Christian—between body and soul. In this tradition the body was the husk and prison of the divine soul, and although they were mutually dependent they were also in conflict, for the crass body weighted the eternal soul with cares and appetites, with flesh amd blood from which character was formed, and the soul's reward depended on how well it survived its earthly trial. That trial was essential to the salvation of the soul—and the embodiment and suffering of the Son was never very far behind such thought—so the beastly in man had a divine function, but such a scheme hardly encouraged one to identify himself with his body. When John Donne describes himself as a "little world made cunningly" he is suggesting praise to the maker and not the product, and because he goes on to emphasize the microcosmic aspects of the body the emphasis is not on its uniqueness but its typicality. The soul was no more help in lending man a sense of his separate and private being, for being eternal and, as it were, lent by God it was the instrument of his connection to all things. It was often even a particle of a universal soul which, temporarily imprisoned in the body, longed for its true home.

In the seventeenth century, with its growing conviction in some places that mathematical models were surer than pretty metaphorical fictions, there was an attempt to place man in a logical or numerical scheme rather than a divine one. Yet it was heretical to deny man his soul, so for some time the term was used although it seemed to have little relation to the traditional dichotomy between the soul and the body. Even though the way toward liberation from the Pauline tradition had been shown by Descartes, Locke, and Berkeley, Hume in 1739 is loath to supplant the word *soul* with another that might be more comfortable for him. So when he states his central principle in the *Treatise of Human Nature* he says that impressions and ideas reach the "soul" through perceptions. It is the soul, not the mind, or the being, or the self. This is the case even though he is insistent that the soul is immaterial, and goes to some length to argue that an object may exist and yet be nowhere. Hume is, unlike Descartes and Locke, a synthesizer, and modestly admits that this is the case. Yet in the mid-eighteenth century he brought together ideas that were ripe for restatement. Even though he felt many were left muddled, his presentation of them turned out to be seminal.

Logic, experimental science, and experience seemed at the close of the seventeenth century to be driving philosophers into the arms of materialism, but prudence and habit made them drag their feet. Their tendency was to see what in the material world could be considered eternal or spiritual, and often appeared less than happy about their conclusions. Descartes sighs that the only evidence that he existed was that he thought, and this seemed a slender recommendation to eternity. In discussing personal identity Locke invites us to cut off our little finger to show that the amputation does not diminish our essential being and to demonstrate that we are not contiguous with our bodies, although it is not suggested that we give an arm or a head to the cause of philosophic proof. Locke's elaboration on this argument was that which most influenced the eighteenth century and was what Hume had in mind in his discussion of the self. Throughout the *Essay Concerning Human Understanding* Locke maintains a safe dualism, and when he discusses the soul it is as though he were raising bits of the material world to its level. Yet the soul is equated with immateriality and consciousness. In book 2, chapter 27, he follows Descartes by saying that consciousness verifies the existence of the self. He then goes on to define what he means by this self: "*Self* is that conscious thinking thing,—whatever substance made up of (whether spiritual or material, simple or compounded, it matters not)—which is sensible or conscious of pleasure and pain, capable of happiness or misery, and so is concerned for itself, as far as that consciousness extends."[2] If the self is material (since we have our choice) Locke makes it sound like a nervous system, as though man were a grand amoeba. But Locke's editor, A. C. Fraser, emphasizes the other side of the quibble and asks rhetorically, "What is this but a definition of a spiritual substance?" It is a good question, for Locke at least allows the possibility of eternity. Locke is also concerned with the self as it relates to a man's civic functions, and so distinguishes between the conscious self and personal identity. The self, when its consciousness is blurred by drink, sleep, or madness, is still responsible for its acts in its personal identity, and so all of these items once more are lumped together. "Personal identity," says Locke, "can by us be placed in nothing but consciousness (which is that alone which makes what we call the *self*)."[3]

There is a similar straddling in Hume's discussion of the self, but his tendency is the reverse of Locke's, for he tries to see what materiality there is in the spiritual rather than what spirituality there is in the material. The *Treatise of Human Nature* begins modestly enough. Not only does he propose to bring together the salient thoughts of his predecessors, and not only does he refer to man's soul instead of using some freethinkers' crasser term, but he always refers to human reason (as though there were also a divine one), and states as a principle that it is impossible to explain "ultimate principles."[4] Such genteel views did not avoid the denial of academic posts to Hume, nor the thunder of such godly critics as Bishop Warburton. When Hume comes to the important section "Of Personal Identity" the term *self* is used in a manner that is different and perhaps original in the language. But once more Hume contends that he is only following and modifying a tradition of philosophic speculation. "There are some philosophers who imagine we are every moment intimately conscious of what we call our SELF, that we feel its existence, and are certain, beyond the evidence of a demonstration, both of its perfect identity and simplicity."[5] What Locke is certain about is that the working of consciousness verifies the existence of the self, and because the consciousness can entertain thoughts about distant times and places (he speaks of our imagining the experience of Noah) he suggests the self arches beyond its mere corporeal materiality. Hume emphasizes the process of thought rather than the thing thought about. He uses the same terms, but in this change of emphasis he is able to divest the self of its pretensions to spirituality. This allows Hume to destroy a concept that he wishes to destroy as though it were another's, when in fact it is largely a dog of his own creation which he is calling a bad name. He goes on: "The strongest sensation, the most violent passion, say they, instead of distracting us from this view, only fix it the more intensely, and make us consider their influence on *self* either by their pain or pleasure."[6] These violent sensations must be felt by something, contend Hume's ghostly antagonists, and that something must be the self, and if the existence of the self cannot be objectively demonstrated it must be accepted as an article of faith. But Hume is in no mood to accept anything on faith, which leads him to his demonstration that the self is no more than (and probably less than) ephemeral perceptions. "For my part, when I enter most intimately into what I call *myself*, I always stumble on some particular perception or other, of heat or cold, light or shade, love or hatred, pain or pleasure. I never can catch *myself* at any time without a perception, and never can observe anything but the perception."[7] Even though the thought that we may be no more than passing perceptions might be less upsetting to our own age than to the eighteenth century, this is a thought which has dogged philosophers ever since, so much so that they have often persuaded themselves that the problem has always existed. The reason for this is that the concept of the self is a Romantic blossom of the earlier theological concept of the soul. The soul, as everyone knew, was many things, but in most sects and theologies it was eternal, immutable, and perfect—it was the flame in the breast lit by God and fueled by faith, or by the Platonist it could be glimpsed through the eye of the beloved, the soul's window. Now Hume seemed to snuff it out with the term *self*, or reduce it to passing human fancies. For Hume mankind is nothing more than "a bundle or collection of different perceptions, which succeed each other with an inconceivable rapidity and are in a perpetual flux and movement."[8] Hume could live with such a conclusion, but others could not. Both the pious traditionalists and the visionary Romantics saw man as distinguished by something else, whether it was God, Reason, Imagination, or the Will. Man as a mere bundle of perceptions would never do, and it did not.

Hume is aware of the unattractiveness of his argument for he plugs all the holes from which he thinks it might leak. He says that when we flatter ourselves that our existence is real we do so by feigning the "continued existence of the perceptions of our senses . . . and run into the notion of a *soul* and *self* and *substance* to disguize the variation."[9] The idea of the soul he can toss out as a cheerful freethinker. Substance had already been disposed of on empirical grounds by Berkeley, but the self is Hume's own trash. It is also, in a way, his invention, and it was the invention rather than the disposal which has impressed everyone who has thought about this matter since, even though they too have often cast off the self. The problem has been whether a person, usually in the form of his mind, can verify his own existence. In one of the fullest considerations of Hume's position on personal identity Terence Penelhum agrees with him that the self is a fiction, but also decides that Hume is misleading when he allows the mind to sit as judge, jury, and defendant in its own case.[10] The problem is perhaps must succinctly posed by Lichtenberg who goes back to Descartes and says that he should have said "It thinks," not "I think"—which moots the whole question of personal identity.[11]

In this century the question of the self has professionally occupied philosophers, psychologists, and anthropologists—while the rest of us have found the term useful and have blithely assumed that it referred to something that our hearer understood. We, I think, are right in our assumptions, but so are the philosophers who almost to a man dismiss the self. It is in the twilight world of journalism and literary criticism that the word and concept wobbles. The philosophers invariably employ and refine the concepts used by Hume. Bertrand Russell even echoes his terms when he settles on a bundle theory of the self, content to dismiss the Platonic criteria so that the self can exist in the ineluctable modality (as Joyce humorously puts it) of perception.[12] Hume's ultimate moral concerns are also echoed by H. J. Paton, who argues that the self wills and feels and so is an activity (on which a moral judgment must be made), but that it in no sense exists.[13] In the past two decades the philosophers have raised a chorus in their own quarters proclaiming that the self does not only not exist, but that it is probably an invidious concept. The case is put in strong terms by Bernard Mayo who says that the problem of the self "is not a genuine problem . . . it is a mistaken notion based on bad grammar."[14] He goes on to approach the question historically and says that the self and the personality are nonprimitive concepts, because "For primitive man, all relations between himself and other objects are personal."[15] For him the world is steeped in animism and magic, so that his relationships with the world are never material or organic, which would create the sense of separateness from which personality derives. In postprimitive society the personality is a concept having to do with our relationship with the world about us, but we flatter (or torture) ourselves when we think that it derives from an independent self. The self, Mayo says, is only useful as a suffix, and "irrelevant to the question of personality."[16]

It would appear to be a simple thing for philosophers to dismiss the self with the heartiness of a Hume if they set their collective minds to it. But they cannot. Hume could set up the self as a hypothesis and then knock it down as a way of attacking the vestry philosophy of such as Bishop Warburton. Hume is marvelously ironic about the certainty that the self is the same as the soul and that both are a commonsensical substance. But Hume could also speak of the passions arising from "good or evil, pain or pleasure." The second pair is consistent with the eighteenth-century attempt to mechanize aesthetics into a science akin to engineering, in which certain colors (for example) were said to elicit specific emotions. But the reference to good and evil, as these existed in a state or tradition or understanding external to man's mind, implies an innocence of which modern philosophers would not be found guilty. For as much as Hume was attacked in his day and in the next century as an atheistical freethinker, he still had a sense of an overarching reason that exists in nature or in tradition and is essentially moral. This is the sense that allows him to write: "Though the rules of justice be *artificial* they are not *arbitrary*. Nor is the expression improper to call them *laws of nature*, if by natural we understand what is common to any species, or even if we confine it to mean what is inseparable from the species."[17] Most men feel and act as though this is correct, but a modern philosopher might be drummed out of the association were he to write in this vein.

And so philosophers who address themselves to the question of the self generally tiptoe around the moral nihilism that invariably lies in the route of their speculations. It might be said that there are three contemporary views of the self among philosophers. One is the identity theory which (as with Hume) sees the self existing in the sensations, and may go on to specify these as mental or neural processes. Another is a behavioral theory which emphasizes the response of the mind and body to its environment rather than the sensations which it receives, but the approach attempts to be purely descriptive and avoids a belief in a "ghost in the machine." A third view is concerned with identity and sees the self as synonymous with the person, or rather sees the self as a fiction which is manifested only in names and pronouns. This approach is often linguistic, and in it self becomes a convenient reflexive. Such approaches have not been without critics who accuse their adherents of moral irresponsibility. For if, as G. Dawes Hicks states it, "instead of experience being the product of the 'self,' the 'self' is rather the product of experience," we exist in a moral vacuum.[18] The question is whether activity implies an agent. Alburey Castell says that beginning with Hume and Kant it did not, but in his work on *The Self in Philosophy*, for ethical reasons the morally responsive agent, the self, is established.[19] This view of the self as a working moral hypothesis or as an act of faith which associates it once again with the soul—from which the eighteenth century tended to divorce it—is stated more fully by Henry Johnstone, who writes, "The existence of the self is a sort of hypothesis used to explain the behavior of persons, but it is almost never used as a hypothesis that we assert that a person exists."[20] He goes on to say that we do not use the self to explain what a person does, taking away with the right hand what was apparently given with the left.

This concept of a working hypothesis or model of the self has become useful for those interested in the ethical and social questions about man's behavior. But as is so often the case, the schema becomes the thing itself. So Freud says that the ego emerges as the result of one's identification with other persons, and "the self arises from tensions in the person."[21] This is a basic tenet of psychoanalytic practice, but for Freud it was no more than a hypothesis—which could be revised as his practice suggested revision. But he also drew charts showing the relation between the ego and id and super ego, almost phrenological in detail, and felt that those who attacked his scheme were heretics, and castigated them as though a law had been violated.

The brethren were then led into arguments, scholastic in their fine distinctions, about terms which they had spun themselves. For example, Jung says that the self includes the ego, which receives impressions and is "the subject of all personal acts of consciousness."[22] And yet he will also say that the ego is consciousness as a whole, as though it could be both the subject of consciousness and consciousness itself. In this vein he writes: "Personality as a total phenomenon does not coincide with the ego, that is with the conscious personality, but forms an entity that has to be distinguished from the ego. . . . the total personality, which though present, cannot be fully known [is] the *self*. The ego is, by definition, subordinate to the self and is related to it like a part to the whole. The self acts upon the ego like an *objective occurrence* which free will can do very little to alter."[23] The self, then, would appear to be the same as the personality, and this includes the ego which is the conscious personality. The self partakes of both consciousness and unconsciousness, the more important part being unconscious. Through both forms of knowing, the self is related to that stream in time and space which Jung refers to as race consciousness and which culminates in the individual. So in one sense the self exists physically without us and psychologically within us. As June Singer states it, "The human psyche is the microcosm which reflects in ways both known and unknown to us, the macrocosm Jung has termed the Self. [The Self] is that center of being which the ego circumambulates; at the same time it is the superordinate factor in a system in which the ego is subordinate."[24] Another way to put it is that the self, for Jung, is a person's symbolization of himself, and this includes much more than the neatly catalogued passions, ideas, and sensations of which Hume writes. Jung, perhaps archly, laments that this is the case. "No doubt it is a great nuisance that mankind is not uniform, but compounded of individuals whose psychic structure spreads them over a span of at least ten thousand years."[25] Yet even this view has implications for Jung that are mainly practical and therapeutic, and the ultimate questions of the existence of a self are left hanging.

The anguish, which we are told is peculiarly modern and based on a feeling of hollowness within, is not well filled by our sages. The psychologists show us how we can make the choices most acceptable to society and our feeling of well-being. The philosophers, at best, can only distract us from the hollowness; they tell us that our sense of an unchanging something within us is a delusion. As Sartre puts it, "each instance of our conscious life reveals to us a creation *ex-nihilo*. Not a new *arrangement*, but a new existence."[26] This leaves us with an abyss under our feet that is very discomforting. When we turn to the social scientists for comfort there is little to be found. For them the personality is a mask hiding something they refuse to acknowledge exists. A typical attitude is expressed by J. Milton Yinger: "The learned repertoire of roles is the personality. There is nothing else. There is no 'core' personality underneath the behavior and the feelings; there is no 'central' monolithic self which lies beneath the various external manifestations . . . The 'self' is a composite of many selves, each of them consisting of a set of self-perceptions, which are specific to one or another major role, specific to the expectations of one or another significant reference group."[27] That "There is nothing else" has both an authoritative and ominous ring about it. Yinger sees no other way, as though he would snort at those who would modestly propose a self as a working hypothesis.

And so I return to the problem of the self—or rather the problem of why the self has been such a problem for the past two centuries. Hume could raise it, but by taking the inevitable steps to be taken in the history of eighteenth-century empiricism, he was led to question the relationship between the consciousness and the soul. Soul was not mind (which could be confused), nor was it the perceptions (which were subject to fits of illusion). And so the soul glided into Cartesian awareness or consciousness, but this made it sound so individual that Hume erected the notion of a self. Yet only for a moment, because consciousness—in which the self was rooted—could not be aware of consciousness. That was a contradiction. And so the self for Hume was stillborn, but others did not notice its demise and it was resuscitated to become the gloomy feeling self that brooded in graveyards, the rational and educated citizen that was assumed by revolutionary constitutions, and it became the Promethean ego of high Romantic fervor. But the graveyards came to harbor Gothic nightmares rather than humanizing dreams; the rational revolutions led to the equality of the guillotine and martial tyranny; the Promethean ego came to be clipped and hobbled by the politics of muddling through and the iron laws of determinism. Since in this broad history something appears to have disappeared it was generally felt that that something must have been something, although disillusionment may be only the process of destroying an illusion. This could have been what Hegel was getting at when he said that the consciousness which was conscious of harboring itself was an unhappy consciousness.[28] The belief in the self then might be considered a form of hypochrondria. If we believe that the self exists, it does so on the basis of our belief in it, just as the illness from which the hypochrondriac suffers is just as grievous as any other illness to the extent that it causes suffering.

It may be impossible to say exactly why this change came about, why the very nature of men's consciousness and the concept of how things were known was altered toward the middle of the eighteenth century. All we can examine are the effects of this change, but as the effects are found in every field the patterns of the shift can emerge. Seeing the patterns from our distance we can know more fully the participants in this change—know them more completely than they knew themselves. First, however, I will briefly examine the manner in which men saw themselves before this shift took place, so that the contrast and revelation can be focused upon. For this purpose I will begin at the beginning and trace the stirrings that have resulted in what we are.

3

Once Upon a Time

The past to which we appeal must be in a sense our
own, precedents set by men conditioned much as we
are, the experience of races or individuals morally akin
to us; its value is proportionate to the degree of continuity by which we are linked to it.
—Sir Leonard Woolley, *Digging Up the Past*

The eye is drawn to that which moves, but the eye itself—though
turning within its socket—looks outward from a relative state of rest.
Except by artificial means (calm pools, mirrors, photographs), we cannot even see our own faces, any more than we can stick our elbow in
our ear. This may be one reason why man's contemplation of himself
comes late in his prehistory, and in what we know of that history
through the analogy of primitive peoples and the life of the infant. The
earliest art depicts animals of the hunt, mainly bison and boars. We
know that what is named is seen, and such cave paintings as we have
in the trans-Pyrenees involve a form of naming. To draw the bison
was evidently a way of capturing it magically with the eye and of
taking on some of its strength, as the artist hoped to sustain himself
with the meat of the beast. This outward and magical power of the
primitive artist's eye is suggested in part by what he did not depict.
His earliest domesticated animals, dogs, and cows, are rarely shown,
and when they are it is in later paintings. Last of all, the primitive
artist depicts himself. His paintings of animals, though usually in
simple profile, often employ size to suggest perspective, and the attention given to form and detail can result in an astonishing realism. But
his depiction of himself is schematic, so the hunt appears to involve
very substantial and fearsomely haunched beasts matched against
fragile stick figures that might be ancestors of the wire and string figures of Paul Klee. The artist might have wished to emphasize the
hunter's vulnerability, or he might not have noticed him as he focused
on the beast.[1]

Sometimes there will appear among the herd a wolf, but if we look
again we see that the wolf carries a spear and has the hind legs of a

man. This form of hunting, also practiced by American plains Indians, suggests the source of totemism and another way in which the primitive mind saw itself as linked to the beast. He himself was an incidental part of a larger undepicted nature. Birds are rarely shown, so although we know they were there they might have been beneath notice. So in a way it might have been with man himself. He could be a fragile twiglike figure, or the sly half-animal covered with the pelt of a wolf. In either case he was probably seen dimly. The Laplanders have the same word for people as for reindeer, and when the researcher expressed his view that this was odd, the Lap's reaction was astonishment that it could be any other way. After all, people could not exist without reindeer; they are linked in life and word.[2] This elemental link between man and nature, this view of man as undistinguished in a larger scene, has been in the very long run the dominant one, and we see traces of it everywhere and in our time. Booker T. Washington, in writing of the backwardness of the freed slave, recounts a story about asking an old Negro how many were sold with him into Alabama. The answer was, "There were five of us; myself and brother and three mules."[3]

The earliest depiction of humans disassociated from the animals with which they contended for survival shows them in schematic forms very unlike the reality lent the animals. Many of these earliest human forms are figurines or dolls that are wide-hipped fertility figures with the clearly incised delta of the pubis. Often the proportions are grossly exaggerated to stress fecundity; sometimes it appears that the shape of the figure is dictated by the material. But in either case the head is usually a mere knob and the arms and feet are missing. In many later cultures such figures will have multiple breasts. It has been appealing to think of the people who made such things as serene in their elemental closeness to nature, but it is probably more honest to think of them as frighteningly aware of their fragility before those huge horned and humped beasts. If we correctly read the testament of these wide-hipped puppets they worried more about sterility than the patriarchs of the Pentateuch. When we impose questions about happiness and even fulfillment on these people, silent beyond their artifacts, we probably raise a question they wouldn't understand.

Another curious representation of man in primitive art are the hands traced on the walls of the same caves where there are the impressive hunting scenes. These tracings are often of small hands, presumably those of children, and often the hand is mutilated in a manner that suggests ritual mutilation. The hand is the part of the body which the person himself most often sees, and since one hand may trace the form of the other this may be the simplest explanation for these hands.

But there could be other forces at work. Those who drew their hands may not have been those who drew the animals. They lived in the same society, and with the hands a different relationship between the depicter and the thing depicted is established, for the tracing creates an intimacy between the object and the symbol of the object that doesn't exist in the pictures of the bison—no matter how convincing they are—and the figurines, which are more statements about fecundity than about women. To put it another way, the tracing of the hand is more of a signature than a picture, and we cannot be sure that some may not be artists' signatures for the painting above, even though (or because of) the possibility that the cave paintings were communal creations. In any case, these small hands—often missing a finger— maintain their fascination and enigma. Hands appear in many magical contexts; the tattooed hand across the face of the American Indian chief, the papal hand which blesses and is kissed, the severed hand of Hussein which appears in brass in the beggars' bowls of Islam. But this dismembered primitive hand could be the dismembered symbol of its possessor, the extension of his symbol-making mind.[4]

Primitive man not only thought of himself (and to phrase it this way is probably to attribute a kind of meditation where there was none, but there is no other way) as an indissoluable part of nature in the natural world, but his own body was evidently considered in segments. Bruno Snell comments on an analogous aspect of primitive Greek art. Early Homeric Greek had no single term comparable to *body*, but there were several terms that referred to the body's parts and characteristics. Early Greek art

corroborates our impression that the physical body of man was comprehended not as a unit but as an aggregate. Not until the classical art of the fifth century do we find attempts to depict the body as an organic unit whose parts are mutually correlated. . . . the Greeks of this early period seem to have seen [man] in a strangely "articulated" way. In their eyes the individual limbs are clearly distinguished from each other, and the joints are, for the sake of emphasis, presented as extraordinarily thin, while the fleshy parts are made to bulge just as unrealistically. The early Greek drawing seeks to demonstrate the agility of the human figure.[5]

Snell also contends that the ancient Greek mind saw the soul as well as the body as fragmented, that *thymos, noos* and *psyche* refer to parts of what was to become the soul. "What we interpret as the soul," Snell writes, "Homeric man splits up into three components each of which he defines by the analogy of physical organs."[6] Such fragmentation of both the body and the soul can be discovered in several early cultures, and is often revealed by the assigning of separate functions to various deities. The Olympian family, and its counterparts in other cultures, was seen as analogous with a human family, but as the person and the family were often helpless before chance and the elements, the gods were most often seen in a state of wrath or destructive lust. The ancients saw the life of a person as hedged by what appeared to be iron laws, but laws which were inscrutable. The earliest gods were gods of the elements and could be as capricious as the winds. Worship, which usually took the form of sacrifice, was a timid bribe. But one bribes anonymously, and there was a prayer that the angry gods might not see or recognize the small and weak. Even the priests approached the gods masked and used pseudonyms. The most influential among the ancients hid themselves.

All of this would appear at first glance to be inconsistent with the confidence of a pharaoh who might identify himself with the sun, or of a Hamurabi who gave the laws on a stela in his own name ("I Hamurabi decree . . ."), or with the Homeric bluster and brag that precedes a battle. And yet in such instances the king and the hero disappear into magic. The king does not become more human by tracing his lineage to the maker of the floods, and his power over his subjects is an inhuman one. He becomes his people's protector and scourge by standing halfway between the human and the godlike divine, so that when things go badly for a people (as they famously did in Thebes under Oedipus) the king must be punished for having failed in his mediation or for losing the magic touch. The bombast of an Ajax involves something else: it is the use of words to make what he wishes to be come true—comparable in its way to the sports fan's noisy claim of his team's supremacy. Much of this does not involve the person's sense of his individuality and uniqueness, but it is rather an assertion of his acquisitive and easily ruffled ego. This sense of our rights and our physical power, a sense that takes us into combat and courts of law and is much of the reason for the haggling in the marketplace, has almost nothing to do with the soul and less to do with what we think of as the self. The ancient about whom we know the most is Alexander. What we know is incredibly mixed with myth and legend, and even the historical facts are the product of speculation and conjecture.[7] Surely Alexander knew very well who and where he was, but he evidently felt that who he was depended on this ego, his name and fame, for he certainly did not give posterity much help in knowing what we might think of as the real Alexander. When he wept at thirty-two in Babylon that there was no more of the world to conquer, it was the ego and not the soul that wept. This scene, true or not, is consistent with the whole lesson of the Greek experience, an experience which has been presented since the Renaissance as humanizing and individualistic. The lesson is that Alexander's hubris was greater than the world is wide, and so he must be brought back to a sense of earthly communitas through a boy's tears. The correlative of this lesson is that the severest punishment for evil is ostracization, for the ancient mind fears separateness more than anything else. Even Hades is peopled with Shades.

It is Heraclitus who, once more according to Bruno Snell, was first to use the concept of the soul in a recognizably modern fashion.[8] For him the soul is the *logos*, which is characterized by depth (which makes it something other than an adjunct of the body), and it is also shared with others. Both attributes suggest a dignity for man that is something other than the merely brutal ego. Yet that dignity depends not on a man's individuality and uniqueness, but rather on his shared immateriality—his manness or *virtus*, in the Roman sense. Even such a sophistication as this does not break down the patterned thought which made men see themselves as types and place themselves in a time almost unrelated to other times. For one of the aspects of our sense of the self is that we see ourselves as unique within a moment of time which is also unique, and we feel that these two singularities create and feed each other. This sense of history and the past was very slow to develop. Ancient men knew that there were events that had happened and that there were events that would happen, but they had little sense that they were connected or that history had a development dependent on discernible forces. There was little reason why they should, for within the memory of those living there had been no change in the way men lived their lives. They were confined in space to the limit of the horizon, and all they saw imitated itself. Time, at the most sophisticated level, depended on genealogy, for one of the things that identified a man was his place in a genealogy, so that a man was not himself as much as he was his father's son.

History, in its earliest written form, is a king list, and this mere chronology was the form that history took for millennia. The earliest is Egyptian, and dates from 2500B.C.; and like many from the Fertile Crescent it is state ancestral memory, often more concerned with establishing legitimacy than with the facts. In such a world eternity and the present are seen as different, but not all that different. "Looking back to the Creation from 1500 B.C., the men of Egypt and Mesopotamia saw its phases 'end-on'—telescoped together into a single timeless process, within which no clear perspective could be discerned."[9] To see ourselves existing in time and not just at the moment is a form of self-definition, and without this sense of history such definition is faulty. Everyone lapses into the fellahin's timelessness at moments, as when he accepts the conventional anachronisms of popular art, but most people in the West do not live their lives this way—like the Greek peasant who points to the cove where Odysseus recently moored ("You can read it in Homer," he insists).

Because our modern sense of history has been so slow to develop, different theorists about history place the change at different periods. Our historical sense involves going beyond mere king lists and glorifying accounts of battles and captured enemy. It involves seeing the forces—economic, racial, technical, and even mythological—that explain events. In other words, it requires a theory of history. Chester Starr writes that a sense of the past begins not with Homer but with Hesiod, and E. R. Dodds identifies the theory on which Hesiod bases his account as that which sees man as fallen from a lost paradise because of his commitment to the city and trade.[10] This is a very rudimentary theory, but it was all that was available in the sixth century B.C. It is comparable to but comes after the theory of history assumed by the Old Testament, which is that Jehovah punishes his Chosen People when they periodically stray from his ways. The figure most often cited as the discoverer of a sense of history is Herodotus, the father of history. Michael Grant identifies the ruling principle as an elegiac one, showing how Herodotus returns again and again to the fall of princes—Croesus, Darius, Xerxes, Alexander.[11] Aubrey De Sélincourt emphasizes a cheerier aspect of Herodotus, for throughout Herodotus' work he contrasts the freedom of the Greek city-state to the slavery of Asiatic empires, and suggests that the merit of freedom is that it produces better fighters.[12] Herodotus probably recited much of his history on the streets of Athens, and surely he knew what his patrons wished to hear, but this doesn't deny his account the ring of conviction. Another aspect of his work is that he presents conflicting accounts of the same event, and although he usually indicates his preference as to the truer account, he invites his reader to decide for himself. This may sometimes be specious, as when one of the tales is absurdly miraculous, but the pretense is scientific. Herodotus claims to have traveled widely to gather the materials for his history, and we have no reason to doubt him. He was a curious questioner, and had a lawyer's nose for an important fact. He was also full of bonhomie and has related wild tales at second and third hand—the sheep of Arabia, for example, have tails so large they must be carried in wagons—and justly confesses to being distracted from the main thread of his story.

At the opening of his history Herodotus announces, in a fashion virtually Homeric, that his topic is the wars between Greece and Persia. But he does not employ the epic invocation nor act as though he is a mere instrument in the hands of Cleo. Indeed, the very first sentence is, "In this book, the result of my inquiries into history, I hope to do two things: to preserve the memory of the past by putting on record the astonishing achievements both of our own and of the Asiatic peoples; secondly, and more particularly, to show how the two races came into conflict."[13] Here it is a matter of "my inquiries" and not the record of a long-known tradition which Herodotus presents. There is an independence and disinterestedness in this opening that even ascribes "astonishing achievements" to the Persians, although the audience is designated as Greek. This evenhandedness sounds very modern, but it should be remembered that Homer is also remarkably evenhanded in his account of the Trojan war. In spite of the personable tone of Herodotus he is not interested in revealing the details of his own life or feelings and so we know almost as little about him as we do of Homer. What is original about Herodotus is revealed in the last clause of his opening, which says that he intends "to show how the two races came into conflict." Such a history could simply be a recitation of accumulated affronts. This is how Homer tells his tale—although he also could ascribe the difficulties to the bickering of the gods. Herodotus recounts the history of difficulties—which mainly begin with the theft of beautiful girls—but leaves the deities out, or includes them as examples of doubtful superstitions. Herodotus also refers to the underlying causes of the conflict, and identifies these as the differing cultures and customs. Everything might have been different if the Greeks had not thought the theft of a woman a reason for contention, whereas the Asiatics took such matters lightly. "Abducting young women, in their opinion, is not, indeed, a lawful act; but it is stupid after the event to make a fuss about it."[14] But the chivalrous Greeks thought the theft of a Helen cause for the launching of a thousand ships. Herodotus gives the Persian version and the Phoenician one, then says, "I have no intention of passing judgement on [their] truth or falsity. I prefer to rely on my own knowledge, and to point out who it was in actual fact that first injured the Greeks."[15] Such silence is more rhetorical than judicious, but the tone is so marvelously personal that it is persuasive. What Herodotus does not do is to connect this history of the theft of women by the Asiatics to their penchant for tyranny, and to contrast this with the Greeks' anger over the violation of a person and their love of liberty. He is more apt to lapse into traditional laments over the fickleness of fate or delight in marvelous tales of bravery or revenge. Herodotus is a presence in his histories, but upon reflection only a ghostly one.

Although Herodotus looked for causes and told his story with charming eccentricity, the result is a strange jumble because there is no firm sense of chronology. One event might lead to another, but these two are more often than not isolated from the rest, and the result is a great junk shop of a book. R. G. Collingwood contends that for the Greeks history was all chronology, and because of their strong sense of the ephemeral nature of events they were essentially antihistorical.[16] De Sélincourt gives Herodotus more credit than this, saying that before him the Greeks "had no sense of the general march or development of human society."[17] The laurel which he passes to Herodotus, this ability to synthesize events through personal investigation, does not extend to a sense of the importance of the private and personal events of a life. "The ancients did not feel—nor perhaps did the moderns before Rousseau wrote his *Confessions*—that there could be any permanent or public interest in the minutiae of personal life. A man's work, or his large acts on the world's stage, were all they thought worth remembering; and, if they wanted more, they were apt to invent a myth which would satisfy their fancy or their sense of fitness."[18] The observation refers mainly to Herodotus, but it is applicable to the other Greek historians, and even the great Roman historians. Even when the emperors wrote history, emperors like Caesar and Claudius, their direction of events does not individualize the narrator so much as it turns him into a fabricating god. Even in the case of Tacitus, probably the greatest of the Roman historians, there is little difference in approach when he is compared to Herodotus—he is only duller.

One reason for this persistent sense that history is mainly a catalog of events, a mere chronology, is that praise of the emperor involves having time begin again with his reign and end with his deification. Some of these units of time were very small—fortunately in the case of such as Caligula—so that a sense of the development of the larger sweep of history against which the historian (and his reader) places himself was lacking. Such a chronological sense was not developed until the First Council of Nicaea was called by the Emperor Constantine in A.D. 325. For this Eusebius collected and matched the classical historians, and set out the various dating systems in a chart of comparables. The ultimate authority was, of course, the Pentateuch, and this eventually resulted in a calendar that counted 1656 years from Adam to the Flood, and 292 from the Flood to Abraham.[19] This could be considered a new myth, but it was a myth that pinned down the sweep of history as it had not been before, and it created a sense of chronology which was related to God's ultimate purposes. Such a system was perfectly adequate for a millennia and a half; indeed it was heretical to tamper with it. Those who did, and some of them were Fathers of the Church, attempted to align such a system with Greek Platonic millenarian thought, but this direction was hardly a one that would lead toward a modern historical consciousness. The system of

Eusebius was tinkered with by Luther, Johannes Kepler, Locke, and Archbishop Ussher, who dated the Creation in 4004 B.C.[20]

If men are to see themselves in a light that is true, or at least truer, an historical sense independent of primitive beliefs is important. It may be that the Renaissance faith in various sciences, especially mathematics, astronomy, and geology in which the dating of the origin of the earth is important, was a form of belief in new myths. The elongation of time which such sciences led to coincided with the tendency of people to muse on the nature of their selves. This elongation of time and a more sophisticated sense of history evolved with relative quickness. As Brèhier puts it, "Historical criticism was born in the seventeenth century from the same intellectual movement as the philosophy of Descartes."[21] By the middle of the next century Diderot, Buffon, Hume, and Gibbon treat historical evidence with an independent eye and scepticism that is virtually modern. This feeling for history is described by Peter Burke as combining the sense of anachronism, and awareness of what constitutes historical evidence, and an interest in causation. Perhaps it is only the first of these three elements that is lacking in Herodotus, but the other two slipped out of historical writing in subsequent centuries. Burke says that these elements developed during the Renaissance, beginning in fifteenth-century Italy, but that they have only "been a part of our culture, by which I mean of the West, since about 1800."[22]

The curious aspect of the Renaissance mind was that it was modern in certain compartments and thoroughly medieval in others. Petrarch has often been referred to as the first modern man, and Burke discusses his *Letters to Classical Authors* as an example of the way in which he was able to convey the distance between himself and those who went before.[23] Yet there is, perhaps because of the epistolary form, a sense that the ancients existed in a single sunlit time, and Petrarch is concerned mainly with the ideas and rhetoric of the ancients, not the inner springs of their personalities. He romanticized the ancients, and the great store of facts he had about them was gained for essentially aesthetic rather than historical pleasure.

There were others, such as Flavio Biondo, whose *Rome Restored* was written in 1440–46, who show a nice use and knowledge of inscriptions and numismatics. Biondo's work is mainly an architectural and topographical description of ancient Rome, and the result shows an objectivity beyond that of the amateur antiquarian. Polydore Vergil was a religious historian who drew attention to the connection between pagan and Christian belief, which required a daring uncommon in the sixteenth century. On other levels, Vasari attempted cultural history in his *Lives of the Painters*, Calvin cast serious doubt on the validity of some of the most sacred relics of the Roman Church, and John Colet did much to establish the manner in which historical documents can be judged in his comparison between the Bible and Suetonius.[24] Much of this was a chipping away at the solid mystery of the past. The great obstacle was the sense that the earth could not be older than pagan myths suggested it to be or Moses appeared to say it was. The inhibitions were understandable, for the extension of science from the fifteenth century onward was in part motivated by the desire—indeed in some circles salvation depended on it—to understand Holy Writ. So the study of languages, geology, geography, or astronomy was a pious exercise. For when Luther, and it was mainly he, set up the Scriptures as an authority superior to the Church, literacy if not scholarship became a pious duty. But such piety sometimes led to frivolous antiquarianism, and sometimes to solid discoveries that extended man's knowledge of the world. But he was still loath to destroy the scheme that gave him his intellectual impulse. Milton, knowing better and prideful of the fact that he knew better, still implies a Ptolemaic scheme for the universe in *Paradise Lost*, for such was less offensive to this epic design and was probably considered less offensive to God. So the true tales of the Old Testament turned into metaphors, and such a figure as Noah, who was a holy precursor of the Messiah in the middle ages, became in the late seventeenth century a marine engineer.[25]

Within the finite cosmologies that persisted into the eighteenth century men knew their place. When time and space have a beginning and an end men are also fixed in status, and the whole message of their culture is to remind them of that place and to warn them that only sorrow can result from any attempt to break the chains that tie them to family, trade, religion, and class. In such a scheme literature and sermon restate old truths, and these truths encourage the audience to think about itself in stereotypic ways. Humor is derived from the eccentric Malvolio who tries to swim against the current of social expectation, and tragic grandeur from Lear who violates the laws of succession. Such a lock-step is consistent with a world in which the final metaphysical solutions had been willed into being, and the person who brooded upon himself was considered ill with melancholy from an excess of black bile in his system.

The frame of this universe was cracked in the seventeenth century by Copernicus, Galileo, Tycho Brahe, and Newton. But new celestial bodies and a new arrangement for the old ones did not do great violence to a Mosaic version of the universe. It was in the middle of the eighteenth century that time was elongated beyond any adjustment with the versions of the Creation given in Genesis. In 1751 J. E. Guettard noticed hexagonal basalt used for paving in the Midi of France. The region was not considered as volcanic as southern Italy which he had just visited. But under the foliage on the mountains of the Massif he discerned the volcanic shapes he had seen in their raw form in Italy. If these mountains were volcanic in origin, it would have taken great periods of time for them to cool and accumulate their present topsoil and green mantle—certainly much longer than the six millennia that were the traditional age of the earth.[26] Another discovery which widened the horizons of eighteenth-century thought was that of the buried Herculaneum and Pompeii. The findings there were published between 1757 and 1792, and each volume added detail and dimension to the Roman classical texts, and the man of sensitivity lived in this wider time by building Roman ruins in his own garden.[27] In 1755 Kant's *General History of Nature and Theory of the Heavens* attempted one of the first evolutionary explanations of the universe, using the discoveries of Newton, Thomas Wright, and Maupertuis. His most astonishing concept was that the universe was still coming into existence. "The future succession of time, by which eternity is unexhausted, will entirely animate the whole range of space to which God is present, and will gradually put it into that order which is comfortable to the excellence of His plan . . . The Creation is never finished or complete. It did indeed once have a beginning, but it will never cease."[28] The language here is such that it might even lull a Bishop Warburton, but the message destroys the Fundamentalist interpretation of Genesis. This Kantian universe is even a precursor of the Einsteinian one which is in a continual state of explosion. Even those who, like Buffon, saw a beginning and an end were willing to state a figure for the age of the earth extended far beyond six thousand years. In the early 1770s Buffon made it 168,000 years, and privately he thought it might be half a million years.[29]

Other writers on the history of historical writing have placed the beginning of a modern sense of history in more recent times. For example, Hendrick van den Berg writes that a sense of the everyday life in the past was invented by Thomas Carlyle.[30] There is a point here, for an historian like Gibbon makes his heroic Roman pioneers a faceless lot, unconvincingly happy in their arduous trenching. Gibbon didn't see the common soldier—only the self-congratulatory official accounts. Again, R. G. Collingwood says that modern techniques in the use of documents were not developed until the middle of the nineteenth century, and J. H. Plumb has placed the beginning of the writing of modern history in this century, for all history prior to this was written—no matter how impressive its scholarship—to glorify a particular thesis or cause.[31] In this sense the writing of history may not yet have begun. The point is that these various beginnings for the writing of history suggest an evolution and not a "big bang" type of creation. Van den Berg is concerned with the social breadth of the historian, Collingswood with the use of documents, and Plumb with disinterestedness where causes are concerned. One could even carry the claims back to Hesiod with his theory of a fall from a pastoral Golden Age. Yet the most impressive claimants for the invention of history—as we now understand it—wrote in the mid-eighteenth century. It is then that all the requirements for an historical sense (the distaste for anachronism, the awareness of evidence, and the interest in causation) became ripe enough that they could be applied to grand historical projects. Many of these—and the histories of Hume and Gibbon come immediately to mind—were immensely popular, which suggests that the placing of the past in a truer light was intriguing to a wide audience. Here a kind of paradox operates. Gibbon might have presented a picture of the Roman empire falling under the weight of Christian superstition and Hume might have given English history a Whiggish reading, but an accompanying objectivity suggested that the causes of events are not simple and that in the grander sweep of history an individual is a smaller speck in eternity than he was under the dispensations of earlier theologies and cosmologies. Yet that helplessness was the conclusion of a Promethean and revolutionary vision. To be able to see how small we are is still to see, and perhaps the new focus on the self in the eighteenth century is a compensation for the realization that the individual is such a mite before the carelessness of natural and historical laws.

4

Biography

Biographies are but the clothes and buttons of the
man—the biography of the man himself cannot be written.

—Mark Twain, *Autobiography*

The forms of history which would seem to come closest to what characters in the past were really like would appear to be portraiture, biography, and autobiography. Yet none of these forms, until the last two
hundred years, end in revealing as much as they conceal. This is, of
course, a modern observation, for the artist of the self in the past
undoubtedly thought that he was telling the whole truth (he often
protests that he does), and if we were to accuse him of leaving much
out—the flaws and eccentricities of the great prince, the amusing anecdotes about the noble orator—he would probably respond that this was
irrelevant; that character consists of what makes a person like others of
his type rather than unlike them. Truth, even the whole truth about an
individual, existed in what was stereotypic rather than in what was
unique.

A book reviewer might now say that a biography of Alexander or
Charlemagne or even Cromwell makes its subject "come to life," or
that "the reader feels he knows" so and so after reading the book. This
is always said admiringly of popular biographies, as though the writer
has overcome the paucity of his material and breathed life into a mute
and distant age. We might suspect that something quite different from
the real person has been synthesized from the dates and decrees and
battles, yet we may still be charmed by the idea of some distant eminent person feeling and thinking much as we do. Such phrases of
praise are rarely used, however, when the subject of the biography
lived within the past two centuries. Here the biographer's task is not
to make Keats, say, "come to life," and to breathe life into inchoate
material. Keats left us so much in an idiom so close to ours that the
biographer's task is to select and arrange, to settle disputes about the
interpretation of the facts, and place once more the subject in his age.
It is not a matter of resuscitation; it is rather one of taming the abun-

40

dance too full of life. It is hard to imagine the necessity of breathing life into Goethe, or Flaubert, or d'Annunzio, or Dreiser. They present us not with an ancient stoical indifference to their lives or with a medieval pious modesty, but rather dissertations on every ecstasy and every scar they have known.

Portraiture is the earliest of these three forms of expression that propose to reveal the nature of a person. Even so, portraiture is very late in growing out of the ancient tangle of pictorial art. The earliest human figures are always shown in terms of a function: as stick figures incidental to a hunting scene in the earliest cave paintings, or the fertility or totem figures where the head is a mere knob or that of an abis, a wolf, or an eagle. Ancient portraiture then begins in magic, and the likeness is usually intended to decieve the beasts or gods rather than to reveal a personality. The Sumerian statue of the god Abu found at Tell Asmar rivets us with enormous black eyes made of butimen, but the rest of the figure is stylized in such a way as to take the figure beyond the human.[1] Such stylization dominates those figures that depict humans, whereas animals are often shown with convincing reality. The famous gold mask of Sargon is remarkable for its sheen and workmanship, but I do not think this idealization of a ruler shows us what the ruler looked like. The statues of seated scribes of Sumer, Akkad, and Egypt hold us with a stare across four millennia, but the posture and shape of the figure obviously is dictated by the workman's material. The "Louvre Scribe" is remarkably lifelike, but other statues of what is undoubtedly the same scribe vary the features.[2] This is probably the result of the material, a different artist, or because precision in rendering the individual was not considered important—the scribe's function was the prime consideration. This is even true of the death masks of the pharaohs rendered in painted wood on their sarcophagi. Here representation is deliberately of the shell awaiting its soul in the afterlife.[3] Most early portraiture is associated with funerary practices, and this is especially true in ancient Egypt, so that "The apparent realism of these royal heads is thus actually a different expression of the idealized ruler."[4]

The influence of artistic stylization and the magical function of portraiture can be seen in classical Greek art, even though we are often struck with the extent to which the best of the Greek artists from the fourth century B.C. on struggled to overcome it. They were the first to treat the whole body of the figure—at least in a freestanding position. This liberated the figure from its material, and so the Greeks were the first to make portraits that had no other magical intent than to fix the subject's appearance in a moment in time. Yet there is an heroic intent in Greek ark which shows the human figure as it might have been but not the individual as he was. James Breckenridge says of Thucydides' description of Pericles, "It has struck many commentators that these text passages have a great deal in common with the sculptured portrait, since they present a list of ideal virtues so depersonalized as to offer no grasp of what an actual man could have been like."[5] This concept of the heroic ideal is impressive in the Greek use of it because it is dedicated to a praise of motion and life, whereas the Roman use of similar idealization was dedicated to ancestor worship.[6] Such idealization and "list of ideal virtues" tends to distort the living model in a manner different from the blank and cocked-head spiritualization of Byzantine or Medieval portraiture, but it is a distortion, for all of its impressiveness of form and expression.[7]

Indeed, the very nature of portraiture—no matter how realistic the intent—results more in a mast to hide the true subject than a transparent image through which or in which we can know the subject. This is the drift of most psychologically oriented discussion of art. E. H. Gombrich, perhaps the most influential of such critics, poses the question of style in such a way that we are led to conclude that artists of differing times and cultures see nature through different systems of stylization. Nature itself does not radically change, but the artist sees it both consciously and unconsciously through the learned stylization of his particular time and place. Even such an artist as Constable, who goaded himself to paint a landscape as though he had never seen a painting, can be shown to manipulate his subject in such a way that it is consistent with the stylization of his age.[8] In addition to the burden and the glory of this stylization is the artist's drive to create, not just imitate. The great painters are those who are able to give us the impression that they have broken out of the prison of stylization, so that we feel we are seeing the scene before us unhampered by tradition. What has actually happened is that an alteration of an old style (and style in any art is never static) is taking place before our eyes, and in looking at the picture we are training ourselves to see what appears to be reality through this altered style.

What is so impressive about Renaissance portraiture, compared to that which went before, is the variety of its subject and treatment. But these portraits are still not of individuals in that they can be divided into certain firm categories. There are the state portraits of such as Holbein, the allegorical or historical portraits of Rembrandt and Rubens, and we might even discern something comparable to the seventeenth-century prose character in the lively studies of such a master as Franz Hals. But even his subjects, caught warty and laughing in a tavern which makes them seem so very real to us, have symbolic objects at hand (a tankard, a pipe, an owl) which suggest a generalized reading of the image rather than a specific one. If there is one category of Renaissance portrait that seems to come closest to breaking the ancient tradition of typology it is the self-portraits, and perhaps those of Albrecht Dürer do this mostly through the haunting absorption with that which lies behind his own image.[9] These self-portraits may be said to prefigure in art the concern with the self that Montaigne exhibits in autobiography. In both cases traditional styles are violently handled, for Dürer plunges ahead of his time, beyond the accepted style of portraiture, and into himself, just as Montaigne shows us the process of his mind's meditation, rather than the daylit and balanced result.

Generally, the Renaissance portrait does not intend to show us a person, but a kind of person. This might even be considered an elaboration of the ancient Egyptian emphasis on the subject's trade, so that we see him not as a person but as a scribe, baker, fowler, and so forth. But in the Renaissance portrait we often know the subject's name, especially if he commissioned the painting. In his study of Renaissance portraiture, John Pope-Hennessy says that one reason for this typology is that the Renaissance had no psychology, so that people were not seen in their complexity, but in their accomplishment or their role in society.[10] They might even be seen through allegory, as in fifteenth-century Italian paintings, which often place the head of the artist's subject on the body of some figure in classical mythology or biblical story. Botticelli, for example, was a Neoplatonist who felt that reality resided not in the thing, but in the symbol, so his subject was delineated through the depiction of his relationship to ancient gods or shepherds.[11]

Gombrich suggests that from the Renaissance on, style appears to become more complicated and subtle, and to the uninitiated the style of his own time virtually disappears, so that, for example, the wildest stylistic experiments during the first quarter of this century have now become domesticated in our commercial art. The lesson that we might apply to the history of portraiture is that likeness in the eighteenth century seemed to usurp the functions of what had before been considered style. For one thing, portraits—even state portraits—became private statements in that the symbols identifying the subject's public function were often removed, and character, rather than function, had to be read in the face. The landscape behind or through the open window in eighteenth-century portraits did not serve to suggest fields to fill or conquer, or merely a setting for the subject as it does in the Renaissance, but rather the mood (usually delicate and meditative) of the subject. The private nature of such portraiture was something that the eighteenth-century artist was aware of, so the portrait was not only a likeness, but became an elaborate cue to the memory of the beholder. Gombrich cites Reynolds's admiration for the way in which Gainsborough could stimulate the memory by certain rough touches that make the canvas seemed marred, but together give the impression of immediacy and truth. "For Reynolds, Gainsborough's frequently unfinished and rather vague indications are little more than those schemata which serve as a support for our memory images; in other words, they are screens onto which the sitter's relatives and friends could project a beloved image, but which remain blank to those who cannot contribute from their own experience. The role which projection plays, and is intended to play, in works of this kind could not be brought out more sharply."[12] To put it in still other words, the eighteenth-century portraitist uses a language which is exceedingly private and suggests merit in individuality, rather than that his subject is the type which may be identified by universally recognized symbols. It is significant that one of the major icons of the American experience is the Gilbert Stuart portrait of Washington, for the American Revolution was led by stable burghers and planters who had great faith that a workable government could result from the leashed conflict of individual interests. That portrait is—in spite of what it has become—individualizing and denuded of any symbol of civil or military power. This a pharaoh or a king who knew his place in God's scheme would not have understood.

When history begins in king lists, time is measured in the accretions of chronicles. The kings themselves are traced to the gods, and biography is beside the point. The story of a man until the last two centuries is stylized for many of the same reasons his portrait is stylized. A person lived through his function, and that was determined by forces over which he had no control (his family, race, religion, class) and which he had no occasion to question. In the same way there would be no reason why he should think that his life would be interesting, or the lives of anyone like him. An inner life did not exist, or if it did it followed patterns that were so universal as to be tedious. In saying this I am attributing thoughts that were probably rarely entertained. In ancient societies the master was by our terms even less human and individualized than the servant. Power not only famously corrupts, but it dehumanizes, and what we know of ancient potentates suggests that they saw themselves in their accomplishments and decrees. These were products of an ego sustained by feelings of divine descent. The result is that we know very little about the ancient great, and what we do know comes to us in the form of artifacts, like mummies and bragging inscriptions that were not intended as biographical document. If the ancients had been concerned with perpetuating the memory of lives they could have been much more helpful.

What lives we do have are incidental to a writer's major purpose, and this was not to write biography, for the view of what constituted a man was very different. The synoptic Gospels give us the works and miracles of Christ, but they do so in anecdotal form, as though Christ existed entirely in his words and gestures. The Gospels are also inadequate as chronology and itinerary, for they famously do not agree at points and they leave enormous gaps in the life. Their purpose is evangelical, and the life of even the Master who came to be the model is incidental to that purpose. There is a similar difficulty with our understanding of the life of Alexander the Great. We might expect to know more about him than any other of the ancients, for he was the first of the Western builders of empire and a virtual troop of historians followed him from victory to victory. Yet the major contemporary accounts of Alexander, those by Clitarchus, Ptolemy, and Aristobulus, have not survived, but what we know of them suggests that each presented his own version of sycophancy. There is an evangelical problem here too, for Alexander excused his conquests by considering them the agent of the spread of Greek culture into barbarian lands. The failure of that undertaking is suggested by the fact that the surviving lives of Alexander—those by Quintus Curtius Rufus, Arrian, and Plutarch— were written at least two centuries after his death, and uncritically mix myth with fact.

What strikes us most about ancient biography is the strange distance between the biographer and his subject resulting from the lists of virtues. Xenophon's portrait of Cyrus illustrates such cataloging. He begins by saying that Cyrus was raised at court and was most eager to learn the arts of war. He was courageous, and this is illustrated by an account of a hunting experience. "There was one occasion when a she-bear charged at him and he, showing no fear, got to grips with the animal and was pulled off his horse. The scars from the wounds he got then were still visible on his body, but he killed the animal in the end, and as for the first man who came to help him Cyrus made people think him very lucky indeed."[13] This last introduces the next virtue on the list, which is Cyrus's generosity, and this is followed by his justice. The incident with the bear is typical of the anecdotes that make up so much of ancient biography, and here Xenophon shows us almost nothing but Cyrus, a horse, a she-bear, and the scars. Nothing is filled in with the kind of detail that would make us see the experience and be convinced by it. The reason for this is that such an experience was exceedingly traditional in accounts of the lives of rulers, so the mere reference to such an experience was intended to stimulate a

panoply of clichéd responses. The ancients contentedly saw themselves and others disappearing into such clichés. Bravery in the hunt
was virtually required for such portraits, but in the case of Cyrus
another incident, recounted by Herodotus, links him with Oedipus,
Moses, and Christ. Because of a dream that predicted the infant was a
threat to the throne, the baby Cyrus was given to a herdsman to be
slaughtered, but of course he was not, and lived to reveal himself.[14]
The tale differs slightly in each infancy of the national savior, but they
are enough alike to make the saviors virtually interchangeable.

We might expect such leveling in portraits drawn a couple of centuries after the death of the subject when legend had time to take over
from fact, or (as in the case of these accounts of Cyrus) the historian
had a special interest in praising the powers of an antagonist who
would be defeated, on the principle that a victory is only worthy over
a worthy enemy. Even portraits of the writer's well-known contemporary tend to be sacrificed to larger purposes. We have a very clear
sense of what Socrates was like from Plato's dialogues, or Pericles from
the speeches given him by Thucydides, but the major purpose of Plato
and Thucydides was not biography, so we must create our own portrait out of bits and pieces. Biography, as independent of such other
purposes, is often said to begin with Plutarch, and in the sense that
anecdote and analysis are not incidental in Plutarch this is true. He is
not mainly concerned with history, nor does he use dialogue to illustrate a philosophic method or position. Plutarch does not write a biographical dictionary or even present a gallery in the *Parallel Lives*. What
happens is simply that the listing of virtues and vices comes to the
foreground, and the clichés of character are not used as flourishes in
an historical narrative, but as the matter of the narrative itself.

One of the curious aspects of classical biography is that it avoids
description, or generalizes it to such an extent that we are in the presence of a swiftly drawn state portrait or a grotesque. Perhaps this is
further testimony to the shell-like quality of classical portraiture,
which for the Greeks suggested an ideal that was removed from the
person, or for the Romans a funerary mask that was vacant of the de-
ceased. The countenance in prose portraits is most often unseen. For
example, Marcus Aurelius admired his adoptive father beyond all
others who influenced him in his life, but he does not think it important to tell us what his father looked like. "The qualities I admired in
my father [the Emperor Antoninus Pius] were his lenience, his firm
refusal to be diverted from any decision he had deliberately reached,
his complete indifference to meretricious honours; his industry, per-
severance, and willingness to listen to any project for the common
good; the unvarying insistence that rewards must depend on merit;

the expert's sense of when to tighten the reins and when to relax them; and the efforts he made to suppress pederasty."[15] Whether the last virtue refers to his own or others' pederasty is not clear, but it is the sole sad humanizing touch in the list. Otherwise this is the portrait of the perfectly restrained and stoical monarch which the portraitist wishes himself to be, but the portrait includes not a hair of his beard. The reason for this is that the body is the seat of the hated passions, and it is best to beat it down with Reason. "A little flesh, a little breath, and a Reason to rule all—that is myself . . . As one already on the threshold of death, think nothing of the first—of its viscid blood, its bones, its web of nerves and veins and arteries."[16] To all this Reason must be the master, so the less said of the diseased corpus the better.

Even when the body later becomes an adjunct to the biographical portrait, it is described in such a manner that it is as stylized as the saints in the niches of medieval cathedrals. An example is the picture which Anna Comnena gives of her beloved father, who is the hero of the *Alexiad*.

Alexius was not a very tall man, but broad shouldered and yet well proportioned. When standing he did not seem particularly striking to onlookers, but when one saw the grim flash of his eyes as he sat on the imperial throne, he reminded one of a fiery whirlwind, so over-whelming was the radiance that emanated from his countenance and his whole presence. His dark eyebrows were curved, and beneath them the gaze of his eyes was both terrible and kind. A quick glance, the brightness of his face, the noble cheeks suffused with red combined to inspire in the beholder both dread and confidence. His broad shoulders, mighty arms and deep chest, all on a heroic scale, invariably commanded the wonder and delight of the people. The man's person indeed radiated beauty and grace and dignity and an unapproachable majesty. When he came into a gathering and began to speak, at once you were conscious of the fiery eloquence of his tongue, for a torrent of argument won a universal hearing and captivated every heart; tongue and hand alike were unsurpassed and invincible, the one in hurling the spear, the other in devising fresh enchantments.[17]

Here there are not only physical qualities mentioned, but they are made specific. Had her father been tall and soft voiced one is sure that Anna could have described these characteristics in such a way that just as much praise would redound on Alexius, but the specifics of stature and voice are there. Anna, however, is concerned with turning these attributes into illustrations of her father's glory. Anyone seated on a fancy throne, with an expert torturer at his bidding, is lent a kind of dignity, but Anna invites us to see through the physical to the glorious force of personality within, a force not dependent on Alexius being the emperor. The machinery of abstraction and typology is, however, working in such a description, so that we get the impression that this portrait is an unconscious distortion of what must really have been. Such dehumanization is even more evident in the portrait which Anna gives of her mother. Here the queen slides into abstractions, and even her hands become ivory. "For the most part her lips were closed and when thus silent she resembled a veritable statue of Beauty, a breathing monument of Harmony. Generally she accompanied her words with graceful gestures, her hands bare to the wrists, and you may say it (her hand) was ivory turned by some craftsman into the form of fingers and hand."[18] The same sort of dehumanization is employed when she describes the enemy, for the despised Robert Guiscard, the Norman, is made a worthy adversary of her father by being described as gigantic (but exactly how big we are not told), and his voice is compared to that of Achilles: "Robert's bellow, so they say, put tens of thousands to flight."[19] Robert's rage is even more fearsome than Achilles', but it is seen through Homer in a stylization comparable to that of Byzantine mosaics.

All accounts of medieval and Renaissance biography divide the subject into two: the lives of saints and the lives of princes. The methods of each are very much the same, for both are anecdotal and strive for the general rather than the particular, and are perfectly clear as to the moral of a life. Donald Stauffer calls these lives static, and explains the difference in this way: "There is one difference immediate and arresting between the medieval conception of biography and our own. We consider the biographer not as one who generalizes, but one who individualizes. *Il ne classe pas; il déclassé.* He seeks, and has sought since Boswell, not the ideal, but the characteristic. This eagerness for particulars would not have been easily understood by the early biographers. During the Middle Ages the office or position, rather than the individual frequently attracts the biographer."[20] What Stauffer says here also applies to classical biography, only in medieval biographers there is an earnestness that is seen only occasionally in ancient writers, such as Marcus Aurelius. The very title of these biographies suggests the weightiness of the subject. As late as 1650 we have an example in Henry Isaacson's *The Life and Death of Lancelot Andrewes, Late Bishop of Winchester, Which May Serve as a Pattern of Piety and Charity to all Godly Disposed Christians.* In the sixteenth century there was a new surge of hagiography from the Protestant writers, as well as court portraits that were occasionally influenced by the discovery of the classical writers. Yet this influence did not alter the moral intent of biography (as the classical models were also often moral and largely generalizing), but did suggest ways in which the details of character could be more arresting. Sir Thomas More's lives of Mirandula and Richard III combine classical and medieval hagiological influences, but most important is More's talent in treating details with drama and irony, so that we get a picture of the times. Yet in both biographies More uses his skill to a moral end, which is more important than creating a full psychological portrait in the modern sense.

Stauffer suggests that the ethical tendency of the Middle Ages destroyed the classical concept of individuality; that all descriptions of persons became like funeral eulogies.[21] More likely the goal of and reason for generalizing the individual into a type had changed. For the classical author it was a matter of an idealized human being unrelated to humanity; for the medieval writer it was a matter of showing the shell of the immortal soul. When these traditions were combined in the Renaissance the details of character gave a sense of real flesh to the portrait, but the didactic intent remained pretty much the same. Stauffer writes, "The two sketches of Colet and More written by Erasmus . . . mark the wide difference between the Middle Ages and the Renaissance. Where the medieval character sketch enumerates superlative and generalized virtues, Erasmus seizes with discrimination the evanescent qualities that form the character of his friends, and records his captured essences. This enthusiasm for the fine distinctions of personality resulted in the character sketches of the seventeenth century."[22] This is all very true, and yet these portraits that seem so vibrant and analogous in their convincing detail to the portraits of Holbein and Ten Enck are relegated to private letters and are still anecdotal. Even Isaac Walton, the most remembered of biographers in the next century, Stauffer calls the last hagiographer.[23] Dryden considered biography inferior to other forms of history, and so it was until Boswell, and so it remains in the eyes of many historians. Because of this, biography was an adjunct to other literary forms; it might come in a prefatory sketch, or it might be the specific matter in a funeral oration. This dependency on other forms was greater than it was in classical times when biography was incidental to history or philosophy or oratory, but it was none the less a dependent form.

It is easy to overemphasize the importance of Boswell's *Life of Johnson*, for as remarkable as that book is—indeed there is none other quite like it—it did not spring full-blown and out of nowhere. The eighteenth century was, in certain classes, a scribbling age which out of sheer energy developed such forms as journalism, the novel, and letter writing. All of these forms contributed to the style and form of biography. The characters that grew out of the journalism of the early decades of the century were more fully drawn than the Theophrastan

characters of the seventeenth century. The scenes that Addison and
Steele create for the *Sir Roger de Coverley* papers involve comic and
characterizing situations in which the earlier types were never found.
This is obviously a source for the eighteenth-century novel, but the
kind of discourse Johnson re-creates in his biography of Richard Savage, and is later the prime matter of Boswell's memories, is indebted
to the early journalism. The novel also was a contributor to biography,
or rather they might be thought of as progressing hand in hand. For
the novel often, in its desire to pretend that it is not art, takes the form
of a biography, and sometimes that of the memoir or autobiography.
Fielding's *Tom Jones* is called a "history," but it could be a biography,
and Sterne's *Tristram Shandy* is labeled *The Life and Opinions*. Even
earlier in the century there are the first-person memoirs in the novels
of Defoe. All of these sources tend to break down the design and
method of earlier biographies. The detached and gentle irony of journalism did not house well with the eulogistic tone of so much biography, but was to be very important in Boswell. The example of the
early novel led the biographer to turn anecdotes into scenes and to
suggest a design to a life that was comparable to plot. But the most
important contribution of these devices to eighteenth-century biography was the sense that a biography might be read for enjoyment,
that our interest in the life of a man might not be to see the pattern of
reward for his virtues and retribution for his sins, but that the life had
inherent interest because of its originality and uniqueness.

To seek such difference in lives the eighteenth-century hack biographer often avoided the former subjects, the lords of the realm or the
saints of the church. Money had long been made from the rhymed
confessions (or if unrepentant, the damned lives) of the condemned,
and these were often hawked while their subjects were carted through
the streets to the gallows.[24] Such works were often simply inverted
saints' lives; titillating, but none the less schematic and moralizing.
Although the form achieved a high and often hypocritical pitch in the
late sixteenth century, it is most famously represented by the lives of
Jonathan Wild by Defoe, Gay (in *The Beggars Opera*), and that of Fielding, for whom Wild offers an occasion for sustained invective against
Robert Walpole in particular and Greatness in general.[25] The age had
almost as insatiable an appetite for the lives of the obscure and infa-
mous as it did for heroic couplets. There were lives of footmen, pirates, and bawds. These were still often cautionary tales, but before
the final caution was reiterated a great deal of vicarious pleasure was
retailed. One of the curious aspects of this growth is that the lives of
the small, which had been so neglected as to be unrecorded, now became clamorously public, and many lives of the great became secret.

Diaries, such as that of Pepys and Evelyn, devoted more to mere record keeping and the judgment of public events than to introspection,
but these were not published for over a century. There were also a
number of family lives written in the form of memorials (and so they
were private eulogies), but they were often kept for the eyes of the
family.

Such biographies would not have had to be published to have been
a direct influence on such as Boswell, for the spirit that created them
was simply more elaborate in his case. Some of these family biographies were published in the mid-eighteenth century. The most interesting instance is that of the biographies Roger North wrote of his
three brothers. One was the Lord Keeper of the Great Seal under
Charles II, another was a merchant dealing with the Levant, and the
third was a dour minister.[26] These biographies give an excellent picture of the age, but they are also marvelously detailed portraits that go
beyond the mere still life of the state portrait. These biographies were
published between 1742 and 1744, the last also the year of Johnson's
life of Richard Savage. North was an antiquarian collector of family
quirks and characters, but his studies are not the anecdotal
hodgepodge that we get from John Aubrey or Anthony à Wood. North
does more than peddle gossip, for the lives of his brothers are
rounded and convincing because he was committed to a concept of
personal biography opposed to the public biographies then in fashion.
North's practice suggests Johnson's own position as expressed in his
essay on biography in 1750:" . . . the business of a biographer is
often to pass slightly over those performances and incidents, which
produce vulgar greatness, to lead the thoughts into domestick
privacies, and display the minute details of daily life, where exterior
appendages are cast aside, and men excel each other only by prudence
and by virtue. . . . There are many invisible circumstances which,
whether we read as inquirers after natural or moral knowledge,
whether we intend to enlarge our science, or increase our virtue, are
more important than publick occurances."[27] Johnson's point is still
that biography should have a moral purpose, even if that is to "enlarge our science," but his concept of what a biographer must consider
is much more involved than it had been before his age. He is not
interested in gossip, such as the tattle that moral men read in Mary
Manley about the court of Anne or in Mrs. Pilkington about Dean
Swift. It is rather that the essential man is not the sum of his public
performances and works, that most men live lives that are reflections
of all lives, and therefore a biographer can increase our knowledge of
the world by attending to private minutia. In consonance with this
view, Boswell quotes Johnson as saying, "They only who live with a

man can write his life with any genuine exactness and discrimination; and few people who have lived with a man know what to remark about him."[28] In *The Lives of the Poets* Johnson had to write the biographies of many with whom he had not lived, and he found that those to whom he talked about his dead subjects were not very helpful. Boswell ascribes this comment to 1776, when Johnson was working on *The Lives*. The observation is also a testament to Boswell's own method, but it is also a warning against the difficulty of his task. Even more important is that the observation suggests that the stereotypes that so dominated biographies were false, and although Johnson himself rarely rose above the typology of his century in his lives, he seems to know what might have been done.

This was, all agree, done by Boswell. Even though the *Life* was not published until 1791, the mood and spirit which created it was formed as early as 1761, when Boswell came to London to seek out his subject. We now know he was an indefatigable diarist as well as a collector of the great and a jotter of their table talk. He confesses that the tour of the Hebrides was mainly a way to get Johnson off to himself, and although there were the pleasures of showing the famous man around his own land, he is more interested in drawing out the conversationalist than in drawing his attention to the glories of Scotland. Johnson, from the advice he gives Boswell about the writing of biography, undoubtedly knew that his young friend was an interested eavesdrooper, and Boswell's book on Corsica would also have hinted at such a biographical project. Boswell's was also not the only life of Johnson, for he had to compete with the published memoirs of Mrs. Piozzi, Sir John Hawkins, and others.[29] What is remarkable about the work is that by 1791 Boswell can begin his opening sentence with the name of his subject, his place of birth, and his birthdate. There is no shuffling about the importance of Johnson or the moral lessons to be learned from his life. The interest in the man has been established for Boswell's audience, but even so the attitude that saw a man's life as inherently interesting for its variety and complexity was more important for Boswell's abrupt assumption of interest.

Still, Boswell's *Life of Johnson* is not the kind of psychological portrait that a modern might expect to result from the intimacy on which the book was based. Boswell tended to emphasize this intimacy, being an avid lionizer of the mighty. He knew Johnson during the last twenty-one years of his life, but during that time they only lived hard by one another for a little over two years, and the three-month tour of the Hebrides in 1776 was the sole sustained rubbing of elbows. Boswell is however able to let us wallow in the minutia of the Great Cam's life as though he and we were constant companions. One result of this is a strange repetitiveness. After the first description of Johnson's figure and huffings we can almost predict when a similar description is due, so when the conversation takes a certain turn we almost know that next will come a broadside against Americans, or a belittling of the moral merit in natural scenery, or a kindly word for a down-and-out friend. The book has not only been described as ideal for the nightstand, but it has often been abridged, and is very abridgeable. These may sound like hard words for a great work; it can withstand them, but we should see the *Life* for what it is. Boswell's talent was like that of the acquisitive antiquarian, and not that of the judicious synthesizer. Therefore he gallops through the first fifty-four years of Johnson's life prior to his meeting with Boswell in 1763 in Davies's bookshop. This is well done, but it is not significantly different from other lives published during the century. After 1763 he can resort to his journals, reenforce these with his subsequent conversation with others of the Club, letters, and Johnson's own writings. Here the work takes on its inimitable character, which is that of a series of lively scenes in tavern, club, or coach. It could also be contended that Boswell's method of disordered accretion of detail is truer to the manner in which lives are lived—at least from the inside—even though Boswell seems to have come to a defense of his method after the fact. There is often little to choose between this disorder and the order of later biographies that tend to break a life upon the rack of phases and chapters. Boswell's organization is simply chronological. This is wise, for the only alternative that might have occurred to him would have been topical bon mots. As private as the parties were, Johnson in his later years must have thought of them as public performances— comparable in a way to Pope's letters or Gide's journals, which the writer knew were destined for the public eye.

Johnson, as biographical theorist, saw man as the sum of public achievements and private quirks and fears. In practice he was very good at dealing with the public achievements; but his subjects not only disappear into their own works, but our interest in Johnson's *Lives of the Poets* is in Johnson more than in the poets, for his marvelously rotund style says as much or more about him than about his subjects. Johnson often includes quirky anecdotes, but Boswell revels in them—too much so, according to some of the contemporary commentators on his work. Their objection to the *Life* was that it displayed too much spite or too much fawning, but Boswell had adjusted a dozen mirrors instead of a single one in which Johnson could be seen. In this he took the next inevitable step in the development of the biographer's art. Yet he still used the objective mirror which left Johnson's private fears a mystery. Boswell could refer to his adolescent depres-

sion and his mature melancholia, or he could quote from his pious
meditations, but our final impression is that Johnson was, as he himself called it, clubbable. The private fears of the age are detailed by
Boswell elsewhere. They are his own, and they are recounted in his
Journals.

5

Autobiography

When Eckhart or Plotinus wrote "I," nothing remained of
their singleness. They leapt abruptly, and with no emotional residue, from the particular into the universal.

—Paul Zweig, *The Heresy of Self-Love*

Things exist before we invent names for them, but when we have
invented the name a shape for the thing is created to which it must
conform. So it is with such literary forms as the epic and the novel.
Homer and the *Beowulf* poet did not think of themselves as epic
poets, but Virgil and Milton did, and they wrote what they did because they took pride in being epical. Much the same is true of the
term *biography*, which did not come into use until about 1660.[1] Then it
was used to describe the type of writing we now consider biography,
although the works themselves were called *lives*, or *accounts*, or *histories*. The term *autobiography* is an even later coinage. It was apparently devised by Robert Southey in 1809.[2] Before this time the form
had been a desultory imitation of the personal narrative (in the coun-
cils of the mighty, on the road, etc.), the religious confession, the informal essay, and technically might be described as the journal, diary,
or memoir. All of these might be thought of as autobiographies after
the fact, but they are not really the same as those that were written
after Rousseau—whose work is slyly called a *confession*. The nature of
autobiography from Saint Paul to Roger North (or even Hume) is very
different from that which runs (to take a couple of antithetical examples) from Casanova to C. S Lewis. Before the fulcrum of the mid-
eighteenth century the point of personal narrative was to make one's
peace with God; afterward it was to make one's peace with himself.

The first person is grammatically a slippery sign and a slipperier
concept. In many languages it usually appears only as an inflection
attached to a verb, as though polite self-effacement were built into the
language. It might also operate as a kind of reflexive pronoun, just to
remove any confusion about the recipient of the action of the verb. On
special occasions it is reserved for God's voice out of the whirlwind or

55

God's priestly or royal emissary. Such a use was dramatized by the Chinese emperor K'ang-hsi, who was the only one in his court who could use the word *chen* or *I*. A comparable situation exists with the royal *We*, or in the presidental reference to his office and himself in the third person. Somewhere between the grammatically functional and the imperial first person there is that *I* which is the feeling, tenderly loved, secularized soul, which we have come to think of as the self.

Bruno Snell says that Sappho was the first to use the first person singular to refer to this something between the grammatically convenient and the royal-egotistical. "Sappho places that which is inwardly felt above external splendour. The notion of Homer and Archilochus, that 'each has his heart cheered in a different way,' had allowed for a number of excellences or ideals, with no priority given to any one of them. Sappho tells us which thing has the greatest value: that which is lovingly embraced by her soul. We find similar confessions in other archaic writings, but Sappho was the first to put this into words . . . She says of her beloved Kleis: 'I would not exchange all the Lydian lands for her'."[3] Here the *I* carries a freight which it had not, and without such a use of the *I*, autobiography is impossible. What is remarkable is how late such a use was to develop, and how timorous writers were in using the *I* in this manner. The tradition of divine inspiration secured the poet's *I* from such a personal emphasis and linked it with the royal prerogative. The invocation to the appropriate muses, because of its long tradition, might be said to be mere lip service, and we suspect that the poet knows who is really writing his verses. Yet poets were willing to hide behind the togas of the Sacred Sisters because they evidently felt comfortable there. Even Milton, who knew very well what he was about, probably seriously believed in his Urania—as much as he believed that he had a special difficulty writing his epic on a wet Atlantic island where his epic wing was dampened. The muses dehumanize the poet into instrument or ego, and that may be why they were sent packing in the eighteenth century, or turned into wispy personifications. At the other end of the scale, the first person may simply serve a grammatical function. Sir Thomas Browne says that his *Religion Medici* is a "private Exercise directed to my self," and he may appear very modern by saying that "there is another man within mee that's angry with mee, rebukes, commands, and dastards mee."[4] Yet as we read on we see that Browne is not concerned with his self, but with his soul, in the tradition of the religious confession. What he means is *myself* and his own spiritual being.

The *I* of the autobiographer is rarely convincing. It is either on the heights of egoism, where history depends upon its acts or decisions, or it is suspiciously too unctuous before God. Boswell has Dr. Johnson say "there are few writers who have gained any reputation by recording their own actions."[5] Then he goes on in his Johnsonian manner and says that there are four types of writers in this class, and labels them all egoists. First, there is Julius Caesar, who relates his own actions. Second, there is Marcus Aurelius, who reflects "on his own life." Third, there are those who relate anecdotes of their life and times. Fourth, there are "old women and fantastic writers of memoirs and meditations." I think most readers know to what he refers in his last two categories, but his description is not very helpful. These, from his vantage, must be tales told by highwaymen and court gossips, and the last by those driven to pious confession. There is in Johnson's tone a dismissal of such works, in spite of the Roman examples, for he is justly suspicious of hungry egos and public penitents.

Yet there is more to the tradition of autobiography than this, even though I have suggested in other contexts that one must look hard for it. Autobiography in ancient times is very hard to find because the ancients did not think of their own temporal beings as significant, so they are of little help to us if we wish to know about their personal lives. Georg Misch has written the standard work on autobiography in antiquity and was able to fill two volumes, even though there are many—Sir Herbert Read is one—who contend that the ancients wrote no autobiography. Read is writing on art and is determined to make the point that the ancients were interested in beauty not likeness, and that since we cannot ultimately "know thyself" it is rash of us to expect art to help us.[6] Misch would concede most of this, and confesses that before Cicero's letters there are "no autobiographies in the proper sense of the word."[7] These letters are not even an autobiography, but they display a convincing "individual consciousness of the self." The argument is very persuasive, for Cicero was impressive when affronted, and when his motives were in question—the subject of many of the letters—he is analytical and eloquent by turns in his defense. But there is a Roman distance. As in the argument for old age in *De senectute*, there is an order too nice for the passion implied. Caesar's work is a campaign biography, in both the ancient and modern senses, so in spite of the "peculiar grace and dignity" (as Johnson phrased it) of his narration, it is hardly a candid book. It is history accidentally told from the viewpoint of the maker of the history. Another kind of ulterior purpose is involved in the personal history of Saint Paul, who was so tremendously influential on subsequent spiritual confessions. The part of the account which is in Paul's own voice is the Epistles, and these are deliberately hortatory and aloof.

The crisis in Paul's experience, the conversion on the road to Damascus, is given in the Acts of the Apostles.[8] The account is in the third person and given from the vantage of Ananias, who performs the persuasive miracle. Even when the disciples of Damascus save Paul from the irate Jews by lowering him over the wall in a basket, it is as though he were a very foreign bundle. We will never know what was going through Paul's mind, and we do not know much more when he later takes over the narrative, for the very nature of the apostolic confession demands a selflessness before the saved and an imperiousness before the antagonist. Sometimes Paul inverted these rhetorical tactics, but either can appear calculated.

Such calculation is dominant in the tradition of classical rhetoric, which makes it difficult for the writer to take himself by surprise, or even appear to do so. An unbuttoned informality rarely comes through in antiquity; occasionally in the Old Testament, in the Greek lyric, and perhaps in Catullus, but it is a quality that is not fostered by the generalizing tendency of all classical literature. In the *Meditations* of Marcus Aurelius, which might also be entitled "To Himself," there is the studied Stoic complacency that enforces a removal from the things of which life is made up. The ideal is the equanimity of the dray horse, and when things go badly, or there is a temptation to intemperance, one must be willed or reasoned back into shape.

Begin each day by telling yourself: Today I shall be meeting with indifference, ingratitude, insolence, disloyalty, ill-will, and selfishness—all of them due to the offenders' ignorance of what is good or evil. But for my part I have long perceived the nature of good and its nobility, the nature of evil and its meanness, and also the nature of the culprit himself, and who is my brother (not in the physical sense, but as a fellow-creature similarly endowed with reason and a share of the divine); therefore none of those things can injure me, for nobody can implicate me in what is degrading.[9]

There were some dark days for the emperor along the Danube, and no doubt such thoughts keep him tranquil in camp and court, but the sentiment has the ring of an Emersonian homily, and sounds a bit compensatory. We might wonder about the unrecorded passions that could have made a better book. Misch treats such documents as steps on the passage from generalizing to individualizing reflection. "Marcus Aurelius expressly puts to himself the question, 'What am I?' But this question of self-knowledge does not concern his own individuality, but has reference to man's nature, and finds its answer through the general distinction between the reason or the rational will, as the centre of the person, and both the body and the soul."[10] This is why there is such a curious, even frustrating, lack of detail in the work, for physical encumbrances are precisely what must be shed if one is to achieve this state of perfect human nature. So those who have the greatest influence on his life remain faceless and flawless. "My mother set for me an example of piety and generosity, avoidance of all uncharitableness—not in actions only, but in thought as well—and a simplicity of life quite unlike the usual habits of the rich."[11] And evidently a very unmotherly austerity.

There is a continuity between the Roman and the Christian view of man that depends both on Paul's Hellenizing the doctrines of Christ and the tendency of early Christianity to adapt itself to local conditions. Because of this, the generality of the ancients became the spirituality of the confessional literature of the church fathers. Misch again puts the case: "The Aristotelians regarded the individual human being as a mere instance of a generality—of the uniform nature of man; and sought to resolve Man's individual character into a combination, varying from case to case, of universal qualities, or 'elements of form,' possessed by him in common with other individuals."[12] Such "elements of form" could have come originally from the articulated figure and the dismembered soul, which Snell says characterized earliest Greek thought about man, as well as the idealized forms that we see in classical statuary. At the end of this period they become, through convenient metamorphosis, the cardinal virtues and scarlet sins of Christian confessionals. This very change might be seen in the writings of Saint Augustine. His early dialogues are soliloquies with reason or *ratio*, which would be perfectly understood by at least the Platonic line of classical thought. Then there is the crisis—actually crises—in his life which leaves him lost and wandering in himself in a fashion that has seemed very modern. He was "the first to perceive the concrete fullness of the inner life," and this led him to write, "I became a great question for myself."[13] Yet those who are most eager to advance Augustine as one of us have their doubts. William Barrett says that he was an "existential lyricist," but adds that this aspect of him was dormant until our times, while the theologian dominated.[14] Misch writes that Augustine is specifically unlike the soul-searchers of the eighteenth century, for whom "the individual had lost that natural confidence in action and judgment, and could only attain it by intellectual effort."[15]

Still, Augustine's consideration of his own life is so full that we can see him more clearly than any person living before the Italian Renaissance. But we must also remember that he is not Boswell, Rousseau, Casanova, or Wordsworth; that he did not tell his life's story for the sheer delight in the discovery and the telling. In one way *The Confessions* is a sort of preamble to *The City of God* in that it establishes his authority through its testament to his salvation and vision, as though an extended examination of himself for its own sake would be unseemly. He is not only aware of the narcissism such a task as his might imply, but he is conscious that God has no reason to care about his transgressions, or that he might earn salvation through an account which would be no news to God. So he writes, "Can any praise be worthy of the Lord's majesty? I have said before, and I shall say again, that I write this book for the love of your love."[16] This is the tone throughout. Augustine treats his life as an exemplum for those who revere him, implying that his salvation was not easily won, and no matter how fallen they might be they can still imitate his strivings. The work is not so much a confession as it is an account of the education of Augustine, and although the work is addressed to God, the real audience is made up of Augustine's penitent readers.

Augustine's work is unlike any other autobiography before Rousseau's in that he is concerned with a process. In this he contrasts with Paul, who experienced a miraculous removal of the scales from his eyes, or with Marcus Aurelius, who writes from an achieved contentment. It is even an account that in this way contrasts to the uniform brag of Cellini or Lord Herbert. Only Montaigne comes close to such a feeling for the process of the growth of the self, yet in his case the form of the essay results in a staccato effect. The process in Augustine's case involves the surrender of his will to the will of God. He begins by wondering how it can be, since God made everything in the world, that he could have been so wicked. He decides that in wickedness his will was being tested by being in opposition to God, and that the surrender of his will to that of God is a difficult process. We are loath to give up what we think of as ourselves, and it takes hard knocks to make us accept the paradox that we are most ourselves when we give ourselves to God. "Or is it rather that I should not exist, unless I existed in you? For all things find in you their origin, their impulse, the centre of their being."[17] It is this idea to which Augustine returns again and again to gnaw on in a style all his own.

I was told that we do evil because we choose to do so of our own free will, and suffer it because your justice rightly demands that we should. I did my best to understand this, but I could not see it clearly. I tried to raise my mental perceptions out of the abyss which engulfed them, but I sank back into it once more. Again and again I tried, but always I sank back. One thing lifted me up into the light of your day. It was that I knew I had a will, as surely as I knew that there was life in me. When I choose to do something or not to do it, I was quite certain that it was my own self, and not some other person, who made this act of will, so that I was on the point of understanding that herein lay the cause of my sin. If I did anything against my will, it seemed to me to be something which happened to me rather than something which I did, and I looked upon it not as a fault, but as a punishment. And because I thought of you as a just God, I admitted at once that your punishments were not unjust.[18]

The prideful will is, however, the last citadel to surrender, and no matter how much he wishes to give himself definition as a man of God, he cannot take the final step. He had first embraced the Manichaean belief that good and evil were two forces external to us, but fought out their differences within us. Augustine had to accept the doctrine that the evil forces within him sprang from his own free will, and this involved a responsibility he was not eager to accept. So he writes, "My inner self was a house divided against itself."[19] At the conversion in the Milanese garden in August 386, he experienced "Bodily actions" that he could not have willed, and this was one of the experiences that led him to see that there was a will stronger than his own, to which his own must surrender.[20] "And all that you asked of me was to deny my own will and accept yours."[21]

Most confessional literature has imitated the stunning conversion of Saint Paul rather than the tortuous one of Saint Augustine. There is a dramatic simplicity in Paul that is easier to reduce to a formula—if not a cliché—but Augustine is embarrassingly specific about his transgressions in order to convince us of the radical spiritual change he had to undergo. He is not, however, as specific as such a scoffer as Byron makes him out to be. There are passages that deal with his sins that seem more concerned with suggesting as many of the seven deadly as he can than in presenting the scarifying details. He draws a moral rather than a picture. Yet the idea of a moral morphology begins even before his memory, for he confesses he cannot remember himself as an infant: "Little by little I began to realize where I was and to want to make my wishes known to others, who might satisfy them. But this I could not do, because my wishes were inside me, while other people were outside, and they had no faculty which could penetrate my mind. So I would toss my arms and legs about and make noises, hoping that such few signs as I could make would show my meaning, though they were quite unlike what they were meant to mime."[22] The willingness begins in the infant animal, but in making this point Augustine details the actions of the infant in a manner brief but clear. Before his time, such a description would be the material for a moral parable, or the vehicle for a poetic metaphor, like the bear licking its cub into the form of a bear. Augustine makes more of the scene. There may even be a touch of rare comedy. Yet the details remain few, for he pretends to address God and not his human flock, and of course God would be disinterested in the details. The famous passage that tells of his youthful theft of pears when he was sixteen is as concerned with the original forbidden fruit as it is with the pears. "There was a pear-tree near our vineyard, loaded with fruit that was attractive neither to look nor to taste. Late one night a band of ruffians, myself included, went off to shake down the fruit and carry it away, for we had continued our games out of doors until well after dark, as was our pernicious habit. We took away an enormous quantity of pears, not to eat them ourselves, but simply to throw them to the pigs. Perhaps we ate some of them, but our real pleasure consisted in doing something that was forbidden."[23] There are many details that a modern writer would include to give texture to the scene which Augustine leaves out, and I suspect most readers fill in the blanks on their own. How many pears, ruffians, and pigs were there? Augustine is not even sure if they ate any of the pears, and he doesn't care, for such questions are for the earth-bound, and he is trying to encourage in us a contempt for the world. Another of his youthful follies was to write a book called "Beauty and Proportion, in two or three volumes as far as I remember. You know how many there were, O Lord. I have forgotten, because by some chance the book was lost and I no longer have it."[24] And could not care less.

Even though Augustine is guilty of fornication, avarice, sodomy, blasphemy, the study of law, and writing poetry (in that general order), the details of these vices are deliberately clouded. Perhaps he wishes to titillate his readers with the details of nothing more naughty than the theft of some rotten pears. Another aspect of this is that he is most specific and dramatic when he is recounting what is presumably the evil which overtakes his student and disciple Alypius. In one of the most memorable scenes, the young man is dragged off to a gladiatorial performance in Rome, after he had forsworn such things. He agrees to go with his rowdy companions, but says he will shut his eyes. Yet he cannot remain master of himself when he hears a roar from the crowd, and opens his eyes with confidence that he will keep control over his passions. "When he saw the blood, it was as though he had drunk a deep draught of savage passion. Instead of turning away, he fixed his eyes upon the scene and drank in all its frenzy, unaware of what he was doing. He revelled in the wickedness of the fighting and was drunk with the fascination of bloodshed. He was no longer the man who had come to the arena, but simply one of the crowd which he had joined, a fit companion for the friends who had brought him."[25] Augustine does not let us see what Alypius saw, yet the experience is one of the most vivid and closely analyzed in the work. The episode might well have happened to another, but it appears to be so deeply felt—even more than the feelings of remorse that

Augustine expresses over his traffic with whores when his concubine returns to Africa from Milan—that we wonder if the experience might have actually happened to Augustine and that he could control it better by projecting it onto the experience of another. In either case, role playing and imaginative projections become a standard device in the autobiographical mode, whether it is the suicide of a young man named Jerusalem that allowed Goethe to objectify his romantic depression in Werther, or the conventional scene of voyeurism in first-person pornographic narratives. The moral of the scene is that Alypius believes that he has mastery over the evil world, but sensation and the flesh hang on his will. Alypius is not fed by his will, but rather imprisoned in the passions of his fit companions. The scene is an appropriate way station on the pilgrimage that leads to the surrender of our will to the will of God, for this is where the education of Augustine must lead us.

One of the most famous works by Benvenuto Cellini is a statue of a naked Perseus with a sword in one hand, and in the other the severed head of Medusa. Although he admired greatly everything he did, his account of his achievements in his *Life* suggests that he particularly liked this piece. Although there is no hint of it in his book, one might wonder if he thought of himself as the demigod of plaited muscles and sharp sword who slew the snaky-haired Gorgon. For Cellini is totally unlike Saint Augustine. He is perfectly confident of his abilities, he is never wrong, and his occasional references to God suggest that God is fortunate to have Cellini on earth to make beautiful objects, and to smite the rascals and fools whom Cellini comes across. There are also the princes and popes whom he serves, and toward them he is humble, if the price is right. Besides, he enjoys dropping names. There are his fellow artists of the century, a few of whom, like Michelangelo and Leonardo, just might be his superiors.[26] But Cellini's main delight is in the tales he tells of his successes at court, in camp, and between the sheets. The reader takes delight in Cellini's delight, but he never expects insight or wisdom from Cellini, and Cellini never offers any.

Cellini defines himself in terms of his family and his city, and beyond that he sees his greatness and immortality depending on his art. Although he says that the book was written to amuse himself—he started it at fifty-eight, dictating to a boy while he worked in his studio—as he proceeds there is a touch of paranoia in his defense of his work and his attack on the critics and his fellow artists. He cannot stomach Vasari, and many of his works are done in a certain medium because someone said it could not be done. He has left enough of merit to testify to his talent, but if some of his works often seem a bit facile compared to the great number of masterpieces of his age, his own *Life* suggests why, for it shows him in his own words waltzing through the world, seeing only himself. He is proud of his family, even though his birth was humble, and traces his ancestry back through his great-grandfather and finds the family name in ancient times. He is also proud to be a Florentine, and will avenge any aspersion cast on a city founded by Caesar. This concern with time and place—which is different from the fixing of the individual at the end of a series of begats—begins in the Italian Renaissance. It can be illustrated in the antiquarian studies of Petrarch two centuries earlier. In Cellini's case it is cause for his pugnaciousness, if no better cause comes to hand. He is perfectly clear that he has been favored by fate, because when he was but three years old he picked up a scorpion and would not surrender it, but his father clipped off its tail and claws without harm, and Cellini presents his survival as miraculous.[27] Since, among other things, he was a part-time necromancer, he believes that he will survive all sorts of scrapes because of the smile of fortune as well as his remarkable skill. He is, for example, heroic beyond measure in a defense of Rome. "I carried on with my work at the guns, and not a day passed without my achieving some outstanding success. As a result my stock with the Pope went up and up. Hardly a day ended without my having killed some of the besiegers."[28] It is a role made for the late Errol Flynn, but Cellini does not play his life with tongue in cheek. On one occasion he entertains a company of important artists whom he delights in naming.

In the middle of it all, a feather-brained young swaggerer . . . happened to pass by. When he heard the noise we were making, he started mocking and hurling insults about the Florentines. As host to all those accomplished artists I took this as a personal affront and so, very softly, without being noticed, I went out and confronted him. He was standing there with his tart, carrying on with his jeering to make her laugh. I went straight up to him and demanded if he was the fellow who had been rash enough to insult the Florentines. He immediately retorted: "I'm that very man." When he said that, I lifted my hand, hit him in the face, and shouted: "Then I'm *this very man*."[29]

Of course this leads to a scuffle, and then a duel in which Cellini's honor is unblemished, because the young swaggerer refuses to show up. The question of honor is terribly important to Cellini. In this encounter it involves his role as host and as Florentine. In others it might be his family. It is only when his art is criticized that we have a sense that something more personal, which might be thought of as his ego, is involved. The ultimate test of this honor is the duel, and Cellini is himself the kind of swaggerer who doesn't avoid them, but also the kind of bully who comes out well. There is the possibility of humor in such material, but Cellini is only capable of practical jokes, such as sneaking up on the taunter and his tart. In another scene a friend of his has come to dinner and brought a whore along. She makes eyes at Cellini (all women do), but he would not steal his friend's woman. Besides, she is thirty years old. So when his friend and his lady retire Cellini seduces her maid who has come along, although she is "thirteen or fourteen." Even Casanova would have found the situation comic, but Cellini simply records that he had a "wonderful time."[30]

A curious aspect of Cellini's account of his life is that the world he describes has no faces and no details. The various scenes he re-creates are vivid in that they have pace and the dialogue is sprightly, but the characters are faceless, and we have no idea what things look like, unless they are made by Cellini and are for sale. It is as though he passes through the world encapsulated in his honor and his ego, and this reduces all else to the flatness of a stage constructed precisely for his heroic acts. This result might seem odd, for Cellini obviously had an eye for form and color, but it is the eye of the merchant-artisan rather than the poet. He never mentions the flora of his Tuscany, unless it is to describe a floral design he is engraving. He must cross the Alps on his way to the court of Francis the First, but there is not a word about the Alpine scenery. The party must cross a treacherous bridge and they are mocked by a Frenchman for walking their horses. The Frenchman then falls into the river, but fortunately Cellini is there to save him. In the account we are only told how wide and deep the river is and how treacherous the bridge, possibly to excuse Cellini from bravely riding across.[31] Throughout the book the world seems made to foolishly taunt Cellini, and he to flail it with his retorts, sword, and art.

Girolamo Cardano, who was an exact contemporary of Cellini, shows many of the same attitudes in *The Book of My Life*, even though his interests and talents were very different. Cardano was a Milanese physician who imagined himself a second Galen, and even the memoir he writes is partly in imitation of Galen's autobiographical letters. He is also aware of the virtue of reflecting on his life in the manner of Marcus Aurelius. There is, therefore, none of the scene painting and braggadocio that we have from Cellini, for Cardano was a solitary and reflective man. He is aware of the contrast between his life and that of a man of the world. "My autobiography, however, is without any artifice; nor is it intended to instruct anyone; but, being merely a story, recounts my life, not tumultuous events."[32] Then he, like Cellini, places great emphasis on his humble but ancient family name, and the identity which he enjoys by being from Milan. Because of the sequestered nature of his life, he presents essays rather than scenes. He writes about dress, gambling, prudence—reducing his life to useful generalities, in spite of his modesty in saying that he has no intent to instruct anyone. Throughout these informal essays Cardano refers to his generalized experiences, and it is clear that although he is old and bitter at the time of writing he once took great pride in his appearance and health. Indeed, there is not a little nostalgic posturing. He is also proud of the way he has been able to save those (especially if they are rich and powerful) who have been given up for dead by other physicians. Still, he muses, they will all die anyway, and his great talents will have been expended for nothing. This is a theme which haunts the book, this longing for some kind of vicarious immortality. Cellini seems confident of it through his art, and his *Life* is mainly a reinforcement of his statues and knickknacks, but Cardano despairs that his son, a murderer, has let the family name die out, and that after him there is nothing.[33] This is surely another reason for his having written his life. His patients are dead, his son is a fool, but the book may live. It has, and what is so very unusual is that it was published during his lifetime and widely read. The first English translation was published in 1573, three years before Cardano's death. Cellini's *Life*, in contrast, was not published until 1728—a most modest occurrence considering the book and its author.

An aspect of autobiographies written before the late eighteenth century is their serious tone. This is a quality that unites such different works as those by Saint Augustine, Cellini, and Cardano. Montaigne is an exception to which I will come, but his case suggests a rhetorical device in those autobiographical works that do indulge in some levity at the author's own expense. Montaigne was able to investigate his own mind and being through many tentative voices which were not wholly his own, so that Montaigne the writer could be amused at Montaigne the living man and, by reserving himself, reveal himself more completely. A comparable situation obtains in the case of Sir Thomas Browne who could show his false starts and absurd beliefs in a prose so delightfully ornate that it becomes a parody of itself. Neither Montaigne nor Browne were writing autobiographies or lives, and perhaps could not have conceived of such a project. The serious writers of lives—aside from their expressed intention to write moral exempla for their heirs—are deadly serious about their task. This is an atmosphere that continues through the eighteenth century, even after the pressures for a purely didactic tale were not so great. The exceptions to this were, I think significantly, those who increased the distance employed by Montaigne between the teller and the tale. The preeminent illustration of this is Laurence Sterne, who teases the reader with heartfelt sentiment, and then shows it to be sentimentality; but then also leaves the question open as to whether the oscillation between the two may be what makes us human. In the *Sentimental Journey* he even reduces that distance between the teller and the tale to such an extent that we are not certain that they are not identical. The more usual and most revealing device is to maintain the distance, as between Goethe and Werther or Wilhelm Meister, or between Byron and Don Juan. Such "standing aside" may not be truly possible until the problem of how the self can know the self is fully articulated in the middle of the eighteenth century.

Yet if there is one writer before this time who used this "standing aside" strategy in order to understand himself—or pretend to allow us to watch him try to understand himself—it is Montaigne. There are also other peculiarly modern techniques used in the *Essays*. First, he addresses the reader as a solitary or a distant friend. He does not pretend that the written word is the shadow of pulpit oratory; or perhaps that the reader is an unacknowledged snoop reading a diary or memoir; or that what we read is a record of a philosophical dialogue. This in itself is unusual, for printing was just over a century old when the essays were published in 1580, and it was less than a century since people had widely read in solitude instead of being read to in an assembly from an exceptionally valuable (and therefore sacred—even if it wasn't scripture) manuscript. This solitary and silent reading was a very Protestant and potentially seditious experience, for there is no control over the imaginings, speculations, and impertinences of the silent reader as there would be in public readings. The invention and spread of movable type is probably the most important mechanical contributor to the idea of the unique self, but other forces—religious and political revolutions, the rediscovery and admiration for classical models of being—retarded the assertion of the self. The intimacy between the writer and the "dear reader," which we tend to think of as beginning in the eighteenth century, assumes a situation which was rarely assumed before that time. When modern novelists and essayists use this tactic it seems to be a coy game in which the feigned intimacy is often a veneer for a writer who lies like a rug; we know it, and we know he knows we know it. This is not the usual situation in the eighteenth century with the legions of writers who addressed "dear readers." They might (I think of Addison, Swift, Fielding) have a final jape at our expense in the last scene, but the "dear reader" formula usually is a sign that the host, an *eiron* with a twinkle in his eye, is inviting us to laugh behind our hands at an *alazon* in the shape of a Ned Softly or a Bridget Allworthy.

When Montaigne begins his book, "This book was written in good faith, reader," he is proposing to be honest and candid, and although there may be ironies at his own expense later on, he is also as honest as he can be throughout. He goes on to say that his purpose is domestic and private, which was much more literally the case with the many didactic autobiographies written in the seventeenth century for family consumption, and not made public for a hundred years or more, and that he will not hide his flaws. "Thus, reader, I am myself the matter of my book; you would be unreasonable to spend your leisure on so frivolous and vain a subject."[34] This is a tone which is genial, candid, and yet ironic. Montaigne wrote at a time when lives were told as exempla. They were either heroic, as in the case of fawning tributes to monarchs or simple saints and brave martyrs, or they were dire warnings, as in the case of stories of the fall of tyrannous princes or the doggereled histories of highwaymen and murders. In all of these traditions, whether they be hagiographical as in the gory lives of John Foxe or the illustrations of the workings of fate as in John Gower's *The Fall of Princes,* the result is a bloodless formula. Montaigne proposes to write in none of these traditions. Indeed, his next line is "A Dieu donc, de Montaigne," and then he gives the date: March 1, 1580. With that Montaigne—or at least the half of Montaigne out of whose experiences the thoughts grow—disappears into his book.

Montaigne says a great deal about himself in his essays, so much that it has been possible to rearrange and patch and come up with a work called *The Autobiography of Michel de Montaigne.*[35] However this is not what he had in mind, for he himself is not the true subject; his experiences and thoughts are simply the material of metaphors which lead to other truths. Bacon, who knew and imitated Montaigne's essays in his own, leaves this element out. In his essays, which so often treat the same subjects, the metaphors are drawn from generalized experience, and Bacon's is a disembodied voice coming from some secularized pulpit. He tells us that we are foolish to fear death any more than the next day, for they are equally unknown. His opening line chides us with childish fears: "Men fear death, as children fear to go in the dark."[36] It is a cliché phrased anew, and this is his purpose. Bacon does not tell us that he himself once feared death, but was able to talk himself out of such foolish fancies. Montaigne tells us little more about himself, but he does present his thoughts on death as though a process were involved. He begins by quoting Cicero to the effect that all philosophy is a preparation for death. Marcus Aurelius or Boethius could have served him just as well. Then he says, "study and contemplation draw our soul out of us to some extent and keep it busy outside the body; which is a sort of apprenticeship and semblance of death."[37] Here there is implied a meditation and struggle with his fears in his tower, and the splitting of the soul from the body—another instance of "standing aside"—still leaves the body to pain and dissolution. Here he and we are involved, while Bacon blithely offers the pap that death is simply a longer sleep. Erich Auerbach says that the method of Montaigne is experimental or inductive, and that through the process he can *see* Montaigne as he cannot see earlier writers.[38]

Yet Montaigne does not give us much of himself to see. Georges Gusdorf has proposed that the reason portraiture came of age in the sixteenth century is that excellent Venetian mirrors came to be widely popular, and for the first time people could really take a good look at themselves.[39] There is no doubt that the great number of self-portraits of the century—memorably of Dürer and one by Parmigianino in a convex mirror (1524), and later a great number by Rembrandt—might have been the result of handy mirrors, or in some cases it might simply have been the availability of a free sitter. Certainly there is not a comparable growth of self-portraiture in prose literature. In the essay on education Montaigne wishes to make the point that children learn best when not goaded by fear, and so cites his own experience: "without the whip and without tears, I learned a Latin quite as pure as what my schoolmaster knew, for I could not have contaminated it or altered it."[40] This may leave open the quality of his tutor's Latin, but that would serve more as a comment on the general state of learning than on Montaigne. There are other little details, such as that his father always had a servant wake the young Montaigne to the sound of music, but this is an embarrassed comment on his class, which culminates with the observation that "all this novel education of mine did for me was to make me skip immediately to the upper classes."[41]

The major spring to Montaigne's archness is a sense of relativity unusual in an age of many dogmatisms. In his famous contemplation of cannibalism he says, "each man calls barbarism whatever is not his own practice."[42] Through a projection of the mind he is able to imagine other ways of doing things and other ways to see the world. This results in a struggle with the character imposed on him by his class, culture, and age. Such refusal to commit himself to the character society expected of him can also be instanced in Erasmus and Petrarch, but in Montaigne this is a stance constantly maintained for purposes of speculation and investigation. It is not that he escapes Renaissance typologies and categories, or that he is immune to the Renaissance penchant for analogical thinking. He is, for example, a dualist who is perfectly clear about the bifold world of body and soul, although he is clearer than most about the mind being dependent on the body. He is sure that there is a mysterious sympathy between himself and the world, and that he too is a little world made cunningly: "This great world, which some multiply further as being only a species under one genus, is the mirror in which we must look at ourselves from the proper angle. In short, I want it to be the book of my student."[43] In the hermetical tradition of a doctrine of signatures one was to look at the world to see how God the Maker signed it and read there what messages He left which might lead to salvation. The old image is here in Montaigne, but his understanding is more of a psychological than a millennial kind. In the end, Montaigne's psychology is social psychology, and his concern with himself is ultimately an attempt to understand others. "I set forth a humble and inglorious life; that does not matter. You can tie up all moral philosophy with a common and private life just as well as with a life of richer stuff. Each man bears the entire form of man's estate."[44] In this, too, we must accept him as being sincere. For as unique as he was, Montaigne sought universal patterns in himself. In this he is very different from, for example, Boswell or Sterne, who sought the being of man in their own quirkiness. The contrast is even more obvious if we think of him in contrast to the later Romantic self-revelers. Montaigne, by describing himself, sought to describe what man was; for the Byrons and the Shelleys it was a matter of describing what man could be.

This difference between the assertive ego, often seen in writers of the Renaissance, and the brooding introspection of Romantic writers, is not always easily seen when their actual words are placed side by side, but it is a difference which results in other meanings. One of the major characteristics of the Renaissance remarked on by all historians is the emphasis placed on individualism. It is certainly there, from the Italian Renaissance with its artistic signatures, through the upheavals caused by the discovery of the New World, and the bitter religious battles that followed the Reformation, down to the dominance of the Atlantic nations run by a practical and merchantile burgher class. Such individuality was based on respect for talent, or property and legal rights, but invariably stopped short of an interest in the drama of an idiosyncratic inner life. At the beginning of the Renaissance, man was everywhere a subject; at the end he was (at least in theory) a citizen—but his private visions were irrelevant to his political role. Yet a correlative of this change was that his own inner life was given a dignity, even an existence, that it had not had previously. At the beginning of the Renaissance, man's place in the world, as described for him by his princes and mediators with God, was perfectly clear. At the end of this period he was often himself responsible for his salvation as well as the material improvement of the world in which he lived. Instead of that sense of timelessness that forms the mind of the primitive, or the man with a hoe, halfway down the row that begins somewhere he can't remember and continues with absolute sameness over the horizon, men began to see that the world changed within the span of their own lives, or even in a few years. The ballad of the pliable "Vicar of Bray" recounts how he could live in one long life under five monarchs and a Protector, and adapt himself to four quite distinct forms of worship between 1640 and 1715. In the same time, the limits of the world were pushed out beyond the known continents, and the white blotches of the unknown on the globe were filled in with pink pretenses and names in Carolingian script. These changes were great and altered much. But the old ways die hard, and man's knowledge of the unknown in himself lagged behind.

The sense of individuality that we associate with a Cellini or a Montaigne was different from the ancient sense of individuality. In classical times there was a sense of the ego, which raised statues of the emperor in the temple and set him next to the gods. This made him in a way nonhuman, as well as inhuman, by making him superhuman. The details of the lives of the Caesars were unimportant for they were not really seen as contributing to the image—indeed they might detract from any godlike victories or strokes of genius. For a Cellini or a Montaigne, as different as they were, the details of life are treated as the integers that add up to a sum. Still, the total is not so much themselves as it is what is typical of their time and place. What makes their accounts seem so modern is that they are specific and secular, but their inner life is a blank or a contrivance—as though they were creating a new hagiography in which they were their own saints.

There are many lives and personal narratives from the seventeenth century, but they almost uniformly strive for patterns that are self-effacing. There are a number of journals of public events, especially from the period of the Commonwealth when events seemed to be moving so very swiftly. These were often private and, like Pepys', written in code or shorthand. The intent was to record and perhaps order events, and sometimes to vent spleen that would better be kept hidden. The other form of personal memoir is the confession, which in Evangelical hands, as in the case of John Bunyan in *Grace Abounding*, followed the tradition of the stunning miracle established by Saint Paul rather than the slow intellectual growth of Augustine. Such works have a purity in their drive, but the movement of the whole is allegorical. The confessor turns himself into a Mr. Christian and keeps at arms' length, or hovers between personal memory and an allegorical abstraction which is given meaning through the biblical analogue. Such a moral purpose is also evident in those memoirs by writers to the manor born who recount their experiences in order to instruct the immediate family. These differ little from the memoirs of the diseased, written by the beloved husband or wife left behind, except that when one's own life is the subject the writer often gets distracted by the delight of telling a tale and momentarily loses his didactic purpose.

One of the best examples of these elaborations on an entry in the family Bible is *The Life of Edward Herbert,* which (and this is a typical provenance) was discovered in the possession of his heirs by Horace Walpole, who connived it away and had it published by Dodsley in 1792. Herbert, who lived a fruitful life as courtier, ambassador, and philosopher, writes that he will tell only the truth about himself for the edification of his own family. He says, "so as my age is now past threescore, it will be fit to recollect my former actions, and examine what has been done well or ill, to the intent I may both reform that which was amiss, and so make my peace with God, as also comfort my self in those things which through God's great grace and favor have been done according to the rules of conscience, vertue and honor."[45] The turgidity of the expression here may be what leads Herbert from his moral purpose, but more likely this announcement of his purpose and intent is largely for the sake of form. Later on he says that there are the senses which are formed in the womb, but are useless there, so must be intended for use somewhere else. This must be the world. Then in the world there are developed the faculties of "Hope, Faith, Love, and Joy [which] never rest or fix upon any transitory or perishing object in this world, as extending themselves to something further than can be here given, and indeed acquiesce only in the perfect, eternal, and infinite."[46] Here analogy, which Vico called the besetting sin of the Renaissance, once more creates a pious equation for the benefit of the Herbert posterity.

Unlike earlier writers, Herbert actually gives us the facts of his life: his genealogy, his schooling, his interests, his successes. Much is left out or glozed over, for in the depression of the interregnum Herbert wished to cast a pleasant glow over his youthful successes, even though these might not fulfill his announced didactic intent. For example, there is a scene (no doubt real, but an echo of one in Cellini's *Life,* which was yet to be published) in which his servant almost drowns, but is happily saved by his master. "The Horse I rode upon [in the water] I remember cost me £40 and was the same Horse which Sir John Ayres hurt under me, and did swimm excellently well, carrying me and his back above Water; whereas that little Nag upon which Richard Griffiths rid, swam so low, that he must needs have drowned, if I had not supported him."[47] Heroism, luck, and bravery must take time for a former scrape and pleasure in the bargain. Montaigne might have wondered by Herbert's servant Dick was not on a fine horse, and he on a nag, but such a moral speculation does not occur to Herbert, for here and elsewhere the world is treated as his oyster. Herbert was also known in his time as a very model courtier who turned the ladies' heads at court and tweaked his enemies' noses in camp. He gives an account of an experience fighting the Spanish at Wezel. A challenge to single combat is sent from the Spaniards, and Lord Herbert accepts it. With a brave gentleman and two lackies he rides into the Spanish camp, but the commander forbids the duel to take place, and invites the English gentlemen to supper. "I finding nothing else to be done did kindly accept his offer, and so attending him to his Tent, where a brave Dinner being put on his Table, he placed the Duke of Newbourg uppermost at one end of the Table, and myself at the other, himself setting below us, presenting with his own hand still the best of that Meat his Carver offer'd him."[48] Honor is saved, and the code of the cavalier is adhered to irrespective of nations or religion. If there is a moral point here for the 1650s when this was written it would have little to do with the Christian virtues. Herbert might be the godfather of the Deists to come, but his own reflections about himself suggest he imagines something out of Mallory. Paul Delaney, after a thorough survey of seventeenth-century autobiographies, sums up the situation this way: "Seventeenth-century autobiography in Britain, far from being a lyrical expression of 'renaissance individualism,' was the servant of didactic, historical, or controversial purposes. Its practitioners devoted relatively little effort to establishing autobiography as a literary genre: caught up in the turmoil of contemporary religious and social struggles, they cared more for the content than for the style of their works, and aimed at functional cogency rather than aesthetic perfection."[49] The purpose of seventeenth-century autobiographies is not self-revelation, and I think that Delaney is quite right in not really criticizing these writers for not doing what they did not pretend to do, and probably wouldn't have understood as their failings if they were faced with them as such. These writers will tell their own histories in an anecdotal form (as does Lord Herbert, or in another fashion the diarists like Pepys and Evelyn), or they will meditate in the first person on the large metaphysical questions of life and death (as does Sir Thomas Browne, or in highly conventionalized ways Bunyan and a legion of eager confessors). But the two approaches were not combined. There are few meditations springing from the materials of the incidents of the author's life. The reason for this is that truth was not seen to lie at the end of this road, for the writer thought of his life as illustrative of general principles, not the source of truth.

The best-known memorialists of the early eighteenth century come through to us as gadabouts and extroverts. They could be querulous in a social age, when people of fashion were trained to be finely attuned to the affront, but they will reflect no more deeply about themselves and society than John Aubrey from whom they trace their descent. Joseph Spence, for example, was widely known as a kind of professional grand tourist, and was a jolly intimate of London literary coffee houses. His *Anecdotes, Observations and Characters of Books and Men* was well known, as books could be in the tight literary circles of his time, even though it was not published until 1768, fifty years after his death.[50] The work is full of gossip which Pope and others found useful, and Spence's descriptions of and enthusiasm for Italian architecture was influential on the English neoclassical style. The work is not a true journal. It is rather a potpourri of chitchat and wagers on the literary stock market. Spence was a collector of people and views and knickknacks, and over the long haul a smashing bore. Even better known were the memoirs and jests of Mrs. Laetitia Pilkington, who tells us in her anecdotal fashion much about the aged Swift. The bulk of her work, which was published in 1748–54, has to do with what so and so said over coffee on such and such occasion. The turns and clever retorts we might suspect of being invented by the writer, but she rarely claims them, as though she is just the hovering pen in the corner. Yet Mrs. Pilkington also presents her *Memoirs* as a cautionary tale of her fall, even though she also has harsh words about "Clergymen & ladies of honour," hypocrites all, who have attacked her unjustly.[51] This brief and perhaps conventional flurry of repentance and righteousness is laid aside for the bright stories to follow. Certainly, Mrs. Pilkington's petulance is nothing compared to the prolonged paranoia of Rousseau's *Confessions*.

6

Rogues and Adventurers

If I can please myself with my own Follies, have I not a
plentiful Provision for Life? If the World thinks me a
Trifler, I don't desire to break in upon their Wisdom: let
them call me any Fool, but an Unchearful one!
—Colley Cibber, *An Apology for the Life of Colley Cibber*

Such unbuttoned memoirs as those of Joseph Spence and Mrs. Pilkington present examples of a fresh and flexible prose, very like that of
the private letters of the period. This is a prose different from that of
the public journalism of the early eighteenth century, although both
styles contributed to the equipment of the novelists who were to follow shortly. One style taught the management of incident; the other of
character. But an autobiographical form even more important to the
novel in terms of structure was the literature of roguery, which in turn
was often indebted to the tradition of the Spanish picaresque. These
rogues' tales left the drawing room to recount the life of mayhem on
the highway and in the inns, but safely ended with a contrite recantation and admonition. They were sometimes in doggerel and were sold
by hawkers at the foot of the gallows where the culprit was to give his
last performance. Because of the very ephemeral and pious nature of
such productions they were inevitably formulaic. But such literature
achieved its highest use and art in the tales of Jonathan Wild, as these
were employed by Fielding and Gay to give the Tory tweak to the
administration of Robert Walpole.[1]

Another form of this literature involved a collection of exciting
exploits in illegal lowlife attributed to one rogue, or retold by him
during his itinerant life. The best example of such a mixture is Richard
Head's life of Meriton Latroon. In the anecdotal memoirs, and even in
the gallows dodgers, there is a feelling of specific time and place; indeed they are much more specific than the religious confessional, in
which the intent is to escape the worldly. Still there is a kind of
empty-headedness to these tales. The characters, whether high or low,
are content to illustrate their social position, just as their literary productions are content to hide in a literary tradition. As sprightly as

75

these accounts are, the first-person method of narration is simply a convenience, and the focus is rarely on the narrator. Incident is all, and any reflection on incident is couched in the most conventional of phrases, for the literature of the period, from Pope to the street ballad, is still reaffirming old truths.

Richard Head's *The English Rogue: Described in the Life of Meriton Latroon, A Witty Extravagant,* which was published in 1665 after Head had been requested to refine it, is an excellent example of this emphasis on incident. Head was a hack with a sharp and inquisitive ear for the tales of London lowlife, and he pours all his discoveries into *The English Rogue,* loosely hanging them on the life of Latroon. Latroon has a wryness toward his life and its viscissitudes that both makes it bearable and serves as a warning against any notion that rogueries result in happiness. Many of the jests and turns have the flavor of street wit so worn that in its day it might not have gained much of a laugh. The work begins in this way: "After a long and strict inquisition after my father's pedigree, I could not find any of his ancestors bearing a coat; surely length of time had *worn* it out."[2] This style might be considered a prose Hudibrastic, and it is used whenever the narrator contrasts his own innocence with the wiles of the world. He sees and we see that everyone in the world is out for himself, but he pretends to be slower to this discovery than the reader. He is the son of a prankster corrupted at Oxford, and finally rusticated for his lewd behavior, who then goes home to amaze the yokels at the fireside with words that sound like Greek, such as "Shoulderamutton" and "Kapathumpton."[3] The rogue-hero is born in Ireland as a result of a dalliance of this prankster, and is then suddenly separated from his parents by insurgents during the Irish rebellion of 1641. From this time on he is on the road with thieves, gypsies, beggars, and finally graduates to the company of highwaymen. Throughout, the narrator presents a virtual encyclopedia of the methods of these trades, and his personal anecdotes are given only to illustrate these evil ways. He gives an account of how a leg can be blackened by a beggar with a mixture of dirt and lye so as to look pathetically burned. He tells how to pick locks, and gives a glossary of gypsy underworld terms. All this is to forearm the wary citizen against being taken, but along the way there are erratic implications that the honest citizen is no better than the dishonest. There is even an admiration and delight in the clever pranks of his colleagues, but rarely in his own pranks, for the narrator remains undescribed, and exists only in the incongruously ornate style assigned to him by a literary hack. Our hero is probably most involved when as an apprentice he steals from his master to support a whore in chambers on the promise that she would be faithful to him. For every favor she allows him he must pay with a stolen "scarf, a hood, a ring, a whisk," and so forth, and when such tribute is not to be had, she rails at him for undoing her. Throughout this experience the whore remains faceless as well as faithless, and Latroon's reactions to the experience are not even recounted. Indeed, the chapter dissolves into "A Short survey of a cunning whore" in which the whole scene is reduced to a stereotypic presentation of the sly apprentice who has so often cuckolded his master and then become the doting cuckold himself and his beloved the conniving shrew.[4]

Head was a hack, but not an ill-read one. Whenever he seems to run out of tales told over a pint, he goes to literature for new comic japes. He has Latroon refer to Ben Jonson's *Bartholomew Fair,* which is a likely source for some of his maker's material. For example, at a nadir of his fortunes he attempts to marry for money, but in consonance with the literary cliché he is deceived "in person and portion."[5] Head also allows his hero to be a poet himself and to pay his victims, both gulls and farmers' daughters, with poems. He will also pillage the classics for atmosphere and dignity: "Though melancholy night had drawn her sable curtains about her hemisphere, yet the coverlet of our optics was not yet laid down to admit our active senses to their usual rest and repose."[6] Et cetera. In this case the reason our hero has not gone to sleep is that he is being entertained by three Amazon highwaymen—or women—whom he eventually must leave because of his sexual exhaustion. This episode is more of an artistic heightening of the adventure rather than a convincing turn of events. It also gives the author a chance to vary his tale by having the ladies tell their own histories (in language exactly like that assigned to Latroon), as we later have a number of chapters devoted to the character of a crooked lawyer. Through all this, the focus is away from our witty extravagant, and when he is himself most involved his role is glozed with convention. The hero is conventionally caught when undone by accomplices, and behind bars recants his evil ways. He also helpfully details all the ways that travelers might avoid being relieved of their possessions. This is not very convincing, since he seemed to enjoy his japes and dalliance so much while free and to recant only when caught. Head doesn't even let Latroon suffer the transportation to which (in August of 1650) he is condemned, for in a dizzy epilogue he goes through shipwreck, is sold into slavery, survives pirates, and in the last scene is happily living with a dusky maid in India.

This conclusion would seem to dilute the recantations that Meriton Latroon professes at the end of his tale. In such accounts written during this period there is a strange mingling of the moral exemplum and

a level-headedness which admits the possibility of good fortune falling willy-nilly to the wicked. Latroon writes that he has "endeavored,
by drawing up a list of my own evil actions, to frighten others from
the commission of the like . . . aiming at nothing more than how I
might completely limn vice in her proper ugly shape."[7] Yet his burdens at the end seem light, if not enviable. Such an ending is not
atypical, and results from that curious shift from the didactic tale to
the true-life adventure, and at this time writers try to satisfy the requirements of both forms. Such exile to a balmy clime occurs at the
end of Grimmelshausen's *Simplicius Simplicissimus*, although the hero's
mood here is more like that of Timon of Athens. A murky morality is
even more clearly seen at the end of Defoe's adventure tales, in which
there is a frittering away of narrative materials that becloud the traditional recantation. In Defoe there is a greater sense of character than in
Head's book. Latroon serves Head as a convenient grammatical and
narrative instrument, a kind of peg on which to hang his tale. Some of
the exploits were probably gained at first hand, others were surely
overheard, and a few culled from earlier literature of lowlife. To all this
Head adds glossaries and sermonettes. The result is a spirited potpourri, but it has little to do with what we normally think of as a
confession, an autobiography, or even an adventure tale. The reason
that Defoe is more successful is that he is able to select or invent
episodes that are consistent to the character and are arranged in an
imaginable chronological order. The main difference is that Defoe
thinks it important to refer to his characters' motivations. These are
always based on the simplest and most mechanical appetites, but they
are mentioned, whereas Latroon is driven by an unanalyzed whim.

The in these works about half-real highwaymen and half-imagined
picaros incident is all and character nothing—or at most little. Defoe
cannot bring Robinson Crusoe back to England but that he must come
by way of Spain, and over the snowy Pyrenees so that he can be
chased by wolves in southern France. Swift appears to both mock and
use this convention of the welter of incident on the way to stranding
Captain Gulliver, but for him to parody the travel adventure was not
also to direct his attention to character, and those moderns who trouble themselves about the psychological complexity of Lemuel Gulliver
are undoubtedly concerned about something that Swift would not
have recognized. Here, too, character is reduced to a type, a character-
nym, and is little more than a grammatical convenience.

The literature of lowlife and the picaresque through the seventeenth century clearly shows how the age saw character as mechanically divisible. The doctrine of the reigning humors supports such division, for it proposes that we are all in our mortal and ungolden state

dominated by blood or phlegm, yellow or black bile. Such theories are holistic and treat man as a mechanically finite entity. The tragedian laments his ruling passions and the satirist is amused by his eccentricities, but neither suggests depths that cannot be plumbed. In literature the results are often magnificent (the high winds raised in Miltonic breasts, the lopsided pretenses of Molière's fools), but we should approach this literature with something other than the modern's concern with the infinite complications of the self.

The picaresque of the seventeenth century offers illustrations of how the character can be analyzed through division. Cervantes implies that humanity can be divided, as are Don Quixote and Sancho Panza, into romantic ideality and practical appetite. His greatness is to mock and revere both extremes, as though the whole work were an embodiment and extension of a single mind. The illustrations are infinite in their variety, but the compass of the work inscribes the varieties of the ideal and the practical. A similar baroque inclusiveness is what makes Sterne's *Tristram Shandy* attractive, although there the major characters are reduced to varieties of romantic ideality, and the harsh practical world exists in the inanimate form of clocks and chamber pots, a clumsy forceps, and a filched sashweight. For all of his famous modernity of technique, Sterne's view of the mind still appears to be old-fashioned and holistic although his dependence on Locke's associationism suggests that the number of its parts are subject to a kind of geometric progression. Sterne's comic assumption is that if one knew all the influences on a mind a person could be wholly known, but that the task is inevitably aborted by weariness and finally death. Sterne forever hovers over the impossibility of completely knowing all there is to be known about a person, but his comic system assumes that the task—at least theoretically—can be completed. In this respect, Fielding, his contemporary, is more romantic and modern, for he extracts comedy from the absurd assumption that characters can be typed by their obsessions.

Cervantes's illustration of the human possibility results in the simultaneous presentation of the alternatives, most simply the ideality of Don Quixote and the practicality of Sancho Panza. Grimmelshausen offers another approach to this presentation of the holistic view of man by presenting his possibilities sequentially in *Simplicius Simplicissimus*. Here the hero goes through a series of radical metamorphoses. The various guises are so different one from another that it is hard to imagine they all belong to the same person. In a sense, they don't, for it is as though Grimmelshausen were trying to illustrate all the varieties of the human condition, and simply pins these on the person of Simplicius. The action takes place during the Thirty Years War, and its horrors and opportunities buffet the hero so severely that his very survival is comic. He begins in the simple state of the raw clay of humanity, so innocent that he doesn't even know his own name. When marauding soldiers come to the farm where he lives, he knows no more than to be amused at the tortures they inflict and amazed at the ingenuity they employ.

My knan was, as I thought, particularly lucky because he confessed [the whereabouts of valuables] with a laugh what others were forced to say in pain and martyrdom. No doubt because he was the head of the household, he was shown special consideration; they put him close to a fire, tied him by his hands and legs, and rubbed damp salt on the bottom of his feet. Our old nanny goat had to lick it off and this so tickled my knan that he could have burst laughing. This seemed so clever and entertaining to me—I had never seen or heard my knan laugh so long—that I joined him in laughter, to keep him company or perhaps to cover up my ignorance.[8]

This innocent will later be a court fool and still later a pious hermit, but he will also be leader of a band of freebooting soldiers, a rhyming courtier, and a quack. In these various guises he may have another name, but we are invited to believe that through these swings from divine simplicity to the depths of world-weary cynicism, he is but a single person. Once more, the concern is with outward events, and the reader must try to discern the nature of the hero from his acts, for there is always a gap where we might expect reflection. The whole tale is held together with conventional and artificial plot devices. The major one is the foundling theme. After Simplicius escapes the marauding soldiers who destroy the only home he ever knew, he wanders to the forest, where is is befriended by a hermit who teaches him how to read and write as well as imbuing him with contempt for the world. Much later this man turns out to be an exiled king and the father of Simplicius, and so another type of human scale is encompassed in a single frame and person. At one point in the story he even becomes a girl. Another organizational device involves characters who reappear during the travels of Simplicius. One is Oliver, who represents the chivalric hypocrisies of court life, and Herzbruder, who represents true Christian piety. Both offer chances for digression and parallel tales, yet these tales do not offer moral alternatives to Simplicius but rather suggest elaborations on his experiences. To put it another way, Oliver and Herzbruder (in spite of his name) are not prototypes of the nineteenth-century doppelgänger used to suggest unplumbable depths of mystery in the human soul; they are simply variations on the describable human condition.

Much can be made of the frontispiece, the "Phoenix Copper," of the original edition of *Simplicius Simplicissimus*. The diabolic comedy of the work is there suggested by a figure which has the tail of a fish, the wings of a bird, while one leg is that of a goat and the other that of a duck. The figure wears a sword, has the pointed ears of an ass, and a horned gargoyle's face. It displays a book which shows the symbols of Simplicius's occupations: a cannon, a crown, a mitre, a goblet, a cap with bells, and so on. On the ground at its feet are various masks, which appear more human than what we must assume is the real face. The implication would seem to be that society and circumstances make us wear masks that appear to be human, but when all are stripped away what we see is a composite beast. At just about the same time, the Earl of Rochester and Thomas Hobbes, in their different ways, were drawing the same dark conclusions. But all of them assumed that man could be known completely. What they described, however, was a far cry from the recoverable god in ruins promoted by Romantic writers just a century later.

Following a line of thought parallel to that of John Locke, and contemporaneously, Defoe elaborates the idea that character (and presumably ideas) is not innate, but rather the sum of environment, and that actions are largely the result of the need to gratify the appetites. We often sense that he would no more like to make moral judgments on these acts than a Balzac or Dreiser, but his age and language are too well equipped with moral judgments that assume an external and eternal truth. Therefore Defoe depicts a Nature that forgives all, but is trapped in a form that demands recantation from his memoirists. The result is a falling between two stools, but before that happens there is such attention to detail that his characters seem much more real than their contemporaries. The characters are still seen from the outside, and the main attention is to how hungers and passions can be gratified in a certain environment. Yet Defoe is astonishingly modern when compared to a writer like Head or Grimmelshausen—or even Swift. Meriton Latroon serves Head as a convenient bearer of the narrative, but with all his poems and seductions and villainies he never comes clearly into focus. On the other hand, Moll Flanders, Roxana, and Robinson Crusoe (and Defoe once termed *The Adventures of Robinson Crusoe* his spiritual biography) are seen completely by the reader, seen so clearly and completely that we feel there is nothing of them left to be seen that they or Defoe do not tell us. Latroon is simply the vehicle as well as the narrator of his tale, whereas Defoe's characters reflect on their stories—yet unlike a modern character they say all there is to be said about them. When Moll steals because she is hungry we accept her explanation as the complete and only explanation, for Defoe does not invite us to meditate on ironies behind the situa-

tion and character. His characterizations are often marvelously detailed, but they are still so curiously flat in their psychological dimensions that most historians of the novel are loath to push the date of the
beginning of the form back to include Defoe. And for this very reason:
there is an essential unreflectiveness and hardness to the surface of his
characters that makes them both predictable and disembodied. When
Roxana sends her husband to bed with her maid, and then watches
the proceedings with amused disinterest, her attitude is very close to
that of the reader toward the story, for we are not led to care about
these characters, because we are not allowed to participate in any
inner torment—or joy—that they might feel.[9] Defoe, and this is his
major point, reduces their contentment to a full belly. In this he an-
ticipates the naturalists of the nineteenth century, although they saw
that the full belly was a more complicated matter and were not so
simple or mechanistic in equating happiness with satiety.

Defoe's achievement depends on his seeing the world in which his
characters exist as one divested of magic. For earlier writers the world
is peopled by types through which a moral drama can be discerned.
The highwaymen that Head's Meriton Latroon meets on the road of
his life are nameless, and their amorality is pure and undefiled by
moral or psychological complications. They are kin to John Bunyan's
Mr. Badman, although Head's world is not accompanied with a rubric
of biblical allusions. Defoe reduced this moral element in his world, so
his characters are what they are and what they seem to be. One measure of this sense of the hard and practical reality of the world is the
reference to money. In Bunyan, coin is but one of many of the vanities
of the world—which can also include houses, wives, and children.
When Latroon is successful he is rewarded with a fine watch or a ring,
and sometimes gold, but we are never told how much the watch is
worth to his fence or how much gold he got. The point is that he steals
and that he is clever in his theft, but the value of the reward is of no
importance. Defoe is not so disinterested in sums. We know, almost
as surely as we know in the case of a character in a novel by a
nineteenth-century Naturalist, how much Moll or Roxana have in their
purse—and what their prospects are for more. Defoe offers us many
specific domestic details, such as those of costume, but it is mainly
through the details of the ledger that the world of his novel is de-
mythologized.

Yet the sense of human complexity that a modern reader expects in
his fictional characters is missing in Defoe. His characters tend to be
as flat and immutable as characters in detective stories. As earlier
writers tend to bleed their characters by linking them to a moral or
mythical significance, Defoe bleeds them by reducing their reality to a

financial statement. There is also a kind of predictability about their fortunes in their grubby lower-middle-class world. This, I think, is even true in the case of Robinson Crusoe, whose difference is that he must purchase his conveniences with ingenuity and labor. A work formerly attributed to Defoe that breaks this pattern is *The Life and Adventures of Mrs. Christian Davies, Commonly Called Mother Ross*. The eighteenth century was fascinated with transvestism. Of course Shakespeare's boy actors dressed as women (and then in the comedies often pretended to dress as men), but the more usual eighteenth-century form of transvestism has the woman dressed as a man. When Latroon overpowers his first Amazon highwayman he gets her down and searches through her garments during a frenzied tussle for the hidden loot, and is so preoccupied that he doesn't notice the unexpected anatomy until there is time for a doubletake. The scene is comic and has no elaborate sexual implications or suggestions that the Amazon is trying to find her true sexual role through her disguise. Latroon is masterful with her (and two others of her sisterhood), although she is perfectly willing to be mastered. "She begged me not to be too tedious in my expressions, nor pump for eloquent phrases, alleging this was no proper place to make orations in. 'But if you will enlarge yourself, let us go to a place not far distant from this, better known, but to few besides myself.'"[10] A raucous time is had by all. Even more dashing examples of such disguise are suggested by the lives of female pirates during the first half of the eighteenth century—two by Defoe.[11] The phenomenon becomes subject for subtle analysis later in the century by Rousseau, whose Sophie memorably appeared to him dressed as a man, and Goethe, who in *Wilhelm Meister* has Mignon dressed as a boy, and Natalia in her uncle's greatcoat when Wilhelm first sees her so that he thinks of her as his angelic Amazon.

The case of Mrs. Christian Davies is one of the more fascinating instances of this eighteenth-century chafing under sexual roles. Her life was published in 1740, a year after her death in Chelsea Hospital where she was a pensioner, and nine years after the death of Defoe, who couldn't possibly have been involved in the project in spite of his many ghostly hands.[12] Christian Davies was a very real person, born in 1667, who fought disguised as a dragoon in the campaigns of Marlborough. By her own account, she was a tomboy who could best the other workers on her mother's farm in any challenge. But she is no less a woman and is assiduously courted by a poor cousin for two years. He finally comes to her when she is alone at home making the beds, swears his eternal love, and takes her precious jewel on the clean sheets. This incident establishes the pattern of her life. Although she is often shown to be capable and masterly, she is also a victim of what is considered a peculiarly feminine passion. After her seduction she is sent to Dublin where she runs a public house and is perfectly happy. But she becomes smitten by her servant, one Richard Welsh, and connives to make him think he seduces her. They marry, have unnumbered and unnamed children, and then he is shanghaied into the army for the wars in the Lowlands. The widow waits for a year before a letter from her beloved Richard reaches her, and with little hesitation she leaves her children in the care of relatives, goes off to the local tavern where an ensign is signing up recruits, and joins a regiment of foot as Christopher Welsh. This course of action is never considered as anything else but a convenient and perhaps safe one, considering the hazards of the road for an unaccompanied lady. There are descriptions of the campaigns of the Duke of Marlborough which are more indebted to the journals than the narrator's witness, but she is convincingly involved in several actions, if not in the reflections on war and bloodshed.

It might be thought that such an isolating experience, one which involves an estrangement from home, family, and even from her sex, might result in deeper contemplation than it does. The narrative was undoubtedly assisted by a ghostly hack, but his hand is not revealed in literary flourishes or moral meditations. There is an allusion to the siege of Limmerick during Christian's childhood where a Captain Bodeaux died most gallantly, but then astonished the victors, for when they stripped him they discovered that he was a woman.[13] This might be an artful prefiguration of things to come, but if it is, it is the sole one. More often the passions are treated in a very conventional manner, as when we have a reflection from Christian on her love for her handsome servant whom she makes her husband. "In a word, I was thoroughly content, and had reason so to be, till love, too often the bane of our sex; love, who has not seldom ruined noble familes; nay, destroyed cities, and lain kingdoms waste; envious of the calm I enjoyed, came to embitter my peace, disturb the tranquillity of my life, and make me know, by experience, the short duration of all sublunary satisfaction."[14] Such eloquence does little to individualize this remarkable Dublin pub keeper. The result is that we have to imagine the complexity of the scrapes she gets into. At one point she returns to Dublin in her disguise, and, like Hawthorne's Wakefield, observes her children from a distance and is not recognized. Back in the wars, she receives a ball in the thigh, but medical attention does not discover her to be a woman, which suggests an observation on the state of eighteenth-century medicine. She finally finds her husband, and then loses him again; finds him once more, but this time with a mistress, and she sabers off a piece of his nose. Christian is finally discovered after she receives a wound in the back of the skull which lays her up for ten weeks. She is more distressed by the discovery than the wound, for now she thoroughly enjoys the military life and is sorry to leave it.[15] Still, this energetic and articulate woman (discounting the hand of some unknown ghost) skims through her life with as little attention to detail as the comrades and doctors who didn't bother to look closely enough to see that she was a woman. There are many tales of carousing in camp, brave encounters with the enemy, and the narrator for her amusement even courts a bawd in Rotterdam. She is fascinated with crime and punishment, even when her information is largely hearsay. There is an account of a celebrated crime of passion in France, and the tale of a soldier who is intimate with a mare. He is hanged, the mare shot, and the mare's owner reimbursed. Such works, of which there were many in the eighteenth century, cleverly mix information—in this case about the wars of Marlborough in the Lowlands—with titillation. But the method of first-person narration is simply a device by which truth is asserted.

In spite of their titles and promises, such works are not really autobiographies, or even lives. Wayne Shumaker may overstate the case when he writes that early eighteenth-century autobiographical portraits are "dim and unfocused"; he might rather say that autobiography offered an occasion to focus on something other than the narrator.[16] This follows a line of ancient autobiographical practice which Shumaker divides into three types: the legal self-defense (as with Socrates), the report on a military campaign (as with Caesar), and the imaginary conversation with Philosophy (as with Boethius).[17] These forms of autobiographical writing persist under various disguises through the eighteenth century. Shumaker puts it this way: "in the last quarter of the eighteenth century autobiography was thought well-bred only when it had admonitory or historical value or explained conduct which, through public misunderstanding, had brought the moral character of the writer in doubt."[18]

Such motivations are used to excuse vanity by autobiographers in our own day, and yet it is oddly genteel to employ them. Such writers are often the mighty of the world, and their account is of how they were able to adapt themselves to the discipline of power. What they were before such adaptation is beside the point, or is the enemy within them. What the reader watches is how the author's image of what he should be obliterates what he was. Such heroism is illustrated by a Helen Keller, for whom the highest achievement is to give audiences the impression that she was not born blind, deaf, and dumb. On a less dramatic level there is Justice William Douglas, who forced himself to climb the Tacoma foothills in order to strengthen weak legs, and ended scaling mountains all over the world. These lives involve an exercise of the will which may be an intimate part of what the author considers his self, but it is also employed to make the individual conform to, or impress himself on, the world around him.

There is another kind of autobiography which tends to celebrate the pristine self and glory in its isolation from society—even its defeat at the hands of the world. There is an analogous development in the novel, which matured almost simultaneously with true autobiographies. The heroes of early fiction achieve their victory through a successful adaptation to society. If they are defeated it is because they are unable to adapt, and their failure is as much an object lesson to the reader as their victory would be. In the literature I have treated so far this can be illustrated by those works in which the sinner ends penitent before the God of society and his assumed reader. The recantation is inevitably a recantation of evil ways, and we are expected to cheer a return of the lost sheep, a cozy readmission of the strayed into our midst. The tacit assumption is that the way in which society works is right, that it always has been correct, and that it will always function in approximately if not precisely the same way. The other side of the lesson involves the life of the scalawag who entertains us with tales illustrating his contempt for society that appeal to our baser antisocial impulses, but then shows us how contemptible these are (or at least ill-advised) by being carted through the streets to the gallows in the last act. A quieter form of the same moral is made in those tales of princes and potentates who overreach themselves and suffer a predictable fall for their defiance of God and society, but tales in this tradition of the fall of princes are rarely first-person narratives.

But the novel, once it finds its form in the middle of the eighteenth century, takes another tack. For in the novel the victory of the hero often involves a definition of the hero as distinct from the society in which he lives, and shows him finally living in successful defiance. With the later Romantics that defiance involves the exaggerated gestures of a tormented and destructive Manfred or a light-giving Prometheus, but in quiet ways apple carts are upset in novels published two generations before Byron and Shelley. One form of this is illustrated in the eccentric, in such writers as Sterne and Smollett. They invite us to laugh at their Uncle Toby and Matthew Bramble, but they also suggest that society should not have such a confined moral center that it cannot allow the eccentric to go his way. Further, they might even imply that eccentricity has a sanity to it that is more moral than the received doctrine. It might be absurd that Uncle Toby lives his life by reliving the grim siege of Namur and now cannot bring himself to swat a fly, but it suggests that he has learned a lesson of sentiment superior to our own.

The other and more pervasive form of social change espoused in the novel involves marriage. Most of these novels, and the novels to come, turn on the question of who will marry whom, and in the end the assumed social aspirations of a middle-class audience are shown to be possible, because the heroine (and sometimes the hero) is raised a notch in class by a trip to the altar. Richardson's heroines are from poor but honest stock, and end as mistresses of the manor. Fielding may be playing ironically with this idea in *Tom Jones,* as he began by mocking other attitudes in Richardson with *Shamela.* In *Tom Jones* there is still the modest violation of class because, although Tom may turn out to be the nephew of Squire Allworthy, his father is still the poor but honest student named Summers. Such crossing of class lines is even involved in the novels of such a conservative writer as Jane Austen. It may be absurd for Emma to allow Harriet Smith to aspire to such an old family as that of Knightley instead of the worthy and more appropriate Robert Martin, but all of her heroines are able to improve their purses, and most their station, through marriage. A Renaissance writer, Shakespeare for example, would find such a resolution comic or absurd, for his matchmaking is invariably confined to a class—or is tragic when it is not.

The sympathetic portrait of the eccentric and the social revolution (or at least evolution) implicit in the novelists' treatment of marriage came about at a time of real political revolutions. But the most radical and dramatic shift in the way in which writers treated their material was when they themselves were the subject. That "dim and unfocused" quality to autobiography, which has been noted in such disparate works as the *Life of Lord Herbert of Cherbury* and the *Life and Adventures of Mrs. Christian Davies,* is not evident in Boswell's *London Journal, 1762–1763* and Jean-Jacques Rousseau's *Confesssions,* which was begun in 1765 and published in 1781, three years after his death. Such works suggest a radical alteration in the way in which men could view themselves. These two works were not, of course, published in the 1760s; Rousseau's confession waited a dozen years, and Boswell's *Journal* had to wait almost two centuries. But the temper which influenced them existed when they were written, and it was the temper of that time which was the tremendous influence on the works which were written in their wake. That they were not published during their authors' lives is significant, for in Boswell's case the *Journals* were first a discipline and an exercise; later they were the raw materials for his book on Corsica, his *Journal of a Tour to the Hebrides,* and finally his monumental *Life of Johnson.* He faced and analyzed the passions and faults recounted in the journal, but he would undoubtedly have felt that to publish these meanderings during his lifetime would be carrying too much on his sleeve. Good-natured he was, but he could also be a good hater and would certainly have been loath to give his candid journals to his enemies for ammunition. Rousseau had enemies galore—when he did not, he made them up— and a major impulse of his confessions is to show their folly and meanness to the world, but he understandbly would prefer to do this as a voice from the other side of the grave.

There is, then, a very different "occasion" for these works. There is also a difference between these works and the predecessors of their type. Many have noted the passion for private diary scribbling that begins with the seventeenth century. These diaries are either very this-worldly or other-worldly; they either serve as the raw material of history in that they give the day-to-day progress of a campaign or the arguments of state, or they are essentially meditative dialogues between the body and the soul. In the first instance, they reflect the dramatic shift which made the individual more a citizen than a subject (and there were several such diaries written during the Commonwealth—a tradition which Pepys and Evelyn continue), and in the second, they reflect the Protestant emphasis on the individual's responsibility for discovering his own steps to salvation. There are elements of both impulses in Boswell's *Journals,* for he both records dispassionately the more or less public literary events of his day (who dined with whom and what they said, and what Johnson said to settle the matter), and contritely addresses his Maker when in a financial or venereal fix. Yet throughout there is a secularization and privacy to his concerns that set the *Journals* off from anything that went before. For in them Boswell attempts to discover, in a manner that we have come to think of as peculiarly modern, what he himself is. The origin of facts may be external to himself, but Boswell is often as interested in the moment of his knowing the fact as in the fact itself, and in this way turns reality into something inside him, something dependent on his own mind and memory. For him wisdom is still external to himself and perhaps eternal, but in making relevant knowledge so dependent on his own experience, Boswell was taking the first step toward establishing the wisdom of the heart as the only true wisdom.

7

Confessional High Tide

Nobody likes to be found out, not even one who has
made ruthless confession a part of his profession. Any
autobiographer, therefore, at least between the lines,
spars with his reader and potential judge.
—Erik Erikson, *Gandhi's Truth*

The most obvious difference between the journal and the memoir as
narratives is that the journalist is lost in the forest of his life when
he writes, and although the facts and feelings he records may be fresh
he cannot judge them with assurance, for he does not know the future
and their implication. The memorialist, on the other hand, because of
the distance in time from the experience, has reason to be hazy about
his facts (as Rousseau often is, and asserts that this doesn't matter),
but he knows how they fit into the larger puzzle of his life, and although he may see his life in a way which contradicts the views of all
others, he still suggests a pattern into which the memories must fit.
Boswell, even as a rather ill-formed young man just turned twenty-
two, writes an invocation and rationale for his journal which antici-
pates just such a pattern. He first quotes Socrates on the merit of
knowing thyself, and goes on to assert that this is best done "by attending to the feelings of his heart and to his external actions, from
which he may with tolerable certainty judge 'what manner of person
he is.' " The quotation is from Saint James, so Boswell is able to give
himself both pagan and Christian authority for the self-indulgence of
his journal, although Socrates and James might have considered such
an enterprise a vanity and a doubtful road to truth. It is those "feelings
of his heart" (as Boswell interprets that phrase) on which earlier writers would choke. Boswell goes on to say that he will record "the
whims that may seize me and the sallies of my luxuriant imagination."[1] This would be sheer frivolity to earlier sages, but Boswell is
here, in a light and self-effacing way, suggesting that everything that
pertains to his life—even in a sense his dream life—is relevant to an
understanding of the whole man. It turns out that there is less evidence of this "luxuriant imagination" than the writer thinks there

might be, but in his youthful pomposity he establishes the principle of knowing himself by leaving nothing out.

Boswell's promised whimsies are balanced by the promise to record his "external actions." Of these there are many; they make up the matter of the journal. The thickness of this record is not unusual, but it differs from the way in which earlier journals obliterate the journalist when the account is of public events, even when the journalist is involved. This is, for example, Pepys' tendency. Boswell in his journal, however, wears his heart on his sleeve. He openly records his unobjective piqué at Goldsmith, or his distaste for Gibbon. He can show himself to be both obsequious and a chatterbox, and his insistence on Johnson's tolerance of people is proved by Johnson's tolerance of Boswell. This is even more evident from the *Journals* than it could possibly have been on the basis of Boswell's *Life of Johnson*. And yet there is an ingeniousness to the *Journals* that makes Boswell all the more fascinating from this safe distance of two centuries. No one before him was so successful at narrowly focusing on himself, and yet giving the impression of a reasonably healthy mind. The reason for this is that Boswell was able to submerse the ego so necessary for such an enterprise in his fascination for the world in which he lived. For Boswell, reality turns out to be the sum of experience, and he himself the sum of his own experiences. It is Rousseau who takes the next step and makes reality and the self the sum of his feelings.

As a child might consciously practice with words or various manners of walking, the young Boswell practices with characters, modeling himself on others or on some image of his own creation. "Since I came up [to London], I have begun to acquire a composed genteel character very different from a rattling uncultivated one which for some time past I have been fond of. I have discovered that we may be in some degree whatever character we choose. Besides, practice forms a man to anything. I was now happy to find myself cool, easy, and serene."[2] He will shortly lose his coolness and on several occasions make an ass of himself, but the idea that he can choose his character and a character independent from his social role and personal accomplishments is a radical one. André Gide says that we, alas, are always imitating ourselves, but here Boswell proposes that he can escape from himself through an act of will and form himself in the shape of any character he chooses. This notion breaks with the earlier typology that saw man's character as determined by his humors, and judged him on how well he conformed to the model of fop, apprentice, king, or priest toward which his education was designed to lead him. Not so Boswell. He kicks over the traces by refusing his father's injunction to study the law, tries to finagle a commission in the guards, and ends as an occasional drunk, frequent fornicator, and literary hanger-on. But throughout this he proposes that he can assume the character that satisfies himself and most pleases the world. At one point he says, "I hoped by degrees to attain to some degree of propriety. Mr. Addison's character in sentiment, mixed with a little of the gaiety of Sir Richard Steele and the manner of Mr. Diggs, were the ideas which I aimed to realize."[3] The imitation of Christ is here laid aside for the persona that impresses the world.

One of the recurrent ways in which this choice of a character is dramatized by Boswell and other writers of the period is to imagine himself standing outside of his skin to watch the empty body perform its role. There is a tradition in dream literature in which the dreaming self rises from the sleeper like a vaporous genii, and is used for the expression of pious visions or social satire. But this typically medieval literary device is not used to refine the definition of the sleeper. It is, as in *Piers the Plowman,* used to comment on social injustice and to discuss the moral discipline that leads to salvation. Boswell's experiences of "standing aside" have little to do with this, for his desire is to examine the fascinating complexity of himself rather than the divine model to which he must aspire. There is also an analogy between his experiences and the homiletic tradition of the dialogue between the body and the soul. Yet that tradition seeks harmony between the warring elements through piety, whereas in the eighteenth century the attempt is to explain disharmony. Boswell was a great theatergoer, and certainly these scenes in which he sees himself from a few paces away are dependent on the theatrical situation. An even more direct source for other writers is a childhood experience with marionettes. Rousseau recounts such an enthusiasm in the *Confessions,* and Goethe repeats the experience in both his autobiography and *Wilhelm Meister.* The device becomes even more eerie in its implications with the introduction of the haunting doppelgänger.

Boswell goes to church with uplifted spirit and hears a sermon on the advantages of early piety. And then he says, "What a curious, inconsistent thing is the mind of man! In the midst of divine service I was laying plans for having women, and yet I had the most sincere feelings of religion."[4] Such a doubleness is not stated in the terms of the traditional dichotomy between the body and the soul, for it is the mind that is strange. Through such reflection Boswell attempts to define the unity that is James Boswell. This assumes that such a unity exists, and that he must cast off the false selves and the demeaning wanderings of the mind. This is often done, paradoxically, by this "standing aside," this imaginative getting out of the self in order to define the self. In the *London Journal* he often frets about his callow-ness and is nervous about being a Scot in London. When he goes into the houses of the great he conducts himself with full consciousness of the impression he makes, viewing himself from the outside. On one occasion he is paid a courtesy by Lady Northumberland, and then: "I could observe people looking at me with envy, as a man of some distinction and a favorite of my Lady's. Bravo! thought I. I am sure I deserve to be a favorite. It was curious to find of how little consequence each individual was in such a crowd. I could imagine how an officer in a great army may be killed without being observed. I came home quiet, laid by my clothes, and went coolly to bed. There's conduct for you."[5] Here is a small drama that begins at Northumberland House and is transferred to the inside of Boswell's head. He first sees those who are envious of him, and then imagines what it would be like to observe the favored Boswell, and reflects on the social inconsequence of each individual in society at large. But this very reflection, as much as the present limelight in which he finds himself, encourages a certain self-satisfaction and coolness of conduct of which he is pleased. Then he leaps to the analogy of the great officer killed unseen on the field of battle, and imagines himself such a great officer who might be snuffed out, yet would still be great. This is "conduct." Throughout the *Journal* there is this constant play between the fragile ego of the narrator and the imaginings of the impression that he makes on others. Boswell is eager to please and often aches to impress, and yet he is also aware of a private self that lives its own life behind the actor's mask he presents to the world.

Boswell presents this relationship between himself and the world in a number of metaphors. They are often drawn from the theater. This is not original—after all, we have famously been described as petty players who strut our hour upon the stage—but the manner in which he uses these metaphors suggests that the conflict between the individual and society is one that takes place in the breast or heart or mind, and not on the stage of history. Nor is its outcome determined by some divine ordering of things. For Boswell's implied vision involves a reality that is causal and material. When he contemplates other influences on his character they may be traditional but they are also causal. He is not, for example, independent of genetic influence. "I have, together with my vivacity and good-humour, a great anxiety of temper which often renders me uneasy. My grandfather had it in a very strong degree."[6] He is also aware of the influence of the unbalance of his humors and will refer to his "warmth and impetuosity of temper," but will dismiss "mystical conjectures" such as the temptations of Satan.[7] Reality is physical and historical, and Boswell sees himself as a complex of experience, memory, genes, mind, and body.

It is such an attitude that leads him to a dogged pursuit of the facts about himself and the world around him. These are interdependent, but the most intense reality is an internal one. This idea is introduced specifically by Boswell as that of his friend Dempster, and it is a fancy he applauds.

He considered the mind of man like a room, which is either made agreeable or the reverse by the pictures with which it is adorned. External circumstances are nothing to the purpose. Our great point is to have pleasing pictures on the inside. To illustrate this: we behold a man of quality in all the affluence of life. We are apt to imagine this man happy. We are apt to imagine that his gallery is hung with the most delightful paintings. But could we look into it, we should in all probability behold portraits of care, discontent, envy, langour, and distraction.[8]

Such an image is consoling to the poor Dempster and Boswell because it makes them essentially equal with the man of quality. But it is also compensatory, because in their hearts they may also covet the carriage and mistress of the man of quality. The same image, they say, might also apply in reverse to the beggar whose mind is filled with a gallery of handsome paintings, but one must assume that Boswell and Dempster covet his paintings rather than his rags. The point is that as much as Boswell would like to make the essential self independent of experience and worldly condition he cannot separate his beloved sensations, memories, and moods from their outer stimuli. His reality is very different from the Platonic one—it is not eternal, immutable, nor perfect.

One of the questions with which the eighteenth century was concerned was the nature of happiness: what it was and how it was achieved. The problem often took the form of the question: Would Sir Isaac Newton be as happy in heaven as a ploughman? The assumption was that happiness is possible, here as well as in heaven, an assumption that the ancients or even most nonwesterners would not recognize. People might have taken satisfaction in their power or accomplishments, they might have felt the serenity of philosophy or the assurance of being saved, but happiness in this vale of tears was not expected, and the most a man could wish for was the avoidance of melancholy. Ecstasy, delight, perhaps contentment, but not happiness. Boswell in the *Journals*, however, is repeatedly concerned with his oscillation between gloom and happiness, and after a fine day in which he shined in social discourse he will record that his gloom is gone. He feels his pulse and takes his temperature, and never fails to tell us how he feels.

This happiness which he seeks to maintain is often connected with the passions, another peculiarly eighteenth-century concern. If man exists in this gallery of the mind, one way to hang pleasing pictures there is to exercise the passions. Of course the passions can be gross and lead to a state of gloom, as when Boswell goes to the cockpit and is shocked at the bloodletting and the anxiety of the bettors. "I was sorry for the poor cocks. I looked round to see if any of the spectators pitied them when mangled and torn in a most cruel manner, but I could not observe the smallest relenting sign in any countenance. I was therefore not ill pleased to see them endure mental torment."[9] Such passions are dehumanizing and make the passionate less than himself, or define him as something less than he should be. Once more Boswell is able to ease himself in the situation by being a spectator of himself and so escape the passion. This is quite different from Saint Augustine on the seductions of the bloody amphitheater in which the reluctant auditor finds himself the prisoner of his senses. Boswell, however, here maintains a private gallery of uplifting pictures in his mind, and is able to stroll within himself. He is less successful where ladies of the street are concerned, although many of these encounters are without passion, as though he must keep his vital juices in balance through a kind of genital phlebotomy. Once he even dallies with two young whores together for the price of a glass of wine.

But the passions are more often sought as uplifting, as though through them a person most fully knows and expresses himself. Boswell presents with approval Sheridan's notion that he judges the capacity for poetic passion in others by the degree of their appreciation of Ossian. "He said Mrs. Sheridan and he had fixed it as a standard of feeling, made it like a thermometer by which they could judge the warmth of everybody's heart; and that they calculated beforehand in what degrees all their acquaintances would feel them, which answered exactly. 'To be sure,' said he, 'except people have genuine feelings of poetry, they cannot relish these poems.' "[10] One of the reasons for this is that the poems of Ossian reveal the "sentiments of delicacy as well as generosity . . . in the breasts of rude, uncultivated people." One must be able to appreciate such simple passions to be a whole person, and yet one can escape through such poetry from under the artificial overlays of civilization. We now think of this notion as mistaken, not only because the poems of Ossian were a fraud, but because the art of primitives is neither rude nor uncultivated. The principle that a person can improve himself—even morally—through such imaginative projections and ticklings of the emotions is consistent with Boswell's project of discovering who he was, and consistent with his hope that what he discovered would be as noble as he hoped it could be.

One aspect of Boswell's nature which he wishes to exercise in London, and through which he hopes to define himself, is what he calls his "romantic genius." There is the lust in him which he vents on the poor whores of the street, but what he is really seeking is the cultivated and passionate woman with whom he may experience the truly uplifting passion.

Indeed, in my mind, there cannot be higher felicity on earth enjoyed by man than the participation in genuine reciprocal amorous affection with an amiable woman. There he has the full indulgence of all the delicate feelings and pleasures both of body and mind, while at the same time in his enchanting union he exults with a consciousness that he is the superior person. The dignity of his sex is kept up. These paradisial scenes of gallantry have exalted my ideas and refined my taste, so that I really cannot think of stooping so far as to make a most intimate companion of a groveling-minded, ill-bred, worthless creature, nor can my delicacy be pleased with the gross voluptuousness of the stews.[11]

The passage is an unconsciously hilarious mixture of yearnings for the pleasures of the flesh and aspirations for delicate feelings, of grovelings before the beauty of woman with pride in keeping (as Boswell unfortuitously puts it) the dignity of his sex up. Shortly thereafter he finds what he thinks is such a prize in his fair Louisa. Yet Boswell's treatment of this central experience leaves Louisa curiously dim. He can record the conversations of others verbatim (or what appears to be verbatim), but Louisa is silent or briefly paraphrased. She is his "prize" and he enjoys contemplating her "person," but when it comes down to describing her it is as though she could be any one of a number of standardized beauties, for Boswell is interested in her only as an instrument to an experience, and is most concerned with his own performance. "Louisa is just twenty-four, of a tall rather than short figure, finely made in person, with a handsome face and an enchanting languish in her eyes. She dresses with taste. She has good sense, good humour, and vivacity, and looks quite a woman in genteel life."[12] If she is to be a picture to be hung in the gallery of Boswell's mind, he doesn't seem to see enough that he might even remember her name in later days, for all these descriptive terms are about as vague as they can be. All he really tells us is that she is taller than she is short—the rest presents a blur. The outcome of the whole affair also casts doubt on the efficacy of passion in making us see ourselves and the world more clearly, for shortly after his night of "delicious feelings" and "sweet delirium" he comes down with the pox. Now he gives her some lines for a little scene he writes depicting his confrontation of the cunning jade with the fact of his disease.[13]

Boswell considered the details of his life important enough to record, but not important enough to make a book out of them. His journal preserved the raw material of other books, and yet there is enough space in them for considering the Boswell who is a quiet presence elsewhere. This is as it should be, for the true Boswell is a private one, and somehow it would not have been right to have published the *Journals* in less than two centuries after they were written. To have placed the living Boswell of the *Journals* before his contemporaries would have created a very different Boswell, and modesty is but one of the reasons the manuscript was consigned to sleep in a croquet box.[14] And yet Boswell's search for the real Boswell is ultimately a failure. When he attempts to be most fervent about his self he falls into highly traditional expressions of pious contrition, and when he most cleverly employs metaphors through which he might see his true self objectively he becomes trapped in considerations of what society thinks of him. His *Journal* is one of the best proofs of Hume's discovery that the self cannot know itself, but Boswell never seems to doubt that a self—as distinguished from soul, or mind, or name—exists.

All commentators have remarked Boswell's assiduousness in pinning down the facts. In writing the *Life of Johnson* he was not content to depend on his own notes and his journal. He certainly was not satisfied to retail the published anecdotes of Mrs. Thrale or Hawkins; they are his competitors and he will take them to task. He ran about London consulting old friends and gathering what documents he could to confirm who was present at a gathering and when it took place. Just such a respect for the fact characterizes the travel literature of the period and the writing about history—although there was still a tendency to perpetuate myths on the part of travelers, and the historians often skewed the past to prove their prejudices. Still, there is a great difference between the use of facts by Sir John Mandeville and Captain Cook, the Venerable Bede and Edward Gibbon. The most obvious reason for this change is that the world in the eighteenth century was looked upon as a very real place, instead of as a metaphor for another more glorious world, and attention to its details was important because this was the only way to learn the ultimate truths. What was true of the outer world was also true of the inner one, and so writers attended to the minute facts about themselves as never before and offer the reader a record of the movement of their bowels as well as of their hearts.

These outer and inner worlds often exist quite independently of each other, and especially in the case of a person who is pleased with the inordinate fancies of his inner one—as was Boswell. When his pride and ego are not involved in the description or account there is a marvelous objectivity, and fortunately this is usually the case when he writes about Johnson, but it is less so when he describes a competitor for Johnson's ear or approval. It is a comparable mechanism at work in his description of his lovely Louisa. She is described as she might have been seen by any London gallant of the time, and what Boswell does is to describe her in such a way that his prize would elicit the envy of his fellow gallants. He does not really see Louisa except as she might be seen through the clichés of gallantry. He is as concerned with what others might think of this experience (even though this is a private journal) as he is with indulging in the experience himself. The two motives are contradictory; we cannot experience and define our selves independent of the world around us, while at the same time we display the uniqueness of our life's experience for the amusement and amazement of an audience. The self, as Hume saw, cannot be aware of itself, and as soon as it is it ceases to be a self because it is lost in the seas of influence upon it. Boswell begins his journal with the observation that the discipline of recording his experiences and emotions will lead him to understand himself. No doubt the process of composition assists his memory of his life, and yet it also distorts that life. Some experiences appear to be sought so that they can be recorded, and even when they are not sought they appear to be experienced with an eye cocked for their eventual recording. The process is proposed as one which makes him understand, but it also distorts that which is to be understood. He looks forward to his passionate assignation with Louisa as an experience through which he might more fully know himself. But when he gets to the inn where his true self is to be plumbed he must register as someone else—a Mr. Digges.[15] And Mr. Digges infects Mr. Boswell with the pox.

The most assiduous hunter of himself during this period, and perhaps of any other, is Jean-Jacques Rousseau. For him the unabashed assertion of his uniqueness becomes doctrine, whereas with Boswell his difference was a curiosity, but both of them felt that truth grew out of their own perceptions, and that such truth was no less true if it did not agree with tradition. This sense is stronger with Rousseau than with Boswell, but Boswell was aware of the differences he had with tradition as they were embodied in Johnson, and was modest enough to hold his tongue (as in the case of his account of their tour to the Hebrides) until Johnson's death. Yet even in his presence Boswell would defend the glories of Ossian or other poets who celebrated dark and primitive emotions. Rousseau, however, made a life of being contrary. Whereas Boswell often wished to be praised or inconspicuous, Rousseau courted conspicuousness, and although he protested that he did not seek antagonists, he made a career out of being damned.

Boswell's account of his world in the journals is a very full and candid one, but (as in the case of his description of Louisa) he tends to see himself as he would have other see him. This is what leads him into those clichés which suggest a favorable impression, but do not really describe. Rousseau's descriptions often work in another way. Instead of viewing his experiences as he imagines others would view them, he projects himself into what he sees as though the whole world were a mirror. In 1728 he arrived as a sixteen-year-old runaway apprentice at the doorway of Mme. de Warens, who was then twenty-eight, and immediately fell in love with this mother figure and later motherly mistress. He says that he has often bathed the ground where they met with his tears and adds that "Whoever delights to honour the memorials of man's salvation should approach it only on his knees." Such excesses are not uncommon to Rousseau, or in his time and place, although this is especially extravagant. Then he describes her on that Palm Sunday: "But what I saw was full of charm, large and lovely blue eyes beaming with kindness, a dazzling complexion and the outline of an enchanting neck. Nothing escaped the glance of the young proselyte. For in a moment I was hers, and certain that a faith preached by such missionaries [as she] would not fail to lead to paradise."[16] There are many vague attributive terms used here, such as *charm, lovely, kindness,* and *enchanting,* but there are also more terms than Boswell would use that give us a clear notion of what she actually looks like. Her eyes are blue, and we are given a fairly clear notion of her face and neck. Another element in this passage suggests a major difference between the strategy of the journal and that of the memoir. When Boswell describes his Louisa, he is not aware that he is to come down with the pox as a result of his transports with her, so his description is influenced by the recency of the delights of seduction. I have suggested that this still does not result in the kind of singleness of focus that Boswell pretends or undoubtedly thought he achieved. Rousseau is separated from the things remembered by forty years, and this both sharpens and distorts the description. Mme. de Warens was his one true love, and his description of her must make her worthy of his devotion, so although he is more complete in his description of her because of the long period of hovering over the beloved, she has also become internalized through his repeated conjuring up of her memory.

In Rousseau's case he is both remembering and remembering his memory. This allows a different kind of "standing aside" from that which Boswell employs when he imagines others envying his fine address and the "complacency" of the noble toward him. In the passage above Rousseau begins in the first person and past tense to re-create the memory of his first encounter with Mme. de Warens. Then, by a process identical to that which turns him into Saint-Preux in *Émile*, he becomes the "young proselyte" in a momentary third person. The experience of this youth is for Rousseau so vivid that the life of the gouty rememberer pales before it. There are two aspects of this. One is that personal memory assumes a glow that makes it more important than the present hard fact. The other is that the intense passions of childhood are more significant than the cool and reasoned judgments of the adult.

Rousseau famously begins his *Confessions* with the claim that he will tell the whole truth about himself, that no one before him has done this, and in addition that no one will again do it. The claim is extravagant, but there is a certain validity to it.

I have resolved on an enterprise which has no precedent, and which, once complete, will have no imitator. My purpose is to display to my kind a portrait in every way true to nature, and the man I shall portray will be myself.

Simply myself. I know my own heart and understand my fellow man. But I am made unlike any one I have ever met; I will even venture to say that I am unlike no one in the whole world. I may be no better, but at least I am different. Whether Nature did well or ill in breaking the mould in which she formed me, is a question which can only be resolved after the reading of my book.[17]

The significant word in all this is *heart*, for truth and facts take on importance only as they are conveyed through remembered, heartfelt passions. Rousseau prides himself on his memory of the details of his life, but the scholars are often able to show that he has the facts wrong.[18] Were he to hear them, his paranoia would be to his mind confirmed, but he would also tell the yapping dogs at his heels that the memory performed by the heart is truer than that of the mind. In writing of his childhood he says:

But now I have passed my prime and am declining into old age, I find these memories reviving as others fade, and stamping themselves on my mind with a charm and vividness of outline that grows from day to day. It is as if, feeling my life escaping from me, I were trying to recapture it at its beginnings. The smallest events of that time please me by the mere fact that they are of that time. I remember places and people and moments in all their detail. I can see the man- or maid-servant bustling from the room, a swallow flying in at the window, a fly lighting on my hand while I am saying my lesson.[19]

These are the facts of the modern novelist, who is sustained by such textures, rather than the anecdotal facts or the details in the public record that formed the material of the memorialist before Rousseau's time. To some, such memories may suggest senility—and he accurately describes that blank between the present and their youth often experienced by the aged—but such details as he cites are presented as realities in themselves, and not metaphors leading toward a pious didacticism. For example, flies had a very limited literary use before this passage was written, even though in a world without screens and insecticides and with open sewage pits there were many. Earlier writers might find meaning in the relation between the spider and the fly, as did Swift, or flies might be accidental victims of wanton boys as man is of Fate, as in Shakespeare, but here the fly is only itself, and a detail which invites us to enjoy the texture of Rousseau's memory and by implication an invication to the reader to delight in his own memory which is a large if not substantial aspect of his self. Such a passage in its natural microscopy is akin to those in Wordsworth that look closely at the daffodil, in Pushkin, who has the bored Eugene Onegin sitting idly in the kitchen of his country estate swatting flies, to Proust and his Marcel drinking madeleine-flavored tea in bed, to Nabokov remembering a bee bumping against the ceiling of his childhood classroom. Literature of the past two centuries is largely made of such remembered sweet-sour details. In that they are sour, they are something like the older tradition of *ubi sunt*, in which the poet laments the death of kings and dogs, but there the lament is general and intended to remind us that all things die, and that we should prepare ourselves for a like dissolution. Rousseau and his Romantic followers add a sweetness to such memories that asserts a new kind of *ars longa* through the record of such personal remembered details.

The other implication of this virtual sanctifying of memory is that it places a great importance on childhood, for these memories are most vivid and moving when they are our earliest. J. H. van den Berg has insisted that the basic nature of man has changed through the centuries, but his major proof is that childhood did not really exist before the eighteenth century, and attributes much of this change to Rousseau who "was the first to view the child as a child, and to stop treating the child as an adult."[20] This was part of his attack on reason and a society that at least pretended to conduct it affairs according to reason. Primitive society was another model for Rousseau of a passionate alternative to the foolishness and injustice that he saw around him, but the life of a savage was mainly for him part of his rhetorical argument (which Samuel Johnson and others took literally). When he speaks of the life of the child, he seems to be speaking literally and about something of which he knows. When he seemed to idealize savages he thought of happy Swiss farmers haying the pleasant lower slopes of the Alps, and was delighted to see them at work from several paces away. But when he thought of childhood he had his own experience to refer to. At eleven he was apprenticed by his Uncle Bernard to the City Registrar to learn "the profitable art of pettifogging," and was a miserable failure. Then he was apprentice to an engraver, "an oafish, violent young man," and ran away.[21] This introduction to the world taught him how to get along in it by destroying his youth and how "to covert in silence, to conceal, to dissimulate, to lie, and finally to steal—an idea that had never before come into my head and one that I have never been able entirely to rid myself of since."[22] This is a picture of the surly apprentice, but the attitude toward him is not that of Rousseau's age (which considered him a bad boy to be beaten into civility), but that of Blake, who sees him bound my mind-forged manacles, or Wordsworth, who speaks of shades of the prison house closing about the growing boy. Rousseau's preapprenticeship childhood, however, is not that of the little child that shall lead us to an instinctive holiness. It is a childhood full of searing trauma that we are to revere for the intensity of passion with which it is filled.

Rousseau's mother died a few days after his birth, and she became sainted to his father, who had reason both to embrace him as the living remnant of his spouse and perhaps to resent him as the cause of his loss. Very early his father read romantic novels to Rousseau, and these were lachymose sessions, but Rousseau says they trained his feelings to know the tenderest emotions. Because of this and other such teary experiences, he says that his was "no true childhood; I always felt and thought like a man."[23] By this he means that his sentiments were finely tuned, and that he was able to feel as a man should be able to. Wordsworth is driving at a similar idea when he insists on the vivid recollection of his childhood memories, and how they make him a true man and poet through his tranquil recollection of them. So when Rousseau says he had no true childhood, he might also say that his whole life, in spite of the dimming of many of his mature memories, might be characterized as childlike. Like Wordsworth, he is aware of a time when a dullness settles on a person and he is never quite the same afterward. Throughout the *Confessions* he points to certain events that mark a turning point. This is another way in which the memorist differs from the diarist, for Rousseau attempts to give his memories a rhythm and form like that of the novel, at least a novel

of Balzacian saturation. Yet he becomes so wrapped up in his narrative that there are several moments that are crowned with the uniqueness of being a turning point. These experiences to which Rousseau
attributes so much seem to anatomize his innermost self.

One of the earliest of these weighty experience involves his being
whipped for neglecting his lessons by the beautiful and astute Mlle.
Lambercier. This happened twice, and Rousseau suspects that it was
only twice because *she* suspected he rather enjoyed the whipping.
"Who could have supposed that this childish punishment, received at
the age of eight at the hands of a woman of thirty, would determine
my tastes and desires, my passions, my very self for the rest of my
life."[24] With this passage Rousseau steals most of the thunder of the
psychoanalytically inclined critics who have lent a hand to his in the
analysis of his character ever since. He knew perfectly well that he
most desired to grovel like a contrite child before older women because it had been made clear to him from the beginning that he was in
part responsible for his saintly mother's death. He is also aware that
another beating shortly afterward at the hands of his uncle was not
enjoyable, and that it released the energetic indignation that made
him oppose injustice for the rest of his life. In this case he was accused
of breaking a comb, and although circumstances indicated that he was
the culprit, he was not, and would not confess. And so he was beaten
by a man, and thereafter would be martyred for the innocent by the
masculine figures of authority. "I feel my pulse beat faster once more
as I write. I shall always remember that time if I live to be a thousand.
That first meeting with violence and injustice has remained so deeply
engraved on my heart that any thought which recalls it summons back
this first emotion. . . . There ended the serenity of my childish life.
From that moment I never again enjoyed pure happiness, and even
to-day I am conscious that memory of childhood's delights stops short
at that point."[25]

This analysis is long after the event and is surely colored by Rousseau's pride in his intervening battles for justice and compassion, but
he does not really disguise to himself the possibility of the distorting
influence of this upon his memory. What is important and original
here is that Rousseau attributes the positive (and perhaps the negative) qualities of his character to such searing childhood experiences,
whereas formal education—as his age and earlier ones knew it—was
designed to suppress whatever was passionate, fanciful, and childlike
in the child. In such an educational scheme, reason (perhaps Divine
Reason, or Right Reason) was the goal, and this existed like a zenith
outside of man and moved above his head as he traveled through life.
With discipline and God's help he might aspire to it, but he could not

attain it, because it was not part of himself. His aspiration involved the suppression of all in him that linked him to the beasts, and education began by erasing the beast in the child. Rousseau was aware of this, too, and wrote *Émile* to make the point.

These singular turning points in Rousseau's life took other forms and taught other lessons. He and his cousin planted a willow tree and built a secret tunnel to take water from an aquaduct his uncle had built to water a walnut tree. They were delighted when their tunnel worked, but Uncle Bernard filled in their tunnel and uprooted the tree. They were mortified and angry, but years later Rousseau can call this his "first well-defined attack of vanity."[26] Later when he is serving in a house in Turin he steals a riband, and when caught accuses a lowly maid, who is dismissed in disgrace. He is anguished by the memory. "But I have derived some benefit from the terrible impression left with me by the sole offence I have committed. For it has secured me for the rest of my life against any act that might prove criminal in its results. I think also that my loathing of untruth derives to a large extent from my having told that one wicked lie."[27] In such a manner Rousseau is able to turn the evil he has done into a victory, but unlike most confressionals in which evil is a *felix culpa* and the victory involves God's redemption, the victory in this case involves an enrichment of character.

But not all of them, for there are things to confess for which the only reward and victory is confession itself. He once traveled from Savoy to Lyon, and there his compansion had an epileptic fit in the street. Rousseau walked away as though he were a stranger.[28] Much later he visited Mme. de Warens, when she was old and poor, on one of his trips between Paris and Geneva. He might have helped her more than he did, he might have overcome her refusal of his generosity, but he did not try. "Of all the remorse I have suffered in my life this was the bitterest and the most enduring."[29] There are many superlatives applied to such experiences, yet Rousseau also appears aware of them as crucial in specific areas. The earliest of these experiences may illustrate lust, the next wrath, and the next vanity, and so on. But Rousseau refuses to think in these terms, and if he were to he would (in spite of his association of his willow tree with vanity) be apt to think of the childhood experiences in terms of the seven cardinal virtues. Even when he sets himself up as a music teacher without knowing anything about music, it forces him to learn something about it, and later permits him to support himself as a music copier, and eventually to make a splash as a composer of opera.[30]

Everything is ultimately turned to Jean-Jacques's advantage because he loves himself, and everything of importance and worth remembering is a reflection of himself. Such an observation might be used as a weapon against Rousseau, and Irving Babbitt or Mario Praz have been delighted to use such weapons, but I do not intend the Humanist's sneer here.[31] For good or ill, Rousseau was the harbinger of ideas that have formed the modern consciousness. And the most important of these ideas is that a person is not to be defined in terms of how he has conformed a primitive self to the demands of his world, but how he has imaginatively restructured his world to conform to him. This is the basis of Rousseau's insistence upon his uniqueness, not his success in relating himself to recognized slots and roles. Jacques Barzun has said that Rousseau was the only eighteenth-century man of genius who was everything socially: a Swiss in France, a hob-nobber with the mighty and the chambermaids, and so forth. His being both an intimate and an outsider encouraged his original bent.[32] The same might be said of Boswell and even of Johnson, but surely such a personal experience of a fracturing of the old orders en-courages the person to find a new center, and for Rousseau and others in his age that center was the figment of the self.

Rousseau's *Confessions* relate a history of intense friendships (with Grimm, Diderot, Hume), and then falling-outs. When he comes to know these friends they are invariably in a position socially and profession-ally much like his own, and Rousseau identifies with them. But in-evitably the paths separate. Grimm is more successful at toadying to the mighty; Diderot prefers the battles for intellectual freedom waged in Paris to the bucolic pleasures of Geneva; Hume turned out to be a philosopher and yet not eccentric. Rousseau sought to love his idealized self, and his enthusiasms often involve such projections. He continues his description of Mme. de Warens, as he remembered her upon their first meeting, in this manner:

Her beauty was of a kind that endures, lying more in the expression than in the features; and so it was still at its height. Her manner was tender and caressing, her gaze was very mild, her smile angelic, her mouth small like mine, her hair, which was ash blond and extraordinarily plentiful, she wore with an affected negligence that increased her attraction. She was small in stature, almost short, and rather stout, though not in an ungainly way; but a lovelier head, a lovelier throat, lovelier hands, and lovelier arms it would have been impossible to find.

Her education had been extremely mixed. Like me, she had lost her mother at birth, and had seized indiscriminately on any instruction that was offered her.[33]

If the sixteen-year-old Jean-Jacques was not actually in love upon first encountering this vision, he certainly remembers it that way. And there is reason, for he sees her as both a feminized version of himself and as an incarnation of the lost mother of whom (according to his bereaved father) he was the very spit and image. Twice in this passage he indicates awareness of this likeness, for they both have small mouths and both lost their mothers early. Elsewhere Rousseau gives evidence that he thought his manner to be tender and caressing and his gaze mild and (even) saintly—rather than angelic. He was also blond, and in later years wore his hair with an "affected negligence" that was usually described as disheveled. He, too, was short and tended toward a plumpness (as Boswell is pleased with his "stoutness") much esteemed in his age. She is as a mirror which reflects himself feminized at a moment in 1728, and in the depths of her image he might also see the lineaments of the mother from whom he came.

Some of the chaff from the critical Freudian mills is concerned with Rousseau's latent bisexuality. The analysts note his aversion to homosexual encounters as extreme, but of course Rousseau notes this too. It is not his sex that is deviant, I think, but his whole way of seeing the world, for he does not even pretend to objectivity—or rather calls the wisdom of his heart a superior objectivity. The question about what is to be done with the runaway Jean-Jacques soon arises, and Mme. de Warens's handyman suggests that he be sent to Turin to seek his fortune. The enamored vagabond is understandably not eager to leave, and so he describes Claude Anet (who was Mme. de Warens's factotum and, Rousseau is to learn later, her lover) as an "oafish fellow."[34] In this passage he is not named, but it can be none other. Later, when Rousseau returns and shares the favors of Mme. de Warens's maternal bed with Anet, he must idealize the *ménage à trois*. Then he refers to Anet as "faithful, honest," and a self-taught botanist who is a wise and restraining influence on both Mme. de Warens and Rousseau.[35] Theirs is a "unique bond," so when Anet dies before his time the remaining pair are thrown into passionate grief.[36] This odd description of an odd relationship springs from Rousseau's idealization of the object of his passions, and he loves Anet as though he were an older sibling, perhaps as he might have loved his real older brother, who disappeared into Germany as a youth and was never heard from again.

Rousseau's assertion of his difference extends to his calling things by unusual names. I have already suggested that he considered his subjectivity truly objective, and that his sins were turned into lessons if not virtues. He had the eighteenth-century penchant for anatomizing his perceptions and feelings, and this process leads him to the use of terms that appear to be used in ways more specific than we might use them. There is *heart, brain, mind, reason, memory, imagination, soul, sense, passion*—all terms that had a peculiar gravity for his age. Rousseau sees himself as truly existing in his heart, his passions, his feelings, and his memory. Yet external cirucmstances do not allow him to see the truth or pattern in the messages from these that he would wish, and he attributes this failure to the falseness of the world, his own shyness, and a haphazard personal history.

It is not unusual for man to be seen as a mixture of elements, for he has long been seen as a compound of body and soul, human and animal, or an imbalance of the four humors. But in the age of Boswell and Rousseau it becomes a more mysterious mixture. Boswell says that men "are made up of contradictory qualities," and is curious, if not pleased with the result, when they are observed in Dr. Johnson or in himself.[37] The mixture that Rousseau observes in himself results in more torment. "In me are united two almost irreconcilable characteristics, though in what way I cannot imagine. I have a passionate temperament, and lively and headstrong emotions. Yet my thoughts arise slowly and confusedly, and are never ready till too late. It is as if my heart and my brain did not belong to the same person."[38] Here is another version of the "standing aside" phenomenon, but in this case the doubleness exists in the same person, like the body and soul of earlier meditative literature. Yet that tradition sought a reconciliation, and even closer to Rousseau's age (as in Rochester or Swift) a reconciliation was sought between reason and common sense. Rousseau resents the manner in which reason acts as an anchor on the passions. This is clearest in his discussion ("I have to tell everything") of his seduction by Mme. de Warens.[39] She begins with a long lecture which is "full of feeling and good sense, better calculated to instruct me than to seduce me, and addressed to my heart rather than to my senses."[40] According to Jean-Jacques, the thought of such a relationship had never entered his head, and he was so distracted by the prospect that he did not attend closely to much that was said, but she gives him eight days to think it over—which whets his appetite more than his reason. It was a poisoned idyll, and Rousseau reflects afterward that the major failing of his "Mamma" was this dependence on sweet reason.

All her faults, I repeat, came from her lack of judgement, never from her passions. She was of gentle birth, her heart was pure, she loved decency, her inclinations were upright and virtuous, her taste was refined; she was born for an elegant way of life which she always loved but never followed, because instead of listening to her heart which gave her good counsel, she listened to her reason which gave her bad. When false principles led her astray, her true feelings always gave them the lie. But unfortunately she prided herself on her philosophy, and the morality she invented for herself corrupted that which her heart dictated.[41]

Here in a single clot are all the terms so beloved by the age, but Rousseau's conclusions are rather different from most of the writers who used them. Boswell, for example, recognized his own "warmth" and "lively spirits," but often had more reason to lament these attributes than the Addisonian "coolness' which he willed on himself. But Rousseau is suspicious of "judgment," "reason," "principles," and "philosophy." Once more he is probably projecting his own image on the world as he does in his description of Mme. de Warens, and his criticism of her might be of himself and the damned heart and brain that live at war in his own person. When he confesses to an error, he usually bases it on a judgment made in the light of reason or philosophy. His anger at his various patrons undoubtedly came from his refusal to be the lackey of the privileged, but it also begins in the reasonable acceptance of a position which will allow him to get on with his life's work. It is also "philosophy" which leads him to set his children out for adoption—and passion which leads him unsuccessfully to search them out in later years. He is fully aware of this tension in himself, but when he acts in accordance with base reason, he seems to be someone else, not himself: "there are times when I am so unlike myself that I might be taken for someone else of an entirely opposite character."[42] What man must do is to purify himself of the vile (usually civilized) dross of reason in his character, and become all heart and pure passion. One of the results of this is that men can escape from the prison of the uniformity of reason and civilization, and grow into their true uniqueness, for unlike reason, which is unitary, individual hearts are infinite in their variety, and the passionate history of any man is unlike that of any other.

Here is the rub. Rousseau's definition of his self involves a refinement that reduces it to a private infinitude. Yet he also wishes to see the world about him from that idealized granule of his essential being. Of course the world often disappoints him, and he is loath to include flaws of the mirroring world in the image of himself. He says that he has "only one faithful guide on which I can count; the succession of feelings which have marked the development of my being," but because the world rarely reciprocates his feelings as he would wish he is left "with a heart oppressed by grief. It can offer me nothing but misfortunes, treasons, perfidies, and sad, heart-rending recollections."[43] The diagnosis has been paranoia, but what he describes is also the Romantic malaise that comes from too great hopes too brutally shattered. When he returns from a trip to Montpellier where he went for his health (and was seduced on the way by a charming mother of ten), he finds his "Mamma" sharing her bed with an itinerant wigmaker. Rousseau is saddened and angry, and says of Mme. de Warens that her "behavior was culpable, but [her] heart was always pure."[44] Once more he might as well be referring to his own recent behavior as much as hers. He has reason to be disappointed with both of them violating what he calls "the laws of virtue," but he prefers to comment on her violation. Such disappointment is sometimes attributed to his own failure of passion. When on his trip through the Midi he visits the Pont du Gard, "the first Roman remains I had seen,"[45] he is sent into a reverie that lasts a couple of hours and dreams upon the grandeur that was Rome. "In spite of my sense of smallness I felt my soul to be in some way elevated, and said to myself with a sigh: 'If only I had been born a Roman.' "[46] Rousseau does not really describe what affects him so, only the transport that he feels. Later he views the Roman amphitheater at Nimes, but it makes much less of an impression on him. He suggests that he might have been exhausted by the vision of the Pont du Gard, or depressed by the modern town around the amphitheater, but in any case he was soon satiated with being a Roman, and, unlike Gibbon later in another amphitheater, was not inspired to write a history of the Empire. The senses which are us can be wearied, the sword wears out its scabbard, and the vision fades.

The accounts from his many visitors insist that Rousseau could be genial and charming in spite of the testiness of his published disputes. But he was not frolicsome, and the *Confessions* take their subject very seriously. This lack of humor leads him to tell tales on himself that are uproarious, although he does not even seem to laugh in retrospect. When in Venice he pays court to Giulietta, a beautiful courtesan. He is depressed by her trade which seems to waste her beauty. "Great men and princes should be her slaves. Sceptres should lie at her feet. Yet here she is, a wretched street-walker, on sale to the world."[47] Her extraordinary beauty overcomes his moodiness as he disrobes her in his memory. She is flawless, until on close inspection he sees that she has a malformed nipple. "I beat my brow, looked harder, and made certain that this nipple did not match the other. Then I started wondering about the reason for this malformation. I was struck by the thought that it resulted from some remarkable imperfection of Nature and, after turning this idea over in my head, I saw as clear as daylight that instead of the most charming creature I could possibly imagine, I held in my arms some kind of monster, rejected by Nature, men, and love."[48] He loses all his passionate impulse, and she with wit beyond her station tells him that he should take up the study of mathematics. Had he done so, or had he remained a musician, he might have found content in perfect models, but he had to get involved with education, government, society, and women.

Rousseau found his world most satisfactory in those situations where there was no flaw in the mirror which the world held up to him. As he aged, he exorcised the impediments to his ideal from his view. He retreated to his hermitage, where the straw in his throat might be limited to his gossipy mother-in-common-law. When he went into society, he insulated himself in his obvious difference. Even as a youth on his first return from Italy he says that "no one of my age had ever come back in as strange a state as I," and similar phrases occur as a leitmotif throughout the *Confessions*.[49] He appeared at a performance of his own play given for a glittering audience which included the king and Mme. de Pompadour. He felt ill at ease because he wore his habitual sack and had a "rough beard and ill-combed wig." He felt that he might have been seated where all could see and mock him. But then "I asked myself whether I was in my right place, and whether I was suitably attired, and after some uncomfortable minutes I answered 'Yes' with a boldness which, perhaps, proceeded rather from the impossibility of drawing back than from the strength of my conviction. 'I am in my proper place.' "[50] This might appear to be an adult's tantrum, but just such gestures were a part of Rousseau's creed and program to show men that their habits and ideals could be different from what they were.

In all of this lies the central paradox. Rousseau was a natural pedagogue. *Émile* is testimony to this, and there are many lessons for us in the *Confessions*. Yet the central lesson is a fie on the world, for it teaches a carelessness toward the world's concerns. In the end, Rousseau is content to close in upon himself and sharpen the faculty of deep and quiet feeling in solitude. Sometimes Thérèse is present, but she (whom he could not even teach how to tell time) only lends a human warmth. He remembers

our little suppers at the open window, sitting opposite one another on two low chairs placed on a trunk which was as wide as the embrasure. In this position the window ledge served as a table, we breathed the fresh air, we could see the distant country and the passers-by and, even though we were on the fourth floor, we looked down into the street as we ate. Who can describe, who can feel, the charm of these meals at which the dishes consisted of no more than a quarter loaf of coarse bread, a few cherries, a little piece of cheese, and a half pint of wine which we drank between us? Friendship, confidence, intimacy, peace of mind, what delicious seasonings they make! Sometimes we sat there til midnight without noticing it, and would never have thought of the time unless informed of it by the old lady. But let us leave these details, which will seem tame or ludicrous. For I have always said and felt that true joy defies description.[51]

Such a passage was impossible in a life written before the middle of the eighteenth century, for life was seen only in outer and measurable events, because a man only truly existed in his acts and works. It might have appeared in a romantic novel as an interlude between adventures, but even there the sharp details would have been missing. French novels of the next century are full of such scenes. They are found especially in Balzac and Flaubert—as in the scenes in *A Sentimental Education* in which Frederic Moreau and his leman, the Marshal, are found gazing down for hours into the Paris street.[52] There the message is that sloth and ennui are inevitable (but none the less a sin), for Flaubert drains his world of all true feeling. For Rousseau, feeling is still possible, and he intends us to see his true self at rest and in harmony with friend, wine, and sunset.

With Rousseau the old Platonic and Christian dualism is altered and dislocated. In him the terms which he inherited from the past take on new meanings, so that the soul becomes a refinement of the feelings and passions, and the body becomes their instrument. This is a secularization of those various forms of religious zeal that swept Europe during the second half of the eighteenth century; that second reformation intended to breathe new life into the old catechisms. All of these movements—Hasidism, Pietism, the Moravian Brethern, Jansenism, Methodism—shared a respect for the fervor of the penitent, and all came into conflict with the old canonical law and its clerical defenders. For these movements, virtue, happiness, and salvation came as a gift from a God outside, who was external to man, and who men recognized through a frenzy of the senses. In such movements there was a reinterpretation of the old dualism, but one not as radical as that in Rousseau. He will refer to God on occasion, but such references seem to be mere rhetorical gestures. He says, for example, "I have never liked to pray in a room; the walls and all the little works of man come between myself and God, I love to contemplate Him in His works, while my heart uplifts itself to Him."[53] Except when he discusses his early religious training, this is the only reference to God in the *Confessions*. Here there is the ever-present reference to his heart, which in another writer would be a pious cliché, but in Rousseau carries the burden of doctrine. The language here suggests that God is transcendent to Nature, yet Rousseau's more usual implication is that God is at most immanent, and the feeling throughout is that any deity exists in a vibration of perception between himself and the natural world. So it is when he views a woman, a Roman antiquity, or a ravine in the Alps.

Northop Frye points out that the reason for Rousseau's impact was not based on the appeal of his educational or political arguments, but "on his assumption that civilization was a partly human artifact, something that man had made, could unmake, could subject to his own criticism, and was at all times entirely responsible for."[54] A more pervasive influence might be described if the word "the self" is substituted for "civilization." Rousseau altered our vision of what civilization might be, but he did not invent the notion that it changed, or that these changes are independent of the actions of great men, wars, or economics. But the self was largely his invention—the self as manifest in the individual's feelings—and these, when undefiled by civilization, are seen as morally good. He made conscience man's guide to happiness and ethical behavior, and, as Louis Bredvold states it, "the acts of conscience are not judgments, but sentiments."[55] This "sentiment intérieur" is virtually synonymous with self, but the self cannot be seen except as it feels, perceives, and acts through the agent of the body—and yet it is not itself the body. Rousseau was much too aware of his partial deafness that resulted in a ringing in the ears, his poor eyesight that made him stoop to see the cowslip, and finally his urinary problems that made travel and public gatherings an embarrassment to identify his poor husk with his transcendent being. Yet the self, as Hume pointed out in 1731, cannot verify itself any more than the mind can contemplate itself. The self cannot be both judge and jury; Rousseau tends to make it both, and sometimes the plaintiff and defendant too. The best he can do—or anyone else since—is to try to catch it unaware by stealing a glimpse of it in the mirror of its feelings and the reflection of its role in the world. If the *Confessions* discovered nothing else, it discovered a method for suggesting the revelation of the self, and ever since memorialists and novelists have used Rousseau's method—and made his method their subject too.

The self was a phenomenon stillborn, perhaps a nonphenomenon or an unhappening. Hume raised the self as a question out of a skeptic's doubts about the soul, and used the models of Lockean epistemology to lay the idea to rest. But it would not die; less serene doubters than Hume resuscitated it again and again, and the assumption of its existence colors subsequent art and thought. Yet self-contemplation always turns into a meditation on ghosts. Boswell projects what he might be and repeatedly sees himself only as he imagines others see him. Rousseau engraves his imprint upon others and nature, and suggests that the emotion he feels is himself. Like joy, this true self defies description. Rousseau's boast that no one after him will do quite what he did in the *Confessions* is not far off the mark, for those who follow him are content to stalk themselves from the covert of their works and in various disguises. Their professed honesty and candidness is always an introduction to indirection and fabrication.

One of the stoniest masks was that assumed by Goethe. Rousseau cast himself in the role of Saint-Preux in *Émile* because of the convenience of a literary form which might (and did) reach the widest possible audience for his pedagogical theories. But Goethe became Werther and Wilhelm Meister in order to discover an aspect of himself. In spite of the pleasant speculations about Shakespeare being Hamlet, such identification between the author and his protagonist does not become common until the last half of the late eighteenth century. Fielding is not Tom Jones in the same way that Sterne is shadowed in Tristram Shandy, or certainly the way in which Byron is Childe Harold. Such Romantic identity between author and hero is so plain that it is the unspoken assumption about these writers, but it is important to say it plainly because the change is significant. Literature becomes in the Romantic period largely an artful circling around the self on the assumption that the truth of a unique individual becomes a universal truth, and knowing thyself is not just a philosophical exercise, but rather a holy quest.

Goethe tells us as much about himself in terms of the facts of his life as does Rousseau, and in terms of the raw facts he is usually more accurate. Both reviewed their lives when they were past the median—Rousseau began the *Confessions* when he was fifty-three; Goethe began his *Dichtung und Wahrheit* when he was sixty-two. Both had established their reputations and knew that there would be an eager audience of admirers (or eager detractors in Rousseau's case), but Rousseau only permitted posterity to judge him, whereas Goethe published his memoirs twenty-one years before his death. The titles of the two works suggest some of the differences between them. Rousseau's title looks back at a long tradition of confessions—and especially to St. Augustine—but also proposes an intimate psychological portrait like none other. Goethe's title, *Poetry and Truth*, might serve for a work on aesthetics, perhaps in the manner of Lessing. Such a title attached to an autiobiography looks ahead to that Victorian notion that the man of letters must be a kind of popular preacher whose metrical homilies are dug out of the moral lessons of his own life. For all his eager exposure, there is a modesty assumed which closets the skeletons and skips the terrors of the night.

Goethe's memoir begins with such modest shuffling that the contrast to Rousseau's extravagant claims might be thought deliberate. As an excuse for such a vain undertaking he reproduces a letter from "a friend" who requests information about the poet's life now that "the twelve parts of your poetical works" have been published. Goethe is pleased to oblige his "well wishers" (which includes himself, for the letter of request is undoubtedly his own composition), and sets out to write an account of only his early years that is longer than Rousseau's *Confessions*.[56] But in spite of this prolixity, he cloaks the most private Goethe behind the public one, and even though he reconstructs some passionate scenes and feelings they are presented through the prism of his own works. The very last scene of the autobiography presents a picture of Goethe tearing himself away from the arms of Mme. Delf to go on his Italian journey. According to this account, his final words were a long quotation from his own *Egmont*: "Child! Child! No more! Lashed as by invisible spirits the sun steeds of time go on with the light car of our destiny, and nothing remains for us but bravely and composedly to hold fast the reins, and now to the right, now to the left, from a rock here, from a precipice there, to avert the wheels. Whither is he going, who knows? Scarcely can he remember whence he came!"[57] It is hard to think of a life lived according to the heroic cadences and allusions of such declamation (and perhaps with Beethoven as background music), but evidently that is the way in which Goethe's audience preferred to think of him—and he knew it. This was convenient, for it allowed him to show himself through the fragments of himself as he walked through the places and dates and the episodes from his works in which, he seems to imply, he has his true existence.

Goethe is fully aware of the game he plays, for he pretends to tell his audience about the real Goethe, and then hides behind his various literary masks. In his foreword he writes in gracious answer to the letter from the inquiring friend:

For the main task of Biography seems to be this: to exhibit the man in relation to the circumstances of his time and to show how far everything has opposed or favoured his progress, what kind of a view of the world and of mankind he has formed from them, and how he, if an artist, poet, or writer, may outwardly reflect them. But for this is required what is scarcely attainable, namely that the individual should know himself and his generation: himself, in how far he has remained the same under all circumstances; his generation as that which carries along with it, determines and forms the willing as well as the unwilling, in such a manner that we may well say that anyone born ten years earlier or later, as regards his own culture and his influence on the outside world, would have been quite a different person.[58]

Rousseau is willing to admit psychological influences on his life—as in the case of those spankings—but Goethe here suggests a much more pervasive environmental determinism. His statement is exceptionally modern, for even though the biographer can only treat his subject within the cultural context, the autobiographer cannot go much further to "know himself" and "how far he has remained the same under all circumstances." For Goethe this is "scarcely attainable"; a notion dismissed by Rousseau in his bombastic prelude, but which seems more sensible as he proceeds. So Goethe's work has the outward appearance of Rousseau's, but there is a restraint and a hiding behind his times that make it very unlike the *Confessions*.

Goethe is largely concerned with his education and his own role in developing a culture which is distinctly German and distinguished mainly from the French. So he often speaks for his generation, as when he recounts the distaste "us youths" had for the chilliness of Voltaire and their enthusiasm for Rousseau, because he too was a child of Nature and felt "disgust for the social life."[59] In many ways this work is a series of reading lists and accounts of the mentors and friends who had an intellectual influence on the young Goethe. The result makes the autobiography a kind of public record or letter to the editor, for Goethe is surely aware how his reader will relate these presumably true personal experiences to the plays, poetry, and novels which were spun from them. The experiences which appear to be the most personal ones—and since these come early in the history they might be considered formative and psychologically important—often involve the young Goethe slipping into roles. He retells an experience on which he had elaborated twenty-five years earlier in *Wilhelm Meister*, and considering the nature of experience it would be hard to say whether he is remembering his own life or that which he created for Wilhelm. In the attic of the Goethe manse in Frankfurt there was a chest of costumes and marionettes, and Goethe was a ringleader in making up plays, generally along classical and heroic lines. When the plays were done, Goethe would simply tell stories to hold his playfellows in a circle. He says they especially enjoyed it when he spoke in his own person.

It was a great joy to them to know that such wonderful things could happen to me, who was one of their own playmates, nor was it hard that they did not understand how I could find time and occasion for such adventures since they knew pretty well how I was occupied and of my goings and comings. Nevertheless, for such occurrences, localities had to be selected, if not from another world, yet certainly from another region, and everything had to happen to-day or yesterday. It was they, therefore, who deceived themselves rather than I who hoaxed them.[60]

Goethe is not as insistent as most memorists that he tells us nothing but the truth. The word is in his title, but there it refers to large philosophical verities and not candidness about personal details. He pretends we believe him, just as his playfellows were delighted to pretend to believe his fancies forty years before. It would be impossible to determine if *he* believed himself, for the habit of spinning tales out of his own experience became so ingrained that he was undoubtedly delighted to hover in the mask of the first person between the delights of being the hoaxed and the hoaxer.

It is in the nature of Romantic genius to reach for truths just beyond the grasp. This is the way with the major English Romantic poets, but it is the case with no one more than with Goethe. We always have the sense with him that he dares to suggest an insight which he cannot quite state, and which is perhaps unstatable. The method is to look into the mire of one's own experience and transform this into fictions in which a kind of spurious control can be exercised. The truth lies somewhere between the mire and the control, and the understanding comes in that electric moment when they meet. This is Goethe's method throughout his career. When he heard of the suicide of a young man named Jerusalem because of unrequited love it gave him a denouement for his own unrequited love for Charlotte, and the result was *Werther*. When he was sixty, he was smitten by Meta Messerschmidt who was a third his age, and the result was *Elective Affinities*. He says that such transformations began with his earliest lyrics which immortalized his love for Gretchen.

> And thus began that tendency from which my whole life long I could not deviate, namely, of transforming into an image, a poem, everything that pleased or troubled me or otherwise occupied me, and to come to some understanding with myself about it in order to rectify my conceptions of external things as well as to tranquillise my inner being about them. For no one was this gift more necessary than for me, whose nature flung him continually from one extreme to the other. All that has become known of me are only fragments of a great confession, and this little book is an attempt I have ventured on to make it complete.[61]

"Little book," indeed! Once more the reader is having his nose tweaked. But there is also in this passage an accurate description of what actually happens in Goethe's works, for in them he presents the paradigms through which we—and even more accurately he—can understand Goethe.

Goethe also refers to his nature which "flung him from one extreme to another." His attitude toward this is quite different from Boswell's or Rousseau's troubling over the split between head and heart that they felt in themselves. Rousseau tries in his *Confessions* to cast out the rule of head in himself, and open the way for the victory of the feelings. He pursues the attack on reason that rose to a crescendo during his age, culminating with such a writer as Blake. In its stead he places his faith on a "sentiment intérieur" which has an innate love of justice and goodness. Its operation reveals the true self in all of its uniqueness.[62] His works illustrate how this sentiment might be revealed, and this is mainly through training the feelings to respond to nature. On the other hand, Goethe attempts to harmonize the extremes he sees in himself. He does this by exaggerating them in his fictions, and in this way he isolates them for placid study. He records that the searing experiences of his life were usually followed by an illness. After Gretchen plays him for a fool, runs off with a young friend, and gets into trouble with the authorities, Goethe falls into a melancholy fever which purges him of his distress, and only then can he turn this experience into poetry.[63] A similar delirium follows his passion for one Annette; once more he is purged, and in a state of renewed youth can compose his scenes. This process requires the repeated assumption of disguises which were part of a strategy resulting in art and self-understanding. Rousseau used disguises too, but his were assumed for the sake of discretion, or were badges of his deliberate eccentricity. When he traveled to Montpellier with Mme. Larnage, who to his astonishment seduces him, he has been cautious enough to present himself as a Mr. Dudding, an Englishman, and through the trip is afraid of meeting a real Englishman, for he doesn't speak a word of English and knows nothing about England.[64] It is a hilarious situation, but even in retrospect Rousseau doesn't crack a smile. When he appears as the disheveled lay monk at the performance of his own play before the king, he tests the affectations of the court. Goethe's disguises are of a different sort.

After telling how he enchanted his playmates with his stories about a fictionalized self, Goethe presents an example. It is a story called "The New Paris," and takes the form of a boy's dream. He dresses for a festival in new clothes, and examines himself carefully before a mirror. "I was curled and powdered, my locks stood out from my head like small wings, but I could not finish my dressing, because I kept confusing the pieces of clothing, and because the first fell from my body when I was about to put on the second."[65] A handsome young Mercury comes and offers him three apples which he must give to the most beautiful youths at the fair, who in turn will then be rewarded with the fairest of the girls for their wives. The apples rise to his fingertips, and turn into a nymph that he tries to grasp, but cannot. On the way to the fair, he passes a garden gate with no latch or keyhole, and which he had not noticed before. The gate is opened from the inside, and there is an old man who guides him about this garden of heavenly delights where the birds shrill the names of Paris and Narcissis. The center is enclosed by a golden railing, and then there is a stream and another golden railing. The old man tells him that he may cross to the middle of the garden, but he must leave his sword and his hat, and that he must disguise himself. He puts on an Oriental costume and looks at himself once more in a mirror. "Now I found myself before a mirror in my disguise quite good-looking, and was better pleased with myself than in my still Sunday clothes."[66] In the mirror he also sees a green whip, and the old man tells him that it is used on those who abuse his confidence. He is led to the center of the garden where there is a palace, and in it three women who are associated with the colors of the apples Mercury gave him. There is also his sweet nymph. He plays with toy soldiers with her; she with Amazons, he with an army led by Achilles. The fight gets out of hand in a childish way, he is driven into the water, and the old man upbraids him for spoiling the game. He is driven out of the garden, and can never find it again.

In this tale there are many elements that appear again and again in Goethe's work: the concern with clothes and disguise, the battle between the sexes, the suggestion of severe erotic punishment for disobedience, and the idea that a truth lies at the center of an idealized aesthetic arrangement. To get to this last, one must disappear into other versions of the self, and in this story Goethe illustrates several forms of such disappearance. The aged Goethe first disappears through memory into his youthful self, and then the youth disappears into the dreamer. The dreamer then disappears into a mishmash of classical allusions, into the disguises he wears, and twice into the mirrors in which he contemplates himself. Such disappearance through disguise is repeatedly courted by Goethe; it is not simply a matter of what I have termed "standing aside," for that involves a momentary separateness through which the person looks back on the self in order to catch it unawares. Goethe so consistently slips into these other roles and disguises that the self remains hidden in a diffusion. Rousseau looks at the world through his own pulse and sees there pieces of himself, as when he notes that Mme. de Warens has a small mouth like his own. For him, he is reality and his self is understood through the fever of his senses. Goethe's fevers precede an imaginative recreation of the outer world, and that is more objective, even though deception is at the heart of the method.

The most significant difference between the autobiographies of Rousseau and Goethe is that Rousseau describes the world around him as it pertains to his remembered feelings, whereas Goethe describes the manner in which he grew to understand the world by entering into it. The works often appear to be more alike than they are, for Rousseau could be described as objective about his feelings (and in the manner of his age and in spite of himself he often searches for reasoned systems of virtue, happiness, government, education, etc.), while Goethe might be seen as subjective about his in the account of the growth of his understanding. The methods of presentation overlap, but there are very different assumptions behind the manner in which they describe the world and themselves. Rousseau describes the world as though he would be the only one to see it in precisely that way at that moment, for its reality is something that ultimately depends on his emotional response to it. We are not told, for example, what the interiors of the houses where he lived looked like. He claims to have been happiest with his Mamma at their little cottage at Chambéry, and even though he considers the place a shrine at which all true devotees of the heart should worship, he tells us almost nothing about it because furniture does not move him. When he recalls those serene suppers with Thérèse on a balcony, there is a little cheese and bread and wine, but the memory is general, not specific, and cumulatively he is remembering wheels of cheese, countless loaves of bread, and a hogshead of wine. The process applies to his aversions as well as his enthusiasms. After a couple of unseemly experiences in Lyons which might have happened anywhere, he describes the city as "the most corrupt in Europe."[67] Rousseau prides himself on his botanical study, but his descriptions of nature suggest a vague green mass—preferably arranged in hilly country rather than on a plain. Goethe is invariably more specific in his descriptions, and although he is given to flourishes of irony and allusion, he describes with a disinterested eye, as though anyone seeing the same scene would see it just as he does. Here he describes the garden of his grandfather, which he would visit with his sister:

The walks for the most part were skirted by vine trellises; one part of the space was given up to vegetables, another part to flowers, which from spring to autumn adorned the borders as well as the beds. The long wall with a southern aspect was used for some well-trained espalier peach trees, of which the forbidden fruit throughout the summer ripened temptingly before us. We rather avoided this side, however, because we could not here satisfy our dainty appetites, and turned to the opposite side, where an interminable row of current and gooseberry bushes opened up to our greed a continuity of harvests till the autumn. No less important in our estimation was an old, high, wide-spreading mulberry tree, as well for its fruit as also because we were told that the silk-worms were fed from its leaves.[68]

In this passage quantities and sizes are left vague, but there is a clarity of arrangement and a catalogue of the objects that convey a clear idea of the garden—certainly much clearer than that of any garden in which Rousseau walked to set his mind in motion. There is also the gentle irony of the allusion to the forbidden fruit, which lends a sweet distance to the memory, rather than the searing immediacy on which Rousseau insists, as in his account of the pirate willow tree.

Even when Goethe remembers a state of passion which might drive him into the forest to brood, his distress does not stand in the way of his memory of the details of the mazy wood. When he hears from a friend that his beloved Gretchen does not love him, indeed, considers him a child, he flees to the forest.

I therefore drew my friend into the woods, and while I fled from the monotonous fir trees, I sought those beautiful leafy groves, which certainly do not extend far and wide in the district, but still are always of sufficient compass for a poor wounded heart to hide itself. In the greatest depth of the forest I sought out a solemn spot where the oldest oaks and beeches formed a large nobly shaded space. The ground sloped somewhat, and made the value of the old trunks all the more noticeable. Round this open circle closed the thickest bushes, from which rocks covered with moss peered forth in their might and dignity and made a rapid fall for a well-watered brook.[69]

There is added here a large helping of pathetic fallacy, but a forester could hardly do more to tell us just what kind of woods this was. The friend says that Tacitus describes the Germans of seventeen centuries before going off into the woods to brood in just this fashion, and such passages as this one have led Teutons to tramp the woods with rucksacks on their backs even since. Rousseau says he likes to contemplate God in all His works, but he is interested in what this contemplation does to him. Goethe surrenders himself to what he sees, and in this way sees it more sharply. For him Nature is not a mirror in which he sees some aspect of himself, but a glass through which he passes into the greenery. The one method might be thought of as centrifugal, the other as centripetal. It is immediately after the loss of Gretchen that Goethe takes to painting landscapes, in part to sublimate his loss, but also to lose himself in the scene. Goethe did not, like Rousseau, become quickly satiated with the contemplation of antiquities. He entered into them with the eye and through his drawings, whereas Rousseau had to depend on his feelings—which could quickly weary.

For Goethe, man's deepest existence involves a perception which hovers between the heart and nature, or between an experience and the art which is based on the experience. After the friend gives the

distressed Goethe the musty reference to Tacitus, the love-sick youth
cries out

"Why does not this precious spot lie in a deeper wilderness! Why may we not
draw a hedge around it to hallow it and ourselves and to separate them from
the world! Certainly there is no more beautiful adoration of the Deity than
that which needs no image, which springs up in one's bosom merely from
intercourse with Nature." What I felt at that time is still present to me; what I
said, I do not know how to recall. But so much is certain, that the indefinite,
widely expanding feelings of youth and of uncultivated nations are alone
adapted to the sublime, which, when it has to be stirred in us by outward
things, without form or moulded into incomprehensible forms, must surround
us with a greatness to which we are not equal.[70]

Rousseau says that the spot where he first saw Mme. de Warens
should be hallowed ground, a golden railing put about it, and that
worshipers should approach it on their knees.[71] He appears perfectly
serious in this suggestion, but as Goethe remembers his similar frenzy
the liklihood that his spot of ground would be hallowed is doubted,
and he suggests that it would be better if God could be worshiped
through a general appreciation of Nature. He is like Rousseau in his
attack on the skepticism and artificiality of civilization, and so prefers
the enthusiasm of youth and "uncultivated nations"—remembering
Tacitus on the Germans. The final implication is (and this is the mature Goethe as well as the distraught youth) that men need the world
to give form and articulation to their praise. For all of his tremors,
Rousseau is a rational anatomist of the heart, but Goethe is a mystic
who sees man and himself existing in his relation to his history, culture, and the world around him. For this reason there is a largeness of
scope to his autobiography—rightly implied by its title—that makes
Rousseau's *Confessions* appear myoptic in contrast. Goethe in writing a
history of his own early years also writes a history of German culture
in the eighteenth century. He shows himself in torment and heartsick
with love, inscribing his name and that of his beloved in the bark of
trees. He will show Nature to be the stimulus to feeling, then mock
himself by going on solitary walks and being eaten by mosquitoes—
"the midges in the best season of the year suffered no tender thought
to arise."[72] And so he slips away through an arch wit from under the
slide in the microscope which he himself has offered us.

8

Travelers East

> But to resume,—should there be (what may not
>   Be in these days?) some infidels, who don't
> Because they can't find out the very spot
>   Of that same Babel, or because they won't
> (Though Claudius Rich, Esquire, some bricks has got,
>   And written lately two memoirs upon 't),
> Believe the Jews, those unbelievers, who
> Must be believed, though they believe not you.
>   —Lord Byron, *Don Juan*

Many streams have come together to encourage a concept of the unique and individualistic self. From one direction they join with tremendous roiling in the revolutions of the last quarter of the eighteenth century. From that time to this, all revolutions have been economic and political in nature rather than religious, and the revolutionaries have been social levelers who wish to change the state of men from subject to citizen. This is a political Protestantism which makes all men equal before the law as well as before their Creator. There was another element in this confluence which denied the concept of man as a mere social integer. This was often, in the eighteenth century, a caverned stream that romantically concerned itself with a secularized soul, and viewed a man as unique and each man as better than all other men. With Napoleon these ideas in all their contradiction became a cataract, if not a deluge, and ever since the great men of the world have attempted to spread the idea of equality and freedom by knocking heads together. Napoleon himself rode gaily over the problems by saying that "Every French soldier carries a marshal's baton in his knapsack."[1] Such fine notions could be entertained—perhaps had to be entertained—because the old props of the individual, like reason, religion, and place, were being knocked away, and something had to replace them. The most significant replacement was the thin reed of the self.

The old supports for the individual might have been illusory; certainly the eighteenth-century critics of reason, religion, and monarchy claimed them to be. Yet men were not willing to be left naked, and even though the romantic self (which only seemed to be manifest in the rights of the liberated citizen and his private passions) might be viewed as no more than an eidolon and ghost, it became an article of faith as firmly believed in as the old Articles. That belief altered the way in which man saw himself and the world around him, but he was rarely aware of this change. The artists of the age often tried to see themselves by slipping out of their own lives and histories into fictional surrogates. This had the advantage of surface modesty, avoided libel, and permitted the play of imagination. It also permitted the writer to circle back upon himself in secret ways, and astonish himself and his creation with insights more illuminating than those of focused philosophy. Somewhere between the old typologies of allegory and the fleshed faces of realism the writer places what looks like a true self, but in fiction—or even in autobiography, as in the case of Rousseau or Goethe—this must always be a shadow of the real self.

Robert Adams points out that the self can be considered both everything and nothing. He uses the metaphor of the pyramid, and says that by subtracting everything that is not his true self a man might be considered as equivalent to the finiteness of the point; but if we consider the true self as the sum of a man's history and culture he might be considered the infinitude of the projected base of the pyramid.

We no more suppose a man is "himself" when he wears formal clothes, puts on the badge of an office, or speaks into a microphone, than when he dresses up for charades. Certain roles in life, we say casually, permit a man to express very little of himself (or, more pointedly, of his self): the locution implies that there is somewhere a full reservoir of essential being that gets drained into various roles in various circumstances. To see the man as "he really is," we must see him in all his roles and then construct what lies behind these different facades, the manipulator of these various puppets.[2]

We can, therefore, Adams continues, subtract all that is not a man, pare down to this essential self, and end with a point of no dimension floating in space. Or we may see the self as the result of an accretion rather than subtraction. "Starting with the very rudimentary set of givens which is ours at birth, we built our selves by accumulating experience: we are what we have been. Adding a book here to a horseback ride there, a fight and an affair, a job as an accountant and a hitch as a justice of the peace, we accumulate over the years a miscellaneous, jerry-built, crudely homogeneous self, which is all most of us need or get in this life."[3] These speculations precede an investigation of the influence of Roman culture and ideals on the eighteenth century, and although Adams presents this discussion of these two forms of self as though it might be relevant to a study of any period of cultural history, I suspect these thoughts occur to him because he is to deal with the eighteenth century, when just such considerations troubled the writers and artists he is about to discuss. Rousseau, for example, attempted to define the self largely through the process of subtraction by stripping away from himself what was false and civilized, so that he could get down to the raw emotions of the heart. Goethe, on the other hand, saw himself as the result of an accretion, and his self as diffused into the experience and culture which formed him, and which he in turn created by his character and work.

Boswell records that Dr. Johnson summed up a discussion of predestination and free will in this manner: "All history is against the freedom of the will; all experience for it."[4] Boswell lets the subject rest, although he appears unhappy with this summation. What is said here about the freedom of the will might also be said about the self, which is certainly mixed up with the question. All theory also argues against the existence of the self, while in practice we assume that it exists. Johnson could also be implying that we hold on to a concept of our own wills being free because that way lies sanity. The same might be said for our private certainty that we exist as unique selves, for it is not comforting to think of ourselves as ciphers in eternity. Yet we are trained by our culture to see, and what we expect to see we do. With such giants of originality as Rousseau and Goethe, we sense and respect a determination to see with their own eyes as no one else had before them. And yet, mixed with their accounts, as impressive and persuasive as they are, there is a tendency toward the elegant flourish and bits of posturing that makes their versions of their lives not wholly convincing. The way in which they saw their lives has directly and indirectly influenced the ways in which we see ours, even though we may be conscious of their conscious manipulations. In both cases, because of the distance in time between the remembering and the remembered experience, they must pretend to catch themselves in memory unaware, and the success of their pretense is what convinces us of the truth of their account. Upon reflection we know that there is a pretense and artificiality involved.

Such pretense may be less involved if we look at the subgenre of travel literature, where the narrator does not consider himself a belletrist, and he most clearly reveals himself because he is not involved in artful affectations. There are difficulties here too in getting at the unvarnished truth of the narrator's self (or his concept of it), but they are difficulties of a different, and in some ways more manageable, kind. I am not here concerned with travelers' lies, or even why they should lie to their assumed audience, but how they see what they choose to describe and how they describe it.[5] The primary qualifications for travelers are a hardiness of constitution, an indifference to boredom, and an indulgence of the manners of others. Getting from here to there does not really depend on an insatiable curiosity or an observant pen; these may even be an impediment. So I here look at the accounts of writers who are very different from such culture-shakers as Rousseau and Goethe. For these very reasons, travel literature is more revealing of what the mass of people really thought, for the traveler was more than likely to be much like his fellow countrymen, except that he had been somewhere else and thought the stay-at-homes might like to hear about it.

I have chosen the travel literature that deals with the Middle East because it neatly spans the period of my concern and because there are elements to it that are generally not in the literature about Africa or the New World. In the Middle East the European traveler encountered a civilization that had accomplished great things in the past, and its accomplishments were still manifest, so the Westerner was forced to meditate on the differences between his culture and the one in which he found himself, and he could not always comfort himself with a conviction of his superiority. This was often not the case with travelers to America or later the Pacific where the traveler could distract himself from what he actually saw with meditations on Golden Ages and doctrines of Noble Savagery. Travelers to anywhere had their reasons for going. It might be to carry the tidings of their monarch to distant places and pave the way for aggrandizement; it was most often a prelude to trade, which sometimes resulted in plunder; and from the middle of the eighteenth century it might be motivated by a truly disinterested desire for scientific knowledge. The travelers to the Middle East often had an antiquarian interest that led them to ruins where they contemplated biblical truths or the accounts of classical historians, and by the beginning of the nineteenth century they were extending our knowledge of the past through a primitive archeology. These added fillips make the literature of Middle Eastern travel curiously different, and finally tend to toss the narrator into a questioning of his cultural, as well as his physical, resources.

It may seem odd that the accounts of these travelers, until the early nineteenth century, are almost entirely lacking in introspection. The character of the traveler might have something to do with this; by the Romantic period the difficulty of travel in strange places had not much diminished, and yet travelers then found time and eye to see their world with a more individualized and passionate view. The accounts of most travelers are written for certain masters. They might be official reports of a diplomatic mission, or they might be supported by subscription or a society, and this influences the tone, generally making it anonymous or at least self-effacing. Many have the quality of a guidebook for the future real or mental traveler, so the result is a selection of verbal picture postcards. Often the actual writer did not see what he pretends to describe. Marco Polo whiled away the hours in a Genoese prison narrating his Oriental adventures to one Rustichello, a writer of undistinguished verse romances, who copied them down with some of his own flourishes.[6] Sir John Mandeville famously copied and invented his travels, and so was not deeply moved to comment on his own individual reactions to sights he did not see. In the late seventeenth century William Dampier (who Swift tells us was a cousin of Lemuel Gulliver) did not write his own account of his voyage around the world, and Richard Waters wrote the account of Admiral Anson's voyage around the world (a work avidly read by both Rousseau and Goethe when they were youths).[7] Captain Cook was a level-headed Yorkshireman, and his sense of plain speaking was offended when he discovered that a scholarly drudge had added pretty tropes and classical allusions to the published account of his first voyage.[8] But these ghosts are easier to identify and dismiss than those ghostly alter egos that creep in between us and the remembered facts in the narrative of more committed literary figures.

Marco Polo's account of his adventures in the East was known to his readers through the Renaissance as *A Description of the World*, and considering the extent of his travels the title was not inappropriate at the time. It also suggests the general geographical intent of the work and this, as well as the conditions under which the work was written, results in a neglect of the continuity of the various travels and a tendency toward anonymity on the narrator's part. It is difficult to determine exactly the role of Rustichello in the composition of the work, although it has been determined that the dedication and certain courtly descriptions are lifted from his own romances.[9] There is also a wavering use of pronouns. The work begins with a description of the conditions of composition, and then continues with such formulae as "I will now describe . . ." in which the *I* could refer to Marco himself, or Rustichello reforming what he heard from Marco. On other occasions the "I" says or does something in the Orient, and this can only refer to Marco, and yet Rustichello has so imposed himself on the narrative that he seems to be hiding in the corner of the room or page. Sometimes the account will slip into the guidebook device of "We shall not touch on India," or, "When the traveller leaves Kerman . . ."[10] None of this brings Marco before the reader in full delineation.

Marco Polo had to be a hardy and prudent fellow to do what he did, and yet there is little of the braggadocio that is common to personal narratives of the later Italian Renaissance. He came from a family of merchants who were situated on the Black Sea. Although he obviously found a certain identity and pride in being a member of an old family, an Italian, and a Catholic, he was from his youth accustomed to strange manners and a babble of tongues. One of his purposes in going to the court of Kablai Khan was to teach, at the great Khan's request, the Monguls something about Catholic belief. For this purpose Marco conducted some priests, but Marco treats his own religion as very light baggage. He is also exceptionally tolerant of strange sexual customs. He is not, for example, aghast at the custom in Kamul that prescribes that the host offer the favors of his wife to his guest for two or three days, although he refers to the practice as cuckolding.[11] He calls some of his hosts idolators, but is remarkably cool in his descriptions of their odd burial practices and even their canabalism.[12] He is also quite indifferent to the miracles he witnesses (such as an entertainment at a dinner of the great Khan's which involves flying dishes) and tales of the miraculous in the past. He refers to the horses of Afghanistan that were descended from Alexander's horse Bucephalus, and so "they were all born like him with a horn on the forehead."[13] He gives us such information for what it is worth, and doesn't insist that we believe in it.

What excites the interest of Marco Polo most are riches for which there might be a market. When he describes the wealth of the monarchs whom he visits, he may refer to them as brutish or tyrannical, but this seems to be suffered because they have lands and cattle and minerals that would command a very good price if he could only transport them to the West. Marco Polo's early readers knew little of the Monguls except that they were infidels and in war were bloodthirsty beasts, so Marco's news that they were peaceful was a piece of revisionist history. He describes the land ruled by Kaunchi Khan in this manner:

He has neither city nor town in his dominion; but his people spend their lives among vast plains and high mountains. They live on the flesh and milk of their herds, without any grain. He has a great many subjects; but he does not lead them into war or battle against anyone, but rules them in great peace. They have enormous herds of camels, horses, cattle, sheep, and other beasts. In his country there are big bears, pure white and more than twenty palms in length, big black foxes, wild asses, plenty of sables—the same that produce the costly furs of which I have told you, which are worth more than 1,000 bezants for one man's fur—vair in abundance and great multitudes of Pharaoh's rats, on which they live all the summer, since they are creatures of some size.[14]

Here are the superlatives of the merchant in the bazaar, for his use of rounded prices and primary colors suggest that the truth may lie somewhere between them and our buyer's skepticism. Most of his energies are spent in describing that which might be marketable, so the accounts of odd manners come through as introductory palaver. When he describes nature there is usually a purpose to the description unrelated to nature as a thing of beauty or scientific curiosity. "This kingdom has many narrow passes and natural fortresses, so that the inhabitants are not afraid of any invader breaking in to molest them," he says of Afghanistan, even though he himself had stumbled through the harsh glories of the Alborz Mountains for hundreds of miles. What he notices is that these mountains abound in game and sheep that "roam in flocks of four to six hundred; and however many of them are taken, their members never grow less."[15] And when he describes the Gobi it is mainly to emphasize the difficulty in getting through it and the scarcity of even brackish water.[16]

There is a kind of purity to Marco Polo's account in that he appears ignorant of earlier travelers, and so must see what he does through his own eyes. The accounts of pilgrims who went to the Holy Land, which date from the seventh century, have two purposes that tend to stand in the way of such innocent description. They first are guidebooks in that they often give the distances and directions from one place of rest to the next, and the sights along the way are only mentioned if they are helpful landmarks. When the narrator gets to his destination everything is seen through the scriptures; indeed, nothing seems to exist except through a biblical reference—which is invariably appended. Sometimes Pliny or Arrian is referred to for dated gossip or history, and sometimes their descriptions are even lifted, but it is the biblical analogues that give real meaning to what the narrator experiences. Other ulterior purposes stand in the way of Renaissance travelers seeing what is there in a modern sense. An early remarkable example of a scientific traveler is Leonhard Rauwolf, a sixteenth-century German botanist and physician, who went to the Levant to collect botanical specimens, and to describe strange diseases and often stranger cures. Rauwolf will comment on the customs he encounters and the hostelries he is forced to suffer, but his eye is generally on the flora, and his concern with its medical use.

The Elizabethan fascination with distant places mixed two interests that were antipathetical; they were interested in trade which they felt would give them a place in the sun enjoyed by the Spanish and Portugese, and they were curious about fantastic beliefs and practices that often made them complacent with their own. Their travel literature was therefore an odd mixture of weights and measures appropriate to a bill of lading, and tall tales heard from superstitious and perhaps humorous foreigners. One such account is that of Anthony Jenkinson, who went on a mission for the Moscow Company in 1561 that took him to Russia and down the Volga, then across the Caspian Sea to the Persian court at Kasvin, where he nearly lost his infidel's head. He later returned to Persia with Sir Robert Sherley to train the troops of Shah Abbas in Isfahan for battle against the Turks. Jenkinson's account of his first voyage is addressed to the Society of Merchants Adventurers. It was published in Hakluyt's *Voyages*, and, because of his original audience, has the asperity of a financial ledger. He still must prepare future travelers for like exploits, and so includes a little history and comments on methods of travel. But his eye is a merchant's eye, and when he describes something he is mainly impressed, as is Marco Polo, with its market value. He describes his reception by the monarch, and then the monarch himself.

The king did sit in a very rich pavillion, wrought with silk & golde, placed very pleasantly, upon a hill side, of sixteen fathom long, and sixe fathom broad, having before him a goodly fountaine of faire water: whereof he and his nobility did drinke, he being a prince of a meane stature, and of a fierce countenance, richly apparelled with long garments of silke, and cloth of gold, imbrodred with pearles and stone: upon his head was a tolipane with a sharpe ende standing upwards halfe a yard long, of rich cloth of golde, wrapped about with a piece of India silke of twentie yards long, wrought with golde, and on the left side of his tolipane stood a plume of fethers, set in a trunke of golde richly inameled, and set with precious stones; His earerings had pendants of golde a handfull long, with two great rubies of great value, set in the ends thereof: all the ground within his pavilion was covered with rich carpets, & under himselfe was spread a square carpet wrought with silver & golde, and thereupon was layd two sutable cushions.[17]

How such a sight would have warmed the avaricious heart of Marco Polo; and how such rich decadence fleshed out the bombast of Marlowe's scenes of Oriental pomp. It must be granted the Jenkinson had little occasion to observe the character of the king, as he was limited by the situation and a foreign language, but on any occasion he rarely goes further than such terms as "fierce," or "meane stature." For him a person exists in what Dickens's Wemmick calls "portable property," and there is nothing in his account that suggests that he considered himself in any different light. When he is caught in a storm on the Caspian he conventionally surrenders his soul to God, and is saved. When he encounters a tale of a giant who lives on top of a mountain and has "two great hornes, and eares, and eyes like a Horse, and taile of a Cow," he hints that he is skeptical, but "whether it be true or not, I referre it to further knowledge."[18]

In the accounts of travelers prior to the past two centuries, considering they saw so much of it at such close hand, there is very little natural description. In the case of Marco Polo we might think that natural scenes passed from his memory, unlike the scenes of pomp animated by kings and their court. He probably never really saw the mountains and the plains as we might in similar circumstances. The Renaissance saw nature in two ways: it was a symbol of God's presence in that it was signed by its Maker, and in this served to teach man lessons of his mortality and God's divinity, or it served the practical uses of food, fuel, and shelter. Jenkinson confines his observations to the second attitude, so when he makes the difficult crossing of the Alborz range to go from the Caspian littoral to Kasvin, the account is given in a single sentence. "The 21 day we departed from Ordowil aforesayd, travelling for the most part over mountaines all in the night season, and resting in the day, being destitute of wood, and therefore were forced to use for fewell the dung of horses & camels, which we bought deare of the pasturing people."[19] It is as though he passes through this adventure stamped with the identity of Englishman and Protestant (even more than Marco Polo is content in being a Venetian and Catholic), and what lies outside his interest in trade exists in a dream. When he has his audience with the Shah he is asked if he is a Mohammedan or an infidel. He is pleased with his answer, which confounds them: "I was neither unbeleever nor Mahometan, but a Christian."[20] He is dismissed by the despot, but perseveres and is eventually able to pave the way for a treaty with gifts to the Shah's underlings, playing a game beneath a Christian but not an English merchant.

Jenkinson's prose is serviceable, but I think that the attraction of his account lies in his subject matter, and that those who praise Hakluyt's collection as an English prose epic are more enthusiastic about its literary qualities than they need be. The first English traveler to go to far places mainly for his own amusement, and who took obvious pleasure in recounting his adventures, was Sir Thomas Herbert, who traveled in the Middle East and elsewhere from 1626 to 1634. The form of the work is one that combines a chronological itinerary with essays on religion, language, history, and customs, and this allows him to broaden the narrow interests of the commercial travelers and pilgrims who went before him. Herbert is also very aware of his identity as an Englishman and a Christian in a heathen land, but he bothered to learn something of the language of the people he visited, and attempts to describe their culture in an objective manner, going beyond the brightness of their precious metals and gems. Jenkinson, for example, describes Islam as proceeding from "false filthie prophets,"[21] but Herbert presents lengthy if uncomplimentary injunctions of the Koran, and tells how the Prophet's body rotted in the sight of his disciples beyond the appointed hour of his resurrection. He also denominated the Prophet as false and filthy, but he is willing to learn more about Islam than Jenkinson bothered to. Herbert's curiosity is impressive, but he still remains cocooned in his identity, and the facts which he presents seem rarely to be drawn from personal experience. He is also a stylist who is fond of ornamenting his account with classical allusions, handsome metaphors, and a gentle irony—elements that never appear in Jenkinson and rarely in the works of other Elizabethan travelers. He gives an account of the cruelty of Shah Abbas and the story of his jealousy of his own son whom he blinded out of fear of usurpation. "And by this excessive impiety, Asia lost her chiefest jewell, Mars his darling, and Persia her incomparable treasure, now undone, blind, imprisoned, and hopeless of any joy or honour ever after. . . . his Army were of long time implacable, but when they saw it was past remedie, and the King would in time, serve them with like sauce, if they continued refractorie, they retired, and buried in murmure and forced silence, what their hearts fully and freely discourst upon."[22] Here there are very pretty turns of phrase and Herbert is right to be proud of them. The touches of irony serve him well in a long section in which he describes the cruelties of the Shahs, which he does, he says, to show Englishmen how fortunate they are to live under a just government and a humane and Christian king. But when he describes the fratricidal intrigues of the court one is reminded of the bloody Tower and the normal practices of the Tudor kings and queens. Herbert never hints that his account may be instructive to Stuart kings, and perhaps he doesn't intend it to, and yet he notes that the man-eating dogs to whom the Shah throws his enemies are imported from England.[23]

Herbert is one of the first to give an account of the ruins of Persepolis. He finds them impressive, but there is none of that brooding on the fickleness of fame and the glories of the past that we associate with Sir Thomas Browne, and he certainly is not given to the sort of meditation on himself that Rousseau indulges in. He accompanies his description of antiquities and monuments with drawings in that curiously flattened perspective of medieval and Renaissance illuminations. This is not a matter of talent, or lack of it, but of style, so that when Herbert presents the great maidan of Isfahan as though it were an enlarged medieval fortress it is both a matter of his knowing what his readers' associations were and of he himself seeing it that way. His drawing shows this center of "half the world" in absolute symmetry, even though the enormous Shah's Mosque is perceivably asymmetrical to the maidan so that it turns toward Mecca.[24] Such rough edges to his observation extend to his phonetic spellings, as when he mysteriously renders Isfahan as "Spawhawn."

Herbert shields himself from this world about which he is at the same time so curious. He gives an account of an affront to the English ambassador to whom the Shah sent only a servant to guide to an audience, and is deeply proud that the ambassador, Sir Dodmore Cotton, disdained the service offered and came escorted with his own troop.[25] He doubts the former grandeur and size of Isfahan, and like other travelers of the period measures its size by the time it takes him to ride around its circumference, as he measures the size of palaces with the vague measure of his pace. And like others in his period he describes people in terms of their clothes, and is rather disappointed to find the Shah dressed in simple garments, and suggests that there is some hypocrisy in this. "His attire was very ordinary, his Tulipant, could not out-value fortie shillings, his coat red Callico quilted with Cotton, worth very little, his sword hung in a leather belt, its handle or hilt was gold, and in regard the King was so plain attired, most of the Court, had like apparell on for that day. Yet the Plate and Jewels in that House argued against povertie, a Merchant then there, imagined it worth twentie millions of pounds." Such ledger-keeping might be thought beneath a gentleman of Herbert's interests and assurance, but he is not free of the kind of evaluation common to the merchant adventurers. His eye for natural beauty is attracted by fertilized and fruitful hills. He comes closest to expressing an appreciation of nature when he describes Damoan [Hamadan?]. "It was a rich and puissant Countrey in the Worlds infancy, but now whither by the al-consuming hand of Warre (here ever acting) or by the Justice of God, for massacring so many good Christians in Chozroes time, tis now a very barren and miserable kingdome, chiefly if you compare it with our Phoenix great Brittaine, who in her selfe exceeds, all the best compacted riches or pleasures, of these Asiaticall Empires."[26] So nature is presented as a patriotic but not a private memory of the green fields of home, and the desolation is attributed to a bloody history or God's judgment.

All of the eighteenth-century travelers in the Middle East look to Sir John Chardin as a master and model. And rightfully so, for he was the best prepared and the most meticulous traveler to go that way up until his time. Chardin was a French Protestant and jeweler who went to Isfahan in 1669, and there he became privy to the court intrigues that eventually dismembered the empire of Shah Abbas. In 1671 he published a short account of the coronation of Soliman the Third. He had been commissioned by Shah Abbas II to procure gems in Europe, returned with his hoard in 1671, and did not return to Europe for six years. During that time he accumulated material as he cooled his heels awaiting payment, and his study was published in Paris in 1686. Because of the persecution of Protestants in France, he came to London where he was appointed court jeweler, was knighted in 1681, and the following year became a Fellow of the Royal Society. He was a man of substance and of the world; his *Journal* shows him to be a man in control of himself and intelligently curious about the world around him. Although his study is called a *Journal*, it is not a day-to-day account of his experiences, nor is it an itinerary. There is a long section which recounts the development of his dealings with the Court officials in his attempts to be paid for the jewels he had procured for the reigning Shah's father. This has all the makings of a drama, or a series of them, but he gives this material as a formal historian might describe the negotiations between sovereign powers. He is concerned mainly with his general observations, and so apologizes for the length and specificity of his account. "Perhaps I may have been tedious in relating so at length my Negotiation with the Nazir; but I chose to do it, because Narratives of this Kind, are better to inform the Intelligent, of the Genius of the Country, than the most exact Descriptions that can be given thereof. The Procedure of all the Oriental States is full as sordid and niggardly; nay, I have seen a great deal worse at the Court of the Great Mongul, altho it be, as one may say, the Center of all the Riches of the World."[27] He rarely uses such strong language, for his coolness would be admired by Boswell, and generally his observations have the acerbity of the laboratory. There is only a moment, according to his account, that he feels panic during these negotiations. Chardin spoke Farsi and dressed in the Persian manner, but he is always perfectly aware that he is an outsider, and he is the first to meditate on the advantages and disadvantages of adopting the costume of his hosts.[28] So he is especially conscious of the necessity of maintaining an air of Oriental indifference when he is told by the Nazir that the Shah was displeased with most of his baubles.

I was in a manner Thunderstruck when I cast my eyes on what the King had set apart, which was not one Quarter of what I brought. I became Pale and without Motion. The Nazir perceiv'd it, and was touch'd thereat; I was just by him, he therefore leaned towards me and said in a low Voice; You afflict your self that the King has lik'd only a small Part of your Jewels. I protest to you that I have done more than I ought, . . . These words pronounc'd with Tenderness, brought me out of the Consternation, into which I had been cast without perceiving it my self; I was much surpriz'd, and very much afflicted that the Nazir had been sensible thereof.[29]

This momentary vision of the flight of wealth focuses his mind on the scene as it does on none other, but he is able to return to his true rational urbane self in a moment, and maintains his poise during the rest of his *Journals*.

Chardin presents verbatim letters of introduction, instructions from companies to their merchants, and governments to their representatives. In all of this he shows himself very aware of his official role as a Frenchman and honest merchant. He is often struck by the wealth of the things he sees, although his descriptions of jewels and fine silver often go beyond the reader's patience.[30] He also describes (and more completely and accurately than does Herbert) the customs, history, government, and economy of the country. He even tells us that barley water was a very successful purge for the troubles he had with the Persian diet. Unlike Herbert, whose reaction to foreign customs suggests that travel narrows, Chardin's reactions to strange customs are not always the predictable ones from a European and Christian. He finds that "There are Europeans of all Nations, who frequently, in the East, give the like Examples of Imprudence, and Irregularity,"[31] although he thinks the European can never match the Persian in cheating and flattery.[32] He thinks that their meticulously arranged marriages may last longer than those in Europe which are not arranged, and speculates that this may be because, once married, a man never sees another woman.[33] As complete as his comments on the manners of the people are, they are colored by the restrained bitterness of his experience as a merchant, and his tabular mind is more adapted to minute descriptions of wine making, the use of pigeon houses for fertilizer, and methods of building. Chardin is a rationalist, so when he recounts odd beliefs and superstitions his incredulity is plain. He also tries to find causes for many differences between the East and West. He attributes the moderate appetite of the Persians to the dry air and their constant smoking—of which he vigorously disapproves. He also insists that the reason for the sparse population on the Iranian plain is not because of the lack of food, for the soil is fertile; rather that the lack of food is due to a lack of people to till the soil.[34]

One of the most dramatic differences between the travel accounts that I have been discussing and modern accounts is the attitude toward corporal and capital punishment. These early accounts contain several references to Oriental cruelty, but these are not given in detail so the emphasis is not on the physical suffering, but rather on the indignity which the victim suffers. The English travelers especially suggest that punishment meted out at the whim of a despot is a bad thing, and that Englishmen should be happy to live under a Christian monarch and a system of law. The writer does not make his point by forcing the reader to participate vicariously in the punishment through detailed description. Jenkinson almost loses his head because the king thinks a Christian's head would make a fine gift for the Turks, whom he was then trying to appease. Jenkinson would like to keep his head because it would be difficult to complete his mission without it, but the process of losing it does not seem to appall him. Herbert clearly does not approve of the use of man-eating dogs, and less of people being thrown to men raised from infancy as cannibals. But it is the indignity of such an end, rather than the pain, that is brought home, as though a ceremonial beheading has a certain pomp which compensates for the loss of life. The indignity is greatest when someone is cut into as many pieces as there are days in the year and the remains are burned in a fire of dog dung. A couple of times Chardin refers in his cool fashion to the bastinado and seems almost amused when it is applied to a mullah because the Great Vizier doesn't like the prose style of his petition.[35] Although the mullah cannot walk afterward there are no screams and no blood. His interest in the mechanic arts extends to the ingenuity of the Persian stocks, which "in Persia is made of three Pieces of Wood square, put in a Triangular Manner, one Piece whereof is twice as long as the other two; the Criminal's Neck is enclos'd in the Triangle, having his Hand at the extream end of the longest Piece, in a Semi-Circle of Wood that was nail'd thereto."[36]

Such indifference toward physical pain seems almost akin to the medieval attitude, which views the body as inconsequential dross and a mere anchor to the soul. These writers, and especially the worldly Chardin, appear reasonably free of such attitudes, but the mind lags behind movements that change the world without our knowing it. It was not until the middle of the eighteenth century that people became aware that animals suffer from being beaten—while it was still an amusement to see soldiers flogged. One of the reasons for this is suggested by the manner in which these writers describe a person. What these descriptions assume first is that a person consists in his garments, which indicate his station and power, and then the mask of his social self is described. Herbert describes others entirely in this way, and never offers more than a word or two to describe the mask. Chardin treats others and himself in this manner, saying that after that moment of distraction when he thinks he might not be paid he recovers himself and is able to assume the polite countenance of the honest tradesman. It is almost as though the body does not exist in a significant way. It is a mere object. It is tall or short, light or dark, and sometimes needs a purge, but it has no real significance where the essential being is concerned. So pain is a mere incident; it is the indignity to station that derives from the form of punishment that is important. How very different this is from the various sufferings inflicted in the Gothic novels of the late eighteenth century, when the hero (usually heroine) was seen to exist essentially in the feelings and sensibilities. This change can be seen in the contrast between Chardin's account of the bastinado and that of Sir [Austen] Henry Layard, who gives a detailed description of the process as practiced at Hebron in 1840 by an Egyptian colonel. Here there is the noose for the ankles, the blood, the cries, the water administered so that the beating can continue, and so forth. "I felt too much disgusted and horrified with these barbarous proceedings to continue to witness them," says Layard, expressing a feeling that would never have occurred to earlier travelers.[37]

Because of British interests in India in the eighteenth century there were several travelers who took the less traveled overland route and left accounts of their adventures. The sea voyage was long and tedious and not without peril. The land route was even more dangerous, but sometimes an adventurer chose it because he was prone to seasickness, or wished to take a self-guided Bible tour, had friends in the Levant trade whom he could visit, or was simply interested in seeing what was between here and there. Many of these accounts are tedious and unobservant, and although they may be more detailed they are essentially like the itineraries of the holy pilgrims of a millennium before. One difference is that these English travelers based their self-satisfaction on a superior technology and reason rather than on a superior God, so although they were not the less self-satisfied when they saw the practices of foreigners, they were more willing to make comparisons. An example of such an account is that of Edward Ives, a physician with the East India Company, who took the overland route in 1754. Ives was a rationalist and freethinker, if not the village atheist at home; so with a ponderous irony he contrasts the regular devotion of the Turk to the hypocracies of English Christians, implying that if one is to worship a God it doesn't make much difference which one, but if you are going to do it, it might as well be done regularly. He is attracted to antiquities, but his description of them is generally cursory and intended to suggest that the Bible got the story wrong.

The main interest of Edward Ives is medicine, so that he is very specific in his descriptions of the cures used in the Middle East for semitropical diseases, and although he dismisses the superstitious ones, he is willing to investigate those that seem to work. But for all his liberality of mind, it is closed to what is not British when people are concerned. Chardin wore Persian dress for convenience and probably because he thought that he might ingratiate himself in this way, but Ives insists on wearing his English togs to signify the might of Britannia's rule. This became an issue in the literature of travel in the late eighteenth century, and there are discernible steps in the argument. While floating down the Tigris on a raft Ives is greeted by a sheik, but he feels that his Majesty's self-appointed representative is above returning the greeting—and for his discourtesy is robbed of most of his belongings.[38] James Morier was conscious of the convenience of Persian garb at the beginning of the nineteenth century, as Alexander Laing was of Arab dress when he crossed the Sahara in 1825. The next step is Lord Byron having his portrait painted in Albanian dress to signify the true tasting of a foreign culture, and the later grandstanding of Henry Layard, Richard Burton, and T. E. Lawrence. But Ives would not stoop to such playacting, even if he is inconvenienced by his English frock coat. When in Baghdad the counsel tells him that it would be rash to walk in the street dressed as he is, and Ives writes, "We are in this great city prisoners in a very strict sense; a circumstance, somewhat mortifying to the free *British* spirit."[39]

A very different traveler from Edward Ives is George Forster, who published an undeservedly neglected account of his travels in 1798. In the first instance, he reverses the experience of most such accounts by traveling from Bengal to England. He left Calcutta in August of 1782, and after going through Kashmir, Kabul, Herat, and Meshad, he crossed the Caspian and went up the Volga to Moscow, and arrived in England in July of the following year. The account uses that spurious epistolary style affected by Richardson and Cleland to give it an air of familiarity, and within the long letters there are raw journal entries, full character sketches, longer accounts of hairbreadth escapes, and long reviews of the bloody and depressing histories of India and Persia during the eighteenth century. In the introduction he excuses his lengthy narrative by saying that the study of different peoples is in itself interesting. Further, in a worldly manner he says that such study "qualifies domestic prejudice," but that Englishmen can "see through a comparison that excommunicates a fond pleasure to the heart, the unrivaled excellency of their laws, constitution and government; they see these rare gifts brightly reflected on their national character, which still avowedly maintains its pre-eminence amongst the nations of the European world."[40] This must be very pleasant for his readers to know, but in Forster's protestations of the truth of his narrative and his avoidance of a "figurative and loose style" he says that he "felt no impulse of partiality for any sect or body of men." Such protestations rarely come in the earlier travel literature of this kind. There are many protestations of truth, but few of absolute disinterest.

Forster generally lives up to the standard he sets himself, for he finds men that are foolish and wise, honest and dishonest, brave and cowardly wherever he goes, and their being Christians or Mohammedans appears to have little to do with it. He is critical of Islam, but unlike the earlier writers he does not refer to the prophets as filthy or worse; his criticism is based on his experience with base Mohammedans. "What think you, my friend, of these Mohometans, who, if they wash and pray at the five stated times, abstain from wine and the flesh of hogs, and utter a string of Arabic ejaculations which they do not understand, believe that they are procured the divine license to violate the laws of justice."[41] Such a criticism has to do with the character of the believer and not the belief, and the assumption is that religion ought to make men better rather than assure their salvation. He himself aspires to dignity and honor, but this appears to derive from something unrelated to his being a Christian or an Englishman.

Unlike earlier travelers, he is willing to put off his identity when that serves his purpose. This is an expedience, but he does it so often and assumes so many disguises that the choice seems almost arbitrary. He knows some Hindi and perhaps Urdu, but he begins his travel as a Georgian Moslem because he is fair (and, he tells us, five feet ten inches) and it is safer to be a Circassian than a Scot. Later he prefers to be a Turk when he encounters a real Georgian. With Armenians he presents himself as a Christian of vaguely European origin, and when he gets to Kashmir, he prefers to be a Spaniard because English officers were impressed into military service to train the native troops. Still later in Persia he pretends to be an Arab, until a Hadji addresses him in Arabic and he is unmasked. When other travelers of the period were discovered in false native garb they usually covered themselves with the Union Jack and bullied their way through, but Forster seems to have a world of identities to choose from, which adds spice to the suspense and an independence to his character.

When earlier travelers employ the journal form, the date and place of the entries serve only as occasions to move to the general as quickly as possible. It is as though what they saw would be seen in approximately, if not precisely, the same way by anyone else in like circumstances. Even when Chardin gives his lengthy account of his troubles in peddling his jewels to the Shah, he presents an analysis of the debates rather than the debate itself, and even this he apologizes for, saying it is simply illustrative of bargaining in the East. Forster establishes a completely different atmosphere. He is apt to apologize for making a hasty generalization, as though his view of a situation might be incorrect because it is clouded by the fatigue or passion of the moment. When he says in the introduction that he will attempt to avoid the "figurative and loose" style of other travelers, he may be suggesting that they lie not only because of their love of metaphor and the sloppy organization of their observations, but because they too hurriedly leap to conclusions. He dramatizes this on several occasions where he himself is concerned. When in dire need of money in Herat he goes to an Armenian merchant in expectation that a fellow Christian will give him help, but the merchant hears his story out and walks away without a word. Forster is again hopeful when he encounters a Russian ship captain on the Caspian, but when the captain hears that he has no passport and that his own cargo might be confiscated if he takes Forster to Baku he treats him like a pariah. His point would seem to be that all we know must be based on our experience, and even that is fallible.

Still, his observation is precise and minute. For him the date and place of the journal may be an occasion to present history or a remembered incident, but it is mainly an occasion to recite the events of the day. He often begins with an observation on the weather, and there are often topographical notes and a record of the distance traveled, but most of his observation is directed at people, and his descriptions often employ a typically eighteenth-century irony. On the bleak Afghan plain he must share a camel with a wet nurse and infant.

In traversing so inhospitable a tract, little matter of information or amusement can occur to the traveller. But had he been journeying over a land stored with every gift and every beauty of nature, a companion like mine would have destroyed his joy and have converted his Eden to a desert. The nurse of the crying child was the immediate reverse of a handsome woman; on this score she was not responsible, and had she been moderately clean, I had no right to complain, and might even have derived entertainment from her talk which flowed with a strong current. But trusting wholly to this qualification for a passage through life, she seemed to despise every other care. Her hair was a complicated maze of filth, which had never I [sic] been explored by comb, and from whose close vicinity I received a severe visitation; nor was her face while I knew her, once touched by water.[42]

Here we see Forster seeing the people in his world through a novelist's wit, with all its ironic understatement and allusion. At this point in the journey Forster is posing as a Georgian Christian, and shortly after he has to suffer a ranting Mohammedan pedant who will not share any bread with an infidel.[43] That evening Forster is shaved, and the barber is told by the zealot that he must purify his instruments, Forster insists that the coin in payment must be washed too.[44]

Such encounters, or his version of them, suggest that Forster was an avid reader of Fielding and Smollett, for he often casts himself as well as the characters he meets in the eighteenth-century picaresque mold. The situation suggests it, but although the narrator may see others as grotesques or kindly philosophers he himself is not a heartless rogue, although on many occasions he must use roguish tricks to escape with his skin. He may be aware of this, for although there are very few literary references, two that he repeats are to Quixote and Gil Blas. His descriptions of nature, however, are more indebted to the late eighteenth-century school of sentiment, rather than that of the picaresque into which nature is dragged for mere stage setting. At one point he apologizes for the disorder of his remarks: "From a glaring deficiency of method, in the arrangement of my remarks, I am often fearful that but faint traces of a general chain will be exhibited. It is not that my ideas flow so thick and strong, as, in confidence of their superior excellency, to contemn reflection or that obedience to order, which is so essential to their utility; it is an habit, perhaps an idle one, that impels me to note at the moment, the train of thoughts which occur."[45] His description of persons is presented with a controlled whimsy that has little to do with the free associative method for which he apologizes in this passage, but such a free flow of image and reflection can be seen in his observation of natural scenes, in which he is perfectly clear about his response and so turns the scene into an inner landscape. He finds the combination of broad river, green mountains, and colorful Hindoo pilgrims at Allahabad on the Ganges a scene that pleases his eye. It is "a situation beautiful as it is commodious; and in the season of the year when the flow of water is spacious and rapid, exhibits a scene of uncommon grandeur."[46] The natural scene itself would normally have been ignored by earlier travelers, even though their eye might have been trained for such scenes by the Dutch landscapes of the seventeenth century or their English imitations. Forster not only describes such scenes, but fixes attributive terms like *beautiful* and *grandeur* to them. When he travels through the cities and villages, he often notes the vermin and filth which was undoubtedly there, but which Herbert and Chardin never mention because it is difficult to extract a neat generalization from such data. Forster gives all the details, and when the eye is dulled by the dry tedium of treeless plains it turns inward and broods.

After crossing the Alborz mountains he descends into the lushness of Mazanderan and toward the Caspian, and this lushness results in delight and memories of home. "The villages all open and neatly built; the verdant hills and dales, encircled by streams of delicious water, presented a scene that gave the mind ineffable delight. The air, though in winter, was mild, and had the temperature of an English climate in the month of April. This change of weather, effected within so short a space of time, arises from the low situation of the province, its near vicinity to the Caspian sea, and the shelter of the adjacent mountains."[47] Such a description attends to the facts of this pastoral scene, but Forster also suggests his response, and we are forced to see what he sees through his experience. It is not only a matter of the scene itself, which was increasingly the subject of the poets of his period, but such descriptions illustrate a new way of seeing, in which the object is almost incidental to its perception, and its significance found in a personal memory.

Before tourists traipsed the world harnessed with cameras, they studied drawing so they could sketch what they saw, and several of the travel narratives of this period are graced with engravings of the result. I have mentioned the curious representations in the case of Sir Thomas Herbert whose drawings were especially schematic and architectural. In his case there is an odd compromise with the third dimension, so that he can compress grand monuments onto a page and somehow make them look as though they would not be out of place in the London exchange. When he introduces cuts of landscapes, they are essentially maps with the suggestion of elevations and intended as guides to navigators.[48] His illustrations of fauna look like something out of the emblem books of a century before, so that his shark has the head of a crocodile with a half-devoured man protruding from the mouth, and in the watery distance there is an ominous black funnel cloud.[49] Such illustrations are like that drawing of the plated rhinoceros made by Dürer, who never saw the beast, and which served encyclopedists into the eighteenth century.[50] The point of such whimsical representations would seem to be that Nature is profligate, and what the artist saw was not the object before him but the clumsy hand of natural history or the vengeful one of God. Well into the eighteenth century, travelers chose either artifacts or people as their main subjects for illustration. The artifacts were usually palaces or ruins, and the drawings were descriptive of their construction and design; the aesthetic elements or the play of light upon surfaces was not rendered. If any implications were suggested, it was the comforting one for Europeans that this alien and infidel culture exists amidst decayed grandeur. When people are the subject, the attention is given to the dress and occasionally to household articles. The faces are those of foreign mannequins, but they are not so foreign that they could not belong to any dark Mediterranean or Celtic type. Thomas Herbert's presentation of Persians native to the Gulf even mutes this aspect of the foreignness, for the oval faces might adorn the figures in an English family portrait of the Elizabethan period. But beyond this, the figures in their nakedness and pleasant proportions undoubtedly owe more to images of a Golden Age and Nobel Savagery than they do to what was really seen. The engraving also has the descriptive quality of Herbert's drawing of the Great Maidan at Isfahan, for here there is no setting, and perspective is sacrificed for what passes as accuracy of description. The woman is seen full-front in a dancing posture that is indebted to Renaissance depictions of the Graces or Springtime dances; the man is seen from the right side, unrelated to the dancer, and in a posture often used to depict military uniforms. Then on the right and out of proportion there is the picture of the nose jewel. The whole is seen from no one point in space and at no specific time so that the eye of the artist remains anonymous. Here the traveler sees across a cluttered bridge between what he knows to what is there before him, but before the late eighteenth century he gives no indication that he is aware of this.

A different approach is dramatically seen in the engravings made from the drawings of James Morier, illustrating his account of a journey to Persia in 1808. Forster describes pastoral settings with attention to his own emotional reaction to them, almost in the manner of a Cowper or even a young Wordsworth, but in Morier the reader is made even more aware of his sensitivity to lights and shades, and his drawings are clearly intended to suggest a mood. They are still descriptive, and his subjects are those that appeal to an anthropological or archeological interest, but the perspective is convincing, and the whole frame is filled with rivers and mountains and sky so that the viewer can both analyze the exotic custom and enter into the mood of the entire scene. There is, for example, an engraving of a Persian gentleman smoking a kaleoon or nargileh while he rides. Beside him walks a servant, who carries the water jar with its basin of burning charcoal at the top. Behind, there is another servant on horseback, who has additional water in his cannister, and from his saddle swings a brazier with more burning coals. The dress is meticulously rendered, and the faces seem more indebted to those on the Achaemenian friezes at Persepolis than to any European types. All of this is descriptive, and that is clearly its intent; but in the background, is a small mosque on a rise, a few cypress trees, a body of water, barren mountains beyond, and a sky with nicely arranged cumulus clouds. The sky might be by Constable who said, "when I sit down to make a sketch from nature the first thing I try to do is to forget that I have ever seen a picture."[51] Such an attitude would never have been entertained by Sir Thomas Herbert, whose stylization refers to other pictorial representations, not to objects

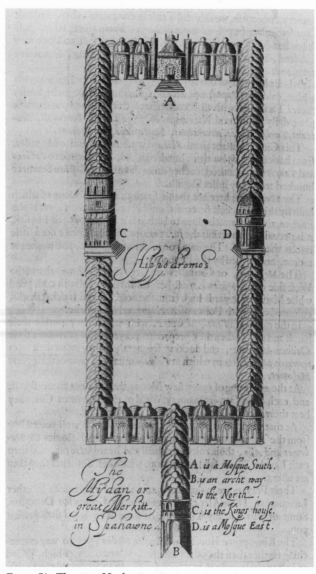

The
Mydan or
great Merkitt
in Spahawne.

A. is a Mosque South.
B. is an archt way
  to the North.
C. is the Kings house.
D. is a Mosque East.

From Sir Thomas Herbert
A Relation of Some Yeares Travaile (1634)

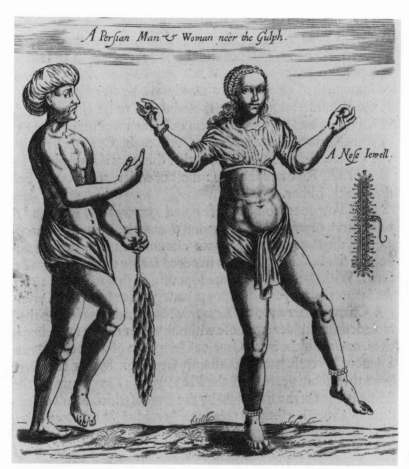

From Sir Thomas Herbert
A Relation of Some Yeares Travaile (1634)

Ruines of
Persæpolis.

Mardash

From Sir Thomas Herbert
A Relation of Some Yeares Travaile (1634)

From James Morier
A Journey Through Persia (1812)

From James Morier
A Journey Through Persia (1812)

From James Morier
A Journey Through Persia (1812)

in nature. He would seem to be a transmitter of external, eternal, and
cultural symbols that have no dependence on himself. His illustrations
of Isfahan and Persepolis deliberately avoid the suggestion of the moment or the point in space from which they were seen. Morier, on the
other hand, is no Constable, but his representation of a scene suggests
that he saw it at a particular moment, and from an imaginable point in
space.

James Morier is best known for his picaresque novel *Adventures of
Hadjji Baba of Ispahan*, which he wrote after several years' residence in
Persia as secretary to the English ambassador. The work is so convincing in its depiction of Oriental manners and attitudes that Persian
readers did not believe it when it became known that the author was
English. His earlier journal of his experience with a British mission to
the court of the Shah has an official air, and when he describes official
functions and the travel of the mission he uses the plural, but as a
mere underling he can often slip off to indulge in his own private
investigations. These include almost everything that interested the
omnivorous Chardin, but Morier sees his experiences through the
specific entries in his journal, and is much less apt to indulge in the
European and Christian sneer at peculiar customs. Chardin speculates
that the Oriental's habit of inaction and his sitting for hours on his
heels is the result of a meatless diet, his use of tobacco, and his indo-

lence. Morier notes how awkward such a posture is for an energetic Englishman, but simply attributes the difference to custom. "We chose to be uncomfortable," he writes, "and to imitate their fashion."[52]

Morier has the antiquarian's fascination with ancient history, and is drawn to the antiquities of the land, armed with tape measure and the artist's pen. He not only describes the ruins with a great deal of accuracy, and politely corrects the mistakes of Herbert and Chardin and others along the way, but he also speculates on what might have been, with a freedom from biblical tradition that was not theirs. He introduces his description of Persepolis by recording an emotional response which, although reined, is reminiscent of other Romantic reflections on ruins. "Our first, and indeed lasting impression were astonishment at the immensity, and admiration at the beauties of the fabric. Although there was nothing, either in the architecture of the buildings, or the sculptures and relief on the rocks, which could bear critical comparison with the delicate proportions and perfect statuary of the Greeks, yet without trying *Persepolis* by a standard to which it never was amenable, we yielded at once to emotions the most lively and the most enraptured."[53] He then takes his "Chardin and Le Brun" in hand and measures this rapture against the monument itself and compares his measurements with earlier ones. His drawings are exceedingly accurate, and if he had not been drawn away by the press of other business might have made some later ones unnecessary.

The descriptions which Morier gives of customs are presented as specific occasions, although they may have been based on repeated exposure; whereas earlier writers treat the same material in just the opposite way. In this manner Morier is able to fill out the picture, as he does his drawings, with more than the costume and forms of address of his hosts.

The room into which we were introduced was very pleasant, and by far more agreeable than any thing that I had expected at *Bushire*. Two pillars, neatly inlaid with looking-glasses, supported it on one side, and thus separated it from a small court, which was crowded with servants. An orange tree stood in the centre of the court. The walls of the room were of a beautiful white stucco, resembling plaster of Paris; and large curtains were suspended around them, to screen in every position the company from the sun. The *Khan* was seated in a corner, and having taken off our shoes at the door, we paid our respects severally, and then settled ourselves according to our rank.[54]

Only after this does he describe the compliments exchanged, the passing of the water pipe, the sherbert, and then again the pipe. In this introduction to the scene he economically says much about the culture he is describing, without condescension and with a completeness that suggests the tactile qualities of the experience. The brilliance and elegance of the scene is depicted, whereas a Chardin would crassly mention only those objects to which he could assign a price. Morier mentions the servants essential to such a society. They are as absent from earlier accounts as they are from a novel by Henry James, or are mentioned only in connection with a real or imagined affront.

In his description of landscapes, Morier adheres to the eighteenth-century opinion that they had to have variety in order to please the eye; a variety that should include a range of textures, colors, and animation. His trip presented him with many monotonous and dreary views, but he is attuned to them (as with Forster—it is not just a matter of an unseen and unmentioned blank), and is ready with pen to catch the moment when the scene takes on a rhythm. "To the east of [Bushire] there is a small elevation, which happily destroys the equalities of the buildings, and renders it no inunteresting subject for a sketch, when enlivened by its concomitants, water and shipping."[55] That elevation and those dhows are just the sort of thing that the eighteenth-century man of feeling would note, and he would note them because they would serve like a pinching of the self, and remind him that he existed in the delicacy of his perceptions. Such connoisseurs of the picturesque who collected pleasant views a generation before—and the Reverend William Gilpin represents them best—attempted to reduce the picturesque to a formula, and that elevation and those concomitants in the view of Bushire satisfy such formulae. By the turn of the century, the term came to be applied to a great variety of scenes, and the standards became less those mechanical ones in which eighteenth-century reason and sensibility came to overlap, but rather the quality of the emotion of the beholder. Forster says the view of Moscow's spires "shooting through extensive plantations" exhibits a view which is "picturesque and magnificant."[56] Claudius Rich, describing the Zagros near Hamadan in 1820, writes after an ascent: "From the top we had a fine view of the plain, winding among beautifully-shaped hills covered with dwarf oak, the background being formed by the high mountains of Persia, whose outline was also extremely picturesque."[57] Mrs. Rich kept her own journal of this trip, and describes the more modest western slopes of the Zagros in this fashion: "The view from the summit of the hills, though not rivaling that from the top of the Jura, was still very agreeable to one who loves anything at all approaching to the picturesque, and who has so long been deprived of every thing of the kind."[58] Here the scene is mainly used as a stimulus to a certain kind of memory, and the picturesque is not so much derived from the properties of the scene, but from something rattling about inside the head of the viewer. And again, Sir Henry Layard, in 1839, frequently describes the bleak deserts of western Syria as picturesque.[59] Such notions would dumbfound Gilpin, fresh from the banks of the verdant Wye.

Morier's descriptions suggest a way station between the mechanical analysis of the picturesque conducted by the scene collectors who hiked bucolic English roads in the 1770s, and those later writers who measured the picturesque by the intensity of the palpitations it created in the viewer. He describes Shapur with its ponderous funereal pile, the Shapur river, and the mountains beyond. "The opening betwixt the two grand masses presented a landscape the most varied, the most tranquil, the most picturesque, and, at the same time, the most sublime that imagination can form."[60] Here certain terms —*tranquil, picturesque, sublime*—fall into place with a kind of predictability, but what he sees conforms to a pattern created by the heightened imagination. Reason might have a role in later tranquil analysis, but it is the imagination of Morier that is touched, and it is ours that he wishes to stir.

In *Don Juan* Byron mentions the bricks from Babylon about which Claudius Rich had published two papers. In the passage Byron was making fun of those scoffers who insisted that the Bible was a pack of lies, so Rich's descriptions of very real ruins was useful in substantiating that the Old Testament told more truth than fiction. Rich was not able to enjoy the reference, for the fifth canto in which it comes was published in 1821, and Rich died in October of that year of cholera in the remoteness of Shiraz.[61] He would have been pleased with the allusion, if not the poem, for in his journal of his travels during the last year and a half of his life he makes reference to the earlier gloomy broodings of Lord Byron with implied applause. In describing unusual electrical storms on a trip from Baghdad to Kurdistan, he refers to "that perfect black, that total absence of light, which Lord Byron has fancied in his horrible dream of the extinction of the sun."[62] An even more romantic mood is supported by Byron when Rich deliberately arranges his arrival at Persepolis to coincide with a full moon, so that he can view the ruins as Darius might have two millennia before. "This may be foolish, but I determined to put off my minute inspection of them [the ruins] till our return, and enjoy for the present the general impression caused by this distant view. Lord Byron would have employed the interval better than I could do."[63]

To earlier travelers such midnight self-indulgences would have appeared lunatic, but Rich was a serious and prolix (considering his poor health and official duties) student of the Middle East. Chardin, compared to him, seems a dilettante, and Morier a fop. Rich, by the time he was a sixteen-year-old schoolboy in Bristol, knew the major Semitic languages, as well as Latin, Greek, and Turkish. He so impressed officials of the East India Company that they sent him to India in 1804, but shipwreck forced a detour through Italy, Malta, Constantinople, Cyprus, Cairo, and Baghdad. At each stop, according to a very loyal sketch of his life by his widow, he mastered the language and customs of the natives. He did not get to Bombay until 1807, and there took little time to woo the daughter of the governor, and two years later took her to Baghdad where he was appointed Resident. His two studies of the ruins of Babylon were published in 1815 and 1818, in time for Byron's notice, but his major work is the posthumous account of his journey to Sulaimaniya, Mosul, and Shiraz which was published in 1836. Here he shows an omnivorous interest, and his fluency in Arabic and Turkish (there are hints that he didn't make much progress in Kurdish or Farsi) and his position as British Resident gained him entree into areas where others were forbidden. In the case of the Kurds, his information is thorough and original, and although he maintains a consciousness of the superiority of British and Christian culture, he is genuinely enthusiastic, suggesting an independence in him that is rare. Forster meets people that he respects for their knowledge or honesty; Morier was fascinated with the Persian ambassador to England whom he knew well, and whose tales contributed to the experiences of Hadjji Baba; but Rich has affection for a whole people. "I quit Koordistan with unfeigned regret. I, most unexpectedly, found in it the best people that I have ever met in the East. I have formed friendships, and been uniformly treated with a degree of sincerety, kindness, and unbounded hospitality, which I fear I must not again look for in the course of my weary pilgrimage; and the remembrance of which will last as long as life itself endures."[64]

The roll of unprepared Europeans who disappeared in the wilds of the Middle East during the first half of the nineteenth century is a long one.[65] Sir Henry Layard was put upon by bandits at every turn during the 1830s, and his experience was typical, but most travelers succumbed to fevers in the head or bowels. This makes Forster's solo feat all the more remarkable. Rich and his bride once rode horseback (she presumably in disguise as a man) from Constantinople to Baghdad, and there was some heartless terrain and tribes between the two cities. On his tour of Kurdistan to avoid the summer heat of Baghdad he had to take his position into consideration, so the trip was conducted with sepoy guards, servants, and other hangers-on to the number of sixty. Mrs. Rich, for the sake of decorum in an Islamic land, traveled separately in a covered litter. As she puts it in her own journal of the trip, a Mohammedan gentleman must display no more con-

cern for his wife than for his baggage.⁶⁶ There was even an English
doctor in attendance with his medicines, yet Rich seems to luxuriate
in his body's frailty, and to adopt the romantic notion that the truly
sensitive person has his nerves strung finely. It is not that he was not
ill, or that travelers before his time were not, but that he is so assiduous in recording his medical report for us. We only know that Chardin
had intestinal problems because he thought it important to tell us that
he thought he had found an effective purge, but Rich makes us hang
upon the information that he is "feeling much better today."⁶⁷ He
often lies under a tree or in his tent all day because (according to his
wife) he is bilious, or (according to him) because of his weak nerves.⁶⁸
Of course there was reason to be concerned for one's health under the
circumstances. The party lost a young German linguist in Mosul, and
Rich himself died at Shiraz, but these reports, as much as the sight of
Persepolis by moonlight, suggest a desire to crush the grape against
the palate fine.

Such tremulousness did not prevent Rich from being an astute observer and an eager gatherer of facts. He recounts Kurdish history
(much of it for the first time), economics, and customs. He lists the
various tribes and includes a glossary of Kurdish words. Even though
he knew best the people of importance, unlike earlier travelers, he is
interested in the lives of the peasants and describes much more than
their curious costumes. He may describe their customs as barbaric or
savage, but he does so without the complete revulsion of earlier
travelers that results in complacent misunderstanding, for he is also
willing to see them as independent, brave, and even dignified. He
attends a Kurdish wedding in disguise, and is enchanted with the
grace and decorum of the occasion.⁶⁹ There is some hankering here for
simpler days and ways, and he compares their dress and music to that
of the highland Scots or rural Irish, but his main motive is to lose
himself—at least tentatively—in another culture. It is tentative, for
when he seems most lost to primitive enchantment, he reminds himself that he is a cultivated European. There is a charming scene in
which he explains to the Pasha of Sulaimaniya how the world is round
and that this conviction resulted in the discovery of America. But he is
also the Gulliver of book 2, for the Pasha asks some very astute questions about the English drive for empire, especially in India.⁷⁰ Rich
says that Islam is a bar to the progress of these people because
Mohammed wrote on everything and closed the minds of his followers
to any other views. He is much taken with the Yazidis, who are Devil
worshipers to the Moslems, and concludes that "Under the British
government much might be made of them."⁷¹ Rich's enthusiasm is
raised to its highest pitch, however, when he is dealing with the an-

tiquities, and his descriptions are minute and accurate, considering that he lived at a time when the Sumerians were unknown and the Assyrians almost hypothetical. Rich had to depend on the Bible and the Greek and Roman historians, so that he walked the ruins with Arrian or Xenophon in hand. It was almost two decades later that Botta and Layard applied the shovel to Nineveh and Khorsabad; Rich simply came before archeology as a field technique was developed.

The observations of nature which Rich offers are of two kinds. As with his meticulous recordings of the dimensions of an ancient site, he records the types of flora he comes across with an exceptionally cool and scientific eye. There is a press for samples which he fills as he goes, and his interest seems most heightened when he discovers oaks in Kurdistan that are much like English oaks. The delight is in the recognition, but he also is delighted with the memory of the cousins of these oaks—as though nature existed for itself, and in an inner eye. This is the other view of nature that he takes, and it sometimes is expressed independently of the scientific one, as when he indulges himself in the view of Persepolis by moonlight and thinks of Lord Byron. At times such emotional reactions are seen through others, as when the party moves up to the green Kurdish hills from the arid plain of the Tigris. "As far as the eye could reach in every direction nothing but fields of barley were to be seen, some yet green, others almost ripe. This sight excited the raptures of the poor *Bagadees* among our party, who would hardly have believed the world could have contained such a sight. Such an expanse of green they had never before beheld!"[72] Such a displacement in the process of describing a scene is even more evident in the journal kept by Mrs. Rich. Although there are moments when she tends to gush, she is a better writer in that she has a nice eye for domestic detail and her characterizations are very convincing. When she treats the landscape, she may brood on the history it has seen. In a high pass in the Zagros she is taken with the green plain and the snowy mountains on the horizon. "It is a most remarkable object; and perhaps from hence some of the most ancient Persian kings, Cyrus or Xerxes, may have surveyed their armies in the plain below; while at the moment I am writing, a company of Indians, in the English uniform, with drums and fifes, are parading on the very same spot, and marching to a Scotch tune!"[73] Such a scene exists in a specific time and place, but the reflection on it involves a view of the broadly ironic twists of history that are her contribution. She is amazed at this and invites us to be amazed through her amazement. The reflection is not the conventional groan of the medieval poet over the fall of princes, for that exists outside of a firm sense of history and time, but here the comment comes from one who knows very well the length of the shadow Cyrus casts, and the causes which bring Indians in English uniforms to this out-of-the-way place, for she has watched her husband pace a nearby battlefield with Xenophon in hand. More often Mrs. Rich internalizes her response, so that what she describes takes on a meaning only through her memory of walks in an English countryside, and the view is important for the very private emotions it creates. When the party first reaches the lush heights of Kurdistan, Rich says that the whole company was in rapture with the flowers and trees and nightingales, for "There is no mind, however brutish, but is affected by the beauties of nature."[74] He is responsible for the whole group, and sees this scene through their response, but his wife sees the scene in a romantic fashion and joins her response with his. "But from our very long privation of such a prospect it appeared like enchantment, and affected us more than the many celebrated spots we had visited either in England, Switzerland, or Italy. We rambled about the valley and through the beautiful grove, gathering roses and wild flowers, till suddenly we came to a *wild rose bush*, for which everything else was abandoned, and we almost worshipped the solitary exile, as it seemed, from England."[75] Here, as is so often the case in Wordsworth and Keats, the landscape is turned into a private feeling and given reality through the memory, as though it only pretended to exist for the eye, but was really painted on the inside of the mind.

In the two centuries that separate the travels of Sir Thomas Herbert and those of Claudius Rich a radical change takes place in the way the traveler sees and relates his experiences. This change begins in the late eighteenth century and accelerates at the beginning of the nineteenth. I have briefly examined accounts of travelers to the Middle East, as a kind of laboratory situation, to show how they treated similar experiences. In this instance, possibly because of the character of the travelers themselves, or possibly because of the difficulty in conveying the strangeness of their experiences, there is a cultural lag, for the kind of ultimate subjectivism that is seen in the account by Mrs. Rich occurs earlier in the truly literary types of the mid–eighteenth century, and even in the accounts of rambles through more familiar European scenery. Herbert usually saw what he expected to see, and so had little reason to express astonishment. The mold which God pressed upon the world was a universal one for him, and the differences between one place and another are not great, for they are the result of the improvisations of puny men. For Herbert, the world moves in a lockstep, and since he himself is one of the marchers there is a kind of anonymity to the presentation of his experiences—they are not in a sense even his. Claudius Rich, however (and in this he is like Chardin), can be admirably objective and precise. He notes the temperature, maps the terrain, and records the traffic of goods between Sulaimaniya and Mosul as though with time and energy he might be able to describe every strand in the fabric of a society. But his observations are particularized, as though truth is always particular; whereas Chardin, with a seventeenth-century confidence in a finite truth which was seen as analogous to mathematical truths, dismisses various aspects of Persian society (its crafts, its diet, its agriculture, etc.) in a series of neat and general paragraphs. Rich also places himself between us and his narrative. We see the particulars he reports through the particular of Claudius Rich, so he favors the reader with allusions to his idle reading, his personal mail, and the state of his nerves and bowels.

9

The Traveler at Home

What man of taste my right will doubt,
To put things in, or leave them out?
'Tis more than right, it is a duty,
If we consider landscape beauty:
He ne'er will as an artist shine,
Who copies Nature line by line:
Whoe'er from Nature takes a view,
Must copy and improve her too.
To heighten every work of art,
Fancy should take an active part:
Thus I (which few I think can boast)
Have made a Landscape of a Post.
　　　　—William Combe, *The Tour of Doctor Syntax*
　　　　　　　　　　in Search of the Picturesque

Before the eighteenth century a traveler was usually happy enough to get to where he was going and forget the tedium of the trip, and if he had to set out the next day for somewhere else he thought of the prospect as a glum necessity. A turn in the garden might have been perfectly refreshing to him at a proper time of year, but a walk in the country would have been out of the question. But by the 1770s the countryside was crowded with men of taste who flocked to the woods and hills in order to collect memories and sketches of views. The history of travelers on their native soil went through the same kind of metamorphosis of attitude that characterizes that of travelers to faraway places. A poem reputed to be the longest in the language is Michael Drayton's *Polyolbion*, an idealized description of almost every nook in England written during the flush of Elizabethan nationalism. Drayton describes real places, but he cloaks them with myth, ecclesiastical and military history, and the purling brooks of verdant spring in such mouth-filling hexameters that few would be tempted to use the poem for their *Baedeker*. Real guidebooks come later, and accounts of journeys to the provinces, such as Johnson's and Boswell's journals of their tour to the Hebrides or that fictionalized tour rendered by Smollett in *Humphrey Clinker* later.

156

An example of the guidebook is the *Journeys* of Celia Fiennes, who toured the home provinces on horseback from 1685 to 1697. Her account was written for "near relations" (as were so many of the elegiac biographies of the period) and the journeys were taken for a "change of aire & exercise," for although still in her twenties when she began she felt oppressed by the foul air of London.[1] She also has a nationalistic motive, for she asserts that it is best to see England first at a time when the English were running off to the Continent.[2] She was undoubtedly an independent and interesting young woman, for in her class (she was the daughter of an eminent dissenting family of Salisbury) it was not quite proper to travel alone, and on horseback, about the country. Yet her journal tells us very little about her, and what we do discover is by accident. We know that she wears a cloak that is not impervious to rain, for she is distressed when she gets soaked through. Her comments on some of the bad food she encounters are not intended to display a delicate stomach, but are warnings to other travelers against certain hostelries. Her purpose is descriptive, but not of herself or of her reflections on the sights along the way. So the work is a verbal map which notes the passing milestones and landmarks. She is, like her contemporaries Chardin and Defoe, uncommonly interested in the mechanical arts, and notes the methods used by the imported Dutch engineers to drain bogs, and how much beer is brewed in a certain town. She is also an observer of antiquities, and in accordance with the reigning quantitative notion of the real she counts the number of stones in Stonehenge, as did Defoe and Evelyn, although each came up with a different number.[3] Much of her description is of stately houses and cathedrals. These are very detailed, but her adjectives run to vague terms like *lofty* and *stately* which convey a general sense of grandeur. Her descriptions of nature are few and used only to give a sense of the setting of a village, or she might complain of the weather, not because it dampens her spirits, but because of the inconvenience of muddy roads.

It could be said that Celia Fiennes and her contemporaries who wrote such guidebooks sought an admirable objectivity consistent with their purpose. Certainly the tradition of such works has been continued by Mobil and Michelin, but in her day there were none of those emtoional accounts of impressive vistas that were added to the guides of the middle of the next century, and which became the incentive to travelers by the 1770s. One way station in this change is the journal of Thomas Pennant, one of those eighteenth-century vestry antiquarians who in 1772 toured Scotland and the Hebrides. He too gives directions and warnings to the traveler, but is more likely than Celia Fiennes to base his injunctions on his own particular experience. Pennant is also encyclopedic in his observations, for he treats history, architecture, business, agriculture, antiquities, superstitions, and describes the paintings in local museums. The work is dedicated to Sir Joseph Banks, and Pennant aspires to be as scientific and objective as his patron, yet he is very apt to suggest his own reaction to a scene or edifice. He begins at Chester, and even before he has need to pack his bags he describes the chapter house with an enthusiasm which demands that the future traveler imitate his feeling. "The beauty and elegant simplicity of a very antique gothic chapter-house, and its fine vestibule, merits a visit from every traveller. The date of the foundation is uncertain, but it seems, from the similitude of roof and pilasters in a chapel in the square tower in the castle, to have been the work of contemporary architects, and these architects were probably *Norman;* for the mode of square towers, with squared angles, was introduced immediately on the conquest."[4] Here we have history and description neatly presented, but we are also nudged toward an aesthetic appreciation of the simple and elegant in a manner that earlier travelers did not use. He also tells us what to think about events in recent history, as when he refers to the Quaker George Fox who captivated his congregation with "grunts and groans," and then "this spiritual Quixot sallied out, and disturbed mankind with all the extravagancies that enthusiasm could invent."[5] When Pennant describes natural scenes he invariably describes the vantage from which the view is seen, and this places him as the lens through which we are to see it, but he also suggests an appropriate emotional response. When he describes Mount Skiddaw and Lake Derwent at its foot, it is as though he were painting a picture, and he even offers us an engraving to supplement his words. One end of the lake where there is a "rude conic hill" and the earth is scratched for a "variety of minerals, the origin of evil by their abuse," is termed "horrible." But the other end is called "a strong and beautiful contrast." "*Skiddaw* shews its vast base, and bounding all that part of the vale, rises gently to a height that sinks the neighboring hills; opens a pleasing front, smooth and verdant, smiling over the country like a gentle generous lord, while the *fells* of *Borrowdale* frown on it like a hardened tyrant."[6] Pennant also presents an account of imports and exports in tabular form, or botanical drawings of highland weeds. Then there are those passages when he breaks through bare fact with elaborate metaphors and mythological allusions. Sir Thomas Herbert is also a fancy travel-writer, but his metaphors invariably show us the moral that lies on the other side of the particular; Pennant intends to make us see the object with emotional clarity, and the moral resides in the object itself. This difference depends on Pennant's awareness of himself—and the reader's acceptance of his awareness—as a mediator between the reader and the object observed. He repeatedly invites "the traveller," to look over his shoulder, and yet the vicarious traveler must look through his ver individual eyes on a certain day in 1772.

Doctor Johnson's feelings about Thomas Pennant were mixed, so although he pointed out to Boswell that "the dog is a whig," he defended him for his "variety of enquiry."[7] Pennant had published his *Tour of Scotland* in 1771, and his work on the Hebrides was in parparation when Boswell was finally able to get Johnson off alone into the northern wilds in 1774. The result of this tour was the two best-known works of actual travel (as opposed to such imaginary voyages as those of Gulliver, Candide, and Johnson's own Rasselas) of the eighteenth century. In some ways, Johnson's *Journey to the Western Islands and Scotland* and Boswell's *Journal of a Tour to the Hebrides with Samuel Johnson L.L.D.* are almost accidentally travel books. Johnson's reportage is often cursory, although he is interested in antiquities and history, for the bulk of the work is an account of conversations (often paraphrased) with northern gentlemen—conversations that often center on the locale, but which might have taken place in a London coffee house. He does not use Pennant's guidebook formula of "the traveller now . . . ," but rather "we then . . . " This tends to personalize the narrative, but what we then do is to sit down to tea and have a conversation rather than view the landscape. The work is read not so much for its comments on travel, which Johnson generally thought a bore, but for the nicely turned aphoristic style behind which Johnson tends to hide. I suspect that most readers have the sense of Johnson's presence in his words, yet what they see is not what Johnson shows them, but rather what Boswell has written about him. Johnson can be crotchety in his own writing, yet he would not report that he called Pennant a dog and a Whig—that must come from Boswell. And it is just such tidbits that make Boswell's report something else than a proper travel book. He is pleased to display his native grounds to the famous Doctor Johnson, but as a collector of the famous he is even more pleased to be seen showing Johnson about. The result is that his journal served to whet his audience's appetite for the forthcoming *Life*, and the itinerary serves as a string on which to bead the anecdotes. Boswell tours not the Hebrides but Samuel Johnson, and the *Journal* has a closer relationship to the gossip of Letitia Pilkington than to the road directions of Cecila Fiennes.

There is a delicate difference between the words *journey* and *journal*, in the two titles. Although the works unfold in the same sequence (and of course Boswell had his own raw journal to work with as well as Johnson's published account), Johnson's account is arranged ac-

cording to place names, and under these heads he discusses methods
of agriculture, geneaolgy, the menu, cottage industry, and so forth, in
his nicely balanced periods. It is as though he were completing the
observations of Pennant and giving his comments a superior orotund
expression. There is an air in his approach of his imposing an order
on the facts that does not derive from the facts themselves, but rather
from some eternal order of the way men live their lives. It is this tacit
assumption that allows him to go from the observation of fact to an
aphoristic generalization with little stripping of the gears of his prose.
He meditates, for example, on the precipitousness of Slanes Castle,
from which one can look out over the stormy sea. "From the windows
the eye wanders over the sea that separates Scotland from Norway,
and when the winds beat with violence must enjoy all the terrifick
grandeur of the tempestuous ocean. I would not for my amusement
wish to see a storm; but as storms, whether wished or not, will sometimes happen, I may say, without violation of humanity, that I should
willingly look out upon them from Slanes Castle."[8] Here, as so often,
Johnson begins with description and then goes to his gruff commonsensical and personal reflection on the object described. This might
suggest the same sort of attitude toward nature that later travelers
record—Mrs. Claudius Rich, for example—in which an object in nature takes on meaning through memory or association, by which it is
internalized. But Johnson's reflection tends to keep the natural object
in its place, and although he here writes of "terrifick grandeur" his
appreciation is a grudging one, and he is willing to let the storm rage
around Slanes Castle while he goes elsewhere. Upon these rocks," he
adds, "there was nothing that could long detain attention," for they
merely exist, and he is willing to let them lie. The next step is the
generalization in which the pontificating author of the *Rambler* once
again describes the effect of the universal mold which the Creator has
pressed on all nature. "But terror without danger is only one of the
sports of fancy, a voluntary agitation of the mind that is permitted no
longer than it pleases."[9] Yes, we say, here once again is something for
our memory book, and it is for such that we read the *Journey*.

These rocks that do not long detain the attention exist on their own
are are of no real use, except perhaps to kick in refutation of Bishop
Berkeley ("Let him deny *that!*"). For Johnson, the mind, and he hoped
the soul, moved on almost independent of the nature around it. For him,
the poet did not rob Nature's pocket (as Coleridge put it), but rather
borrowed to give substance to his expression of abstract truths. Reality
simply was, and truth moved above like a zenith, almost independent
of nature. Not so for Boswell. Instead of imposing a scheme on his
observations, as Johnson uses the scheme of place to arrange his *Jour-*

ney, Boswell calls his work a *Journal*; he surrenders himself to the calendar, and lets the passing days organize his observations. Such a surrender might appear to be a denial of his self—especially when compared to Johnson in his pontifical summaries. But Johnson was merely exercising a learned talent to rephrase old wisdoms that existed without his expression of them. Boswell's surrender to the world about him is also an incorporation of the world into himself, so that his descriptions of nature lead not toward a grand aphoristic generalization, but end with a personal reaction. "We had good weather, and a fine sail this day. The shore was varied with hills, and rocks, and corn-fields, bushes, which are here dignified with the name of natural *wood*."[10] The description is cursory, as it usually is in the *Journal*, because Boswell wishes to get back to what Johnson said on the occasion, but the catalogue is a romantic one and has the kind of variety that was so admired by the writers of this period on the picturesque. Boswell says it was a fine sail; Johnson would have put up with it. There are several passages in the two accounts that show such a difference. Johnson mentions the weather to explain how their passage is detained or expedited; Boswell will often be sprightly on fine days and gloomy on dank ones—except when these might offer occasion for him to be closeted with Johnson. At one point, he himself notes this difference. "The weather was worse than yesterday. I felt as if imprisoned. Dr. Johnson said, it was irksome to be detained thus: yet he seemed to have less uneasiness, or more patience, than I had."[11] For Johnson, weather also simply is, and the soul and the mind move on independently of it; Boswell feels it in his bones and perhaps along the blood, and it essentially exists there.

In "The Decay of Lying," Oscar Wilde says that people never noticed or complained about the fog in London until Turner painted it shrouded in mist. Wilde's point is that life is a pale imitation of art, and it is a good point, for all the facetiousness in the making, but he might have gone further to point out that the weather was barely noticed by writers at all before the middle of the eighteenth century. The weather, as in Johnson, was simply the cause of delay or the occasion for getting something done. But quite suddenly the weather became a subject for minute description, and (in a spirit the Gothic novelists often carried to excess) became a mirror for the writer's feelings. There was the time of day and change of seasons (which are still the major form of meteorological observation in the Graveyard School of poets), but nice barometic distinctions and qualities of haze and light do not become a major preoccupation until the 1760s. This becomes material for workaday journals, as with Boswell, for travelers' descriptions, as in William Gilpin, and for poetry, as in Cowper. The diary of Thomas Campbell, a Scots physician who visited London in 1775, well illustrates this tendency. Every entry begins with a weather report, and like a true scientist he often includes the temperature reading. But he goes on to suggest a very subjective observation. "Fri 3rd—it hailed more than once in the forenoon & it rained almost all the afternoon, so the streets were very slobbery—the atmosphere over London is above measure heavy, impregnated so strongly with coal that the lower part of St. Paul's & the other churches are blackened prodigiously."[12] Here as elsewhere Campbell implies the contrast between the dank London climate and the limpid air of his native heath. He is concerned with matters of health and wholesome air, but the descriptions are so minute that he goes beyond a concern with mere wholesome air.

Such an observation about the weather as Campbell's is a corollary of the aesthetic of this period that became adumbrated from the notion of the picturesque. This aesthetic assumed that there was a science that could describe the process by which a natural scene could affect the heart of the viewer through the agents of the eye and the imagination. The whole process was treated with a curious mixture of rational empiricism and Romantic faith in the sensibilities. The assumption, never fully stated, was that if truth was not external and eternal but rather internal and experiential, it should be possible to describe an arrangement of experience and nature that is morally uplifting. The theory was attracted to the ancient sense that the pastoral life was the ideal one, and the attempt was to systemize its scenes, so as to please the eye and purify the heart. The attitude mines Virgil and Theocritus for its authority, finds support in the natural settings of Milton and Pope, and adopts a moral fervor from such works as the "The Praise and Happinesse of the Countrie-Life" by Antonio de Guervara, the Bishop of Carthage.[13] In this tradition, however, the emphasis is on the advantage of a mind and soul free from the temptations of the city and so the debauchery of society, but untrammeled nature itself has a kind of negative effect.

Not so with the Romantics for whom nature is curative and not just preventative moral medicine, and one touch of the vernal wood (as Wordsworth famously put it) can teach us more than all the sages. The clearest example of the English devotees of the picturesque is the Reverend William Gilpin, who published his *Observations on the River Wye, and Several Parts of South Wales, &c. Relative Chiefly to Picturesque Beauty: made In the Summer of the Year 1770*. Gilpin begins by stating that his travel book will be unlike all previous ones in that they concern themselves with agriculture, antiquities, manners, and so forth—but not his. He even dismisses a "survey of the beauties of nature" as part of his task. "The following little work proposes a new object of pursuit; that of examining the face of a country *by the rules of picturesque beauty:* opening the sources of those pleasures, which are derived from the comparison."[14] Such an assertion of the originality of his task is reminiscent of Rousseau's extravagance in claiming that he does in his *Confessions* what no other man has done, or will do; and Gilpin might have added that brag, too, for no one after him described nature with quite his set of assumptions. Gilpin writes as though the idea of the picturesque involved natural laws pertaining to the relationship between objects in nature and the viewer's perception of them. He assumes that if these laws are followed, the traveler can choose to examine scenes that are most pleasant to his sensibilities, and the artist can depict them on his canvas to the greatest effect on the viewer. He is not concerned with the awe felt at the precipice or the majesty of an Alpine mountain, as were more Gothic-minded Romantics who sought sublimity in the intensity of their emotions. Nor is he particularly moved by the mere prettiness or the neat symmetry of arrangement which so often enchanted writers in the first half of the eighteenth century. He rather treads between these two positions in his attempt to systemize the manner in which the affections gently lead us on.

Gilpin's theory of the picturesque often seems a strange mishmash because it is not so much stated but rather emerges from his observations on particular scenes. He refers (as a lexicographer might put it) to *p.* remarks, *p.* eye, *p.* ideas, and of course to the theory of the *p.*[15] This results in a rather loose aesthetic, but a theory of the picturesque might be abstracted from his comments. It involves a scene which is rural, and shows a variety in its textures. There should be field, forest, elevations, water. A touch of human interest is allowed, but he is not happy with the bucolic subjects of, say Breughel, nor would he be with the starkness of a Millet. The picturesque does not admit allegory nor the ideality of classical figures—as in Rubens. Gilpin sketches as well as describes, and in both he intends the imagination of the audience to fill in the interstices between lines or words. In his dedication he writes, "I am most pleased with the free, rough stile of etching landscape with a needle, after the manner of Rembrandt; in which much is left to the imagination to make out."[16] But, he confesses, he must often help his public, as they have not seen the scenes he has visited. This specificity of scene is important and it appears that he is always striving for a compromise between an insistance on a particular place (as Wordsworth is to be so particular in locating the precise place of inspiration), and suggesting qualities of the scene that will appeal to the feelings and memory of the reader. In this there is an analogy with Wordsworth, who in the very title, often insists on the specific scene of inspiration for a poem, and yet the description is more connotative than denotative and intended to suggest a private and tranquil reflection. Gilpin scorns scenes that lend themselves to a riot of the imagination. He terms such indulgence romantic, and presumably feels that such leads to amoral (if not immoral) passions. He describes Persfield, a manor house on the Wye where the bank is precipitous and the rocks allow only for harsh and abrupt views of greenery. "We cannot however call these views picturesque. They are either presented from too high a point; or they have little to mark them as characteristic; or they do not fall into such composition, as would appear to advantage on canvas. But they are extremely romantic; and give loose to the most pleasing riot of imagination."[17] Pleasing, perhaps, but *riot* is a term that casts doubt on the propriety of such pleasure—as though he might be in sympathy with Doctor Johnson's comments on the terror mixed with the pleasures of the scenery about Slanes Castle. The picturesque depends on nature, but only when nature conducts itself in a seemly fashion. If a plain is offered to our view, even if there are mountains in the distance which might lend a "grandeur of extension," the lack of variety to amuse the eye results in a "bleak unpleasant wilderness."[18] Indeed, nature itself is never "*correctly picturesque*," for it requires some gleaner or antique harvester in the foreground, and perhaps a handy ancient ruin in the middle ground.[19] Nature, however, must not be violated, so it is perfectly proper to have violets at the foot of an oak, but not intermixed in a hedge.[20] A single scene can also be picturesque at one moment and not the next. Water, for example, should be calm or slightly rippled, but waves suggest a confusing torment.[21] Gilpin is also opposed to cloud shadows on mountains, and is particularly unhappy with white objects in a scene, for they usually suggest the unnatural intervention of man—although he allows a beauty to natural white objects in moderation. "In general, the Welsh gentlemen, in these parts, seem fond of whitening their houses, which gives them a disagreeable glare. A *speck* of white is often beautiful; but white, in profussion, is, of all tints, the most inharmonious. A white seat, at the corner of a wood, or a few white cattle grazing in a meadow, inliven a scene perhaps more, than if the seat or the cattle, had been of any other colour."[22] He goes on to say that nature's coloring is never offensive, and when it is (as in the white cliffs of Dover) it suggests the working of some furious element.[23] No, Gilpin would avoid fury, for he prefers the quiet scenes—as Wordsworth prefers the quiet pleasures, and Meredith the quiet smiles.

There is the whiff of the laboratory about much of this aesthetic speculation. It is as though Gilpin had some machine more elaborate than those Claude glasses with which eighteenth-century scene collectors could make every appropriate view look like a painting by Lorrain. The lover of the picturesque does not end, however, with the delicate arrangement of light, hue, and form, or gain ultimate pleasure in mere visual stimulation. All of this scene-collecting is intended to tickle the imagination, so that it is delighted and refined by filling in those interstices between the lines. Gilpin is even attracted to scenes in which the light is so slight that it is almost impossible to tell what is there. This is not because he wishes to encourage the gloom of night thoughts and graveyard ruminations, but because he feels that the imagination is then most exercised. At one point in his trip he descends at evening into a valley toward Monmouth.

Before we reached it we were benighted: but as far as we could judge of the country through the grey obscurity of a summer-evening, this seemed to abound with many beautiful, woody vallies among the hills, which we descended. A light of this kind, tho not so favorable to landscape, is very favorable to the imagination. This active power embodies half-formed images; which it rapidly combines; and often composes landscapes, perhaps more beautiful, if the imagination be well-stored, than any, that can be found in nature herself. They are formed indeed from nature—from the most beautiful of her scenes; and having been treasured up in the memory, are called into these fanciful creations by some distant resemblances, which strike the eye in the multiplicity of dubious surfaces, that float before it.[24]

How very far this is from the cool and anonymous objectivity of the guidebook, or even from the stout generalizations of Doctor Johnson. With such a passage, we have arrived at a point where it doesn't really make much difference what is out there, but rather what is suggested to the well-stored imagination which creates scenes even more beautiful than those in nature. The idea of combining images that the eye perceives and those stored in the memory suggests the associationism of David Hartley, and both Gilpin and Hartley were influential on Wordsworth and Coleridge.[25] What is most significant is that this passage suggests a shift in the center of reality from the object to the process of perceiving the object. In this respect, one corner of the theory of the picturesque is analogus to late nineteenth-century literary impressionism, in which the process of perception becomes the center of the author's focus, so that (as with Stephen Crane) the object in nature turns into a splash of color and repeatedly only "seems to be" something. But there is a significant difference, too, for the literary Impressionists took little heart from the implications of their technique, because the panic or weariness that causes a character to see reality as a blur turns into a comment on his spiritual frailty; whereas, according to the picturesque, the images of beauty that are superior to nature's arrangements are evidences of a higher and purer mind.

The passage on Gilpin's benighting at Monmouth is unusual, and he rarely takes the step that obliterates the real landscape. He is ultimately concerned with the attuning of the affections through the eye, and the discussion is of the process, not the result, so his attention is on the scene before him. As he approaches Tintern Abbey delight is heightened, for it is a "noble ruin," and "esteemed, with its appendages, the most beautiful and picturesque view on the river." The Abbey stands in a secluded valley, surrounded by wooded hills. "A more pleasing retreat could not easily be found. The woods, and glades intermixed; the winding of the river; the variety of the ground; the splendid ruin, contrasted with the objects of nature; and the elegant line formed by the summits of the hills, which include the whole; make all together a very inchanting piece of scenery. Every thing around breathes an air so calm, and tranquil; so sequestered from the commerce of life; that it is easy to conceive, a man of warm imagination, in monkish times, might have been allured by such a scene to become an inhabitant of it."[26] Here there are some terms and ideas (like that "air so calm, and tranquil," "the commerce of life") which ring a bell with any reader of Wordsworth. The Abbey itself is described as a "Gothic pile," which is beautiful in its parts, but Gilpin is dissatisfied with the whole effect. There are a "number of gable-ends [that] hurt the eye with their regularity," and he even fancies knocking some of them off to achieve the right variety and make the object conform to the picturesque image of the imagination. The inside of the ruin pleases him, indeed, "the eye was above measure delighted with the beauty, the greatness, and the novelty of the scene."[27] The picturesqueness is soon destroyed, for the buildings adjacent to the Abbey have been made into hovels for beggars who surround Gilpin and his companion, contesting for alms and offering to be their guides. He describes one old hag who offers to show them the library and takes them to her own dank cell to encourage their sympathy. This is the kind of material that rarely gets into other travel books, and perhaps Gilpin admits it here to show the workings of the sensibilities in the man trained to appreciate picturesque views. His description brings out all the pathos and plight of the squatters, yet he seems to keep his distance and we are not told what comfort he offers. Celia Fiennes says that the poverty of the Scots is due to their simple sloth,[28] and Pennant gives a general description of the misery of cottagers on the Hebribes, yet suggests that there is nothing to be done about it.[29] Not that Gilpin proposes political reforms or even charity, but he obviously wishes to touch his readers' heartstrings so that they might know that he feels deeply, but in a fashion refined by the doctrines of the picturesque.

It would be easy to pursue this line of thought and show that with the English Romantic poets nature becomes mainly, if not wholly, internal landscapes. This notion is behind much that Coleridge has to say about the fancy. Even a poem so specific in its description of objects and atmosphere as "Frost at Midnight" uses that description only as a prologue to the memory of Coleridge's own London boyhood, and the highly subjective regret that his early being was formed by the cries of the cobbled streets instead of the songs of birds. Again, we know from the letters of Keats that many of the poems descriptive of landscape began with very real landscapes that can be found on the map. But, as with the ode "To Autumn," he peoples the stubble fields with creatures of the imagination, abstractions that can exist only in the inner eye, and even moves that imagination about the landscape as though it were free of a body. The point most obviously invites comment on Wordsworth's own poem on Tintern Abbey. To begin with, the Abbey cannot even be seen by Wordsworth for he is a few miles above it, and as Gilpin points out the Abbey is hidden in its valley for purposes of holy meditation. Wordsworth includes some elements in his description that Gilpin would consider with distaste as appealing to an excessive, barbaric emotion. The "steep and lofty cliffs" and the "wild secluded scene" would suggest an unpleasant harshness to the eye, but he would probably approve of the connotation Wordsworth notes between "The landscape with the quiet of the sky." Yet the description in the poem is not as detailed as that which Gilpin offers of similar scenes, and we probably think we see it clearly through familiarity and the connotation. The lines which seem most pictorial suggest that what is described is seen from a distance.

Once Again I see

These hedge-rows, hardly hedge-rows, little lines
Of sportive wood run wild: these pastoral farms,
Green to the very door; and wreaths of smoke
Sent up, in silence, from among the trees!

What we see—and the opening of the poem with its tender memory suggested—is not what Wordsworth sees, but rather we see Wordsworth seeing it. We even struggle with him over the proper phrase ("hardly hedge-rows"). At one point in Gilpin's narrative, he confesses that he can't make out what he wrote in his journal, but this is an embarrassment, whereas Wordsworth's difficulty is a deliberate part of the portrait of his mind.[30] Gilpin was not writing, to use Northrop Frye's term, a poem of process. And when Wordsworth describes the hedgerows as "little lines / Of sportive wood run wild," our delight is as much in the cadence and the fall of the words as in the image the words suggest. But most important, the poem leaves the scene after twenty lines to meditate on kindness and love, and how these are encouraged by the experience and memory of natural settings. It is almost as though Wordsworth set about to state the unspoken goal of the lover of the picturesque—although he can be drawn to bleaker scenes than Gilpin was.

But Coleridge, Keats, and Wordsworth were not writing travel literature—or even less than was Gilpin. Although they would not have written as they did without the analysis of the man of sensibility that we have in Gilpin and his contemporaries, a direct and unbroken line cannot be drawn. Yet the point remains that as soon as nature was seen to have a moral effect on man, and a moral effect unconnected with the Renaissance allegorical doctrine of signatures, nature disappeared. Even Gilpin, who seems so sure that what he describes exists in an old commonsensical way (and his very itinerary suggests this strong sense of place), describes only to illustrate his abstract theory of the picturesque. And, as in his description of going into the darkening valley toward Monmouth, he asserts the supremacy of imagination and memory over the scene observed. It is as though the man of sensibility begins by affirming his own reality and self by observing nature, but as the idea of the self died as an hypothesis in the very sentence in which Hume gave it birth, so does nature as an adequate external mirror of the inner being. At best, this nature serves as another form of the displacement or standing-aside that the autobiographers and novelists use to comment on character. As the doppelgänger serves to suggest a fragment of a character, but is not the character, so nature serves to reflect the observer—but is not that observer. In the end, it is a figment of an enigmatic mind.

There was a tribe of travelers during the eighteenth century who reported seeing things they never saw and knew they never saw. Chateaubriand may be the most famous example.[31] They loved fame, originality, or thought that nature should conform to some private poetic vision, and so they discovered Northwest Passages and a race of giants in Patagonia. Their accounts are fascinating, but the less flighty travelers—like Captain Cook, Joseph Banks, the Bartrams, Mungo Park, Alexander von Humboldt—who measured and recorded and collected and described—assumed that through scientific accretion the cosmos could be known. They illustrate the cool side of Romantic Prometheanism. They felt freed of the analogical science of the ancients and the mathematical pigeonholing of the Renaissance, so that with new instruments and eyes they encountered natural phenomena as it truly was, and explained the role of each phenomenon in the larger organic and interdependent system. Yet as much as they explained they were not able to explain away, for as they extended the domain of facts they deepened the mystery of the whole. There are always moments in their reports when the sedate scientist borrows the pen of the poet, and suggests that he is lost.

The period begins with precise botanical drawings in which there is an assumption that perception is uniform and universal, and the writer's reality is the reality of the camera. He catalogues, but he also interprets, for truth is seen as the accumulation of descriptions of phenomena and objects. At the same time, the school of graveyard gloom and heightened sensibility existed independently, and it saw nature as an Arcadia peopled by allegorical abstractions, or a misty heath on which there was a well-arranged ruin. Such attitudes rarely came together in a single work even though they were both part of the intellectual equipment of some, Rousseau and Goethe, for example. Rousseau prided himself on his scientific attainments, especially in botany, although he laments that his poor eyesight forced him to stoop to see a cowslip. But the laboratory truths are pale beside those of the heart, which may use nature to lend an aura of deep feeling. Rousseau often observes nature not to see it, but to experience the process of observation.

In telling the story of my travels, as in travelling itself, I never know how to stop. My heart throbbed with joy as I drew near to my dear Mamma, but I did not go any the quicker for that. I like to walk at my leisure, and halt when I please. The wandering life is what I like. To journey on foot, unhurried, in fine weather and in fine country, and to have something pleasant to look forward to at my goal, that is of all ways of life the one that suits me best. It is already clear what I mean by fine country. Never does a plain, however beautiful it may be, seem so in my eyes. I need torrents, rocks, firs, dark woods, mountains, steep roads to climb or descend, abysses beside me to make me afraid. I had these pleasures, and I relished them to the full, as I came near to Chambéry. At a place called Chailles, not far from a precipitous mountain wall called the Pas de l'Échelle, there runs boiling through hideous gulfs below the high road—which is cut into the rock—a little river which would appear to have spent thousands of centuries excavating its bed. The road has been edged with a parapet to prevent accidents, and so I was able to gaze into the depth and make myself as giddy as I pleased. For the amusing thing about my taste for precipitous places is that they make my head spin; and I am very fond of this giddy feeling so long as I am in safety. Supporting myself firmly on the parapet, I craned forward and stayed there for hours on end, glancing every now and then at the foam and the blue water, whose roaring came to me amidst the screams of the ravens and birds of prey which flew from rock to rock and from bush to bush, a hundred fathoms below me.[32]

Such a passage is strikingly specific—much more so than the descriptions in travel books of this period. They would not even bother to describe the gorge, although it might be mentioned as a warning to the timid traveler. Rousseau not only chooses to describe this awesome scene, but the description is used to explain his own sense of physical existence through his imagining that it could cease to exist, and this results in a powerful excitement of the mind. Doctor Johnson would pass on after a moment. Rousseau stays to enjoy his vertigo after he makes sure that the parapet is secure, yet it is the excitement and not the depths that impress him, and once more truth takes root in the feelings.

Rousseau prides himself on being an extreme case in these as well as other matters. Yet I have noted how Claudius Rich, who thought of himself more as scholar than a belletrist, indulged himself by arranging to see the ruins of Persepolis for the first time by the light of the moon, and how he stayed awake until dawn brooding on their shadows. A traveler even less given to flights of poetic feeling is Meriwether Lewis, a complete product of the practical and laconic frontier. Both he and William Clark attribute their success to experience in the wilds and a cool head—destiny or the deity have little to do with it. On rare occasions, however, Lewis especially will use the language of eighteenth-century natural description more usual with the poets. When he first sees the Rocky Mountains in the distance, he terms them "beautiful and picturesque," and "an august spectacle."[33] This is restrained enough, considering the trials that the party had passed through, but when he sees the great falls of the Missouri scientific description turns out to be wholly inadequate, as though there was a truth and significance beyond mere dimensions.

After writing this imperfect description, I again viewed the Falls, and was so much disgusted with the imperfect idea which it conveyed of the scene, that I determined to draw my pen across it and begin again; but then reflected that I could not perhaps succeed better than penning the first impressions of the mind. I wished for the pencil of Salvator Rosa, a Titian, or the pen of Thompson, that I might be enabled to give to the enlightened world some just idea of this truly magnificent and sublimely grand object which has, from the commencement of time, been concealed from the view of civilized man. But this was fruitless and vain. I most sincerely regretted that I had not brought a camera obscura with me, by the assistance of which even I could have hoped to have done better, but alas, this was also out of my reach.[34]

Thompson, or Rousseau, would probably not have been able to convey a clearer sense of the details of the scene than does Lewis, but they might have (especially Rousseau) been able to convey their own sense of emotional stimulation. Lewis assumes that with a different talent he might be able to convey a uniform impression of the scene to his readers, but what he does by stating his inadequacy is, through a kind of inversion, to convey a sense of his own heightened feelings. The result is that he too suggests that a phenomenon in nature is something more of a cluster of facts, that it takes on a meaning which depends ("from the commencement of time, been concealed from the view of civilized man") on his reaction to it.

When Samuel Johnson viewed nature, he was not concerned with what he felt about it, but what he thought, and what he thought was attuned to what others thought—or should think. With Rousseau it is a matter of what one, or really *he*, feels about a scene, and this is increasingly the concern from his time on. It is this very difference with which Sterne plays comically in his *Sentimental Journey*, hovering between the two views, or allowing them to clash in teapot tempests. With such a sane writer as Meriwether Lewis there is a commitment to telling the facts and getting them straight, but he feels the inadequacy of this, yet is not sure that he can plumb his feelings. But he is sure that they are there, and insists that they are what is ultimately important. Another traveler, one who had his head screwed on very tightly and was not at all given to self-indulgent and romantic meanderings, is Henry Layard. He could be blunt and gruff, and this obstinacy came into full play in his political life during the Crimean War. It is a miracle that he was able to escape whole from his early wanderings among the tribes of Luristan. At one point he gives a horrified description of the use of the bastinado, and then immediately criticizes one of his servants before the governor of Isfahan. The next day he is astonished to see the poor fellow barely able to walk, but thinks he may have deserved the punishment.[35] Yet Layard was an unusual nabob, for he could feel a magic in a mysterious Oriental moment and an enchantment in the ruins from the past. Upon leaving Isfahan with a caravan of Bakhtiyari, he is grumpy because they do not get off, and spend the first night in a garden just outside the city walls. The scene induces a strange reverie.

There was nothing to be done but to picket my horse, and to spread my carpet as near to it as possible, so as to be on the watch for thieves. The scene was singularly picturesque. The stars were shining brilliantly overhead, the majestic trees of a long avenue rose clearly above us, a bright fire threw a red and flickering glare upon the countenances of the wild and savage men gathered above it, and the silence was soon only disturbed by the tinkling of the bells of the mules tethered about us. I wrapped myself in my cloak, for the nights were beginning to be cold, and soon fell asleep.[36]

This is the mood to be mined later by Doughty, T. E. Lawrence, and Freya Stark, but in such moments of weakness as this Layard showed the way—certainly Morier, Forster, Chardin, or Sir Thomas Herbert did not write in this vein. Yet Layard's major enthusiasm was for the past. He was largely responsible for the development of scientific archeology, and is mainly known as the discoverer (actually excavator or thief) of Nineveh. He often slept during the period of excavation in the forty-foot trench that went to the pedestals of the giant winged bulls at the gate of the processional way to the throne of Assyrian kings. There he meditated on the mystery of history and how he himself had extended its time. Even the tedious process of excavation assumed a sort of mystery for him. "These long galleries, dimly lighted, lined with the remains of ancient art, broken urns projecting from the crumbling sides, and the wild Arab and hardy Nestorian wandering through their intricacies, or working in their dark recesses, were singularly picturesque . . . In this series of bas-reliefs the history of an Assyrian conquest was more fully portrayed than in any other yet discovered, from the going out of the monarch to battle, to his triumphal return after a complete victory."[37] In both of these passages Layard uses the term *picturesque* in a manner that would arch the brow of Reverend Gilpin. Layard often does, for the word becomes a kind of crutch to express a feeling superior to the raw fact. In his *Early Travels* he uses *picturesque* to describe the ruins of Ammon and the surrounding bleak countryside; the bazaar in Damascus; the medieval castle of El Hosn; a half-ruined village in the high Zagros; a flowered Persian courtyard; mountain peaks; the domes and minarets of a Persian cityscape; and a small mud Persian fortress.[38] Here the science of the picturesque has fallen away, and all that is left is the implied feeling that results from a great range of visual and auditory stimulation.

Such a feeling becomes even more narrowly defined by the Transcendentalists. For a Lewis or a Layard a world of natural objects exists, although they are also aware of the grand and disturbing feelings that these can stimulate. The writers of a truly Transcendental bent often only pretend to describe natural scenes, and their metaphors and play with the process of observation suggest that labeling is mere name-calling and a game for fools. In *Nature* Emerson turns the natural world into the raw material for symbol and metaphor, and the world of things make up a convenient illusion through which we can communicate our deepest thoughts and feelings. Even the sober Emerson plays with our assumptions about the reality of what we see, by asking how long it has been since we have turned our eyes upside down to see the world, suggesting that when the blood runs to our brain we feel the world and so know it more truly than when we calmly count its facts with an upright scientific face.[39]

Thoreau pushes the idea even further. He often counts and tabulates and names so as to give an impression that he is a one-man Royal Society, but as soon as we think that we have another plainspoken Captain Cook on our hands, he tells us that he has traveled much—in Concord. He gives us temperatures, distances, financial accounts, and the Latin nomenclature, and we understand that he is interested in such things if only to keep the mind in tune and agile. But these are really throwaway facts, and there is little reason why we should be interested in them. This point is often made in those magical moments, moments that invariably come in Transcendental works, when nature disappears, as though it were the mask of both the eternity within and without, and which must be stripped away. In the section on the ponds in *Walden*, Thoreau says that a lake is the earth's eye, for it reflects the sky and so mediates between earth and heaven.

> Standing on the smooth sandy beach at the east end of the pond, in a calm September afternoon, when a slight haze makes the opposite shore line indistinct, I have seen whence came the expression, "the glassy surface of the lake." When you invert your head, it looks like a thread of finest gossamer stretched across the valley, and gleaming against the distant pine woods, separating one stratum of the atmosphere from another. You would think that you could walk dry under it to the opposite hills, and that the swallows which skim over might perch on it. Indeed, they sometimes dive below the line, as it were by mistake, and are undeceived.[40]

There is a marvelous specificity in the opening of this passage, for Thoreau places himself as viewer of the scene. It must be a "calm September afternoon" and there must be "a slight haze." Then the reader is invited to invert his head and to imagine walking under the lake (as another walked upon it?), but there is no hint that there might be a nugget of wisdom buried in the description, for Thoreau's prose keeps a straight face and we as dry as the wit. As description the passage is both clear and slightly insane. The reader is lulled by the lucidity of the day and words so that he comes to accept being topsy-turvy, but when we reflect upon the experience we might be troubled. Thoreau has in effect held up a kaleidoscope for us to peer through at a scene, and like a confidence man has convinced us that what we see is reality. In the process, nature, the naturalist's nature, has through a trick of the eye disappeared. Thoreau teaches us to see, and then through such passages he teaches us to see further. That further can be into the unnatural cosmos or it can be into ourselves—vicinities which most Transcendentalists consider congruent, if not identical. In such a scheme, the self is very specific. Thoreau encourages us to make it so by insisting through his example and words on its independence, and states this in terms of politics, economics, and sheer opinion. Yet he also insists that a man is not only his political view or his trade or even his opinions. The whole intent of *Walden* is to go beyond such narrow definitions of man, but to get to a truer definition of man he must resort to wrenched metaphors that can only hint at the great beyond and the greater within.

The traveler must always stand between his experiences and his reader when he writes his report. The very nature of the distance in time and space between a far-off land and his writing desk demands he be a mediator. The lesson of this survey is that travelers who wrote before the end of the eighteenth century seemed to assume that they were transparent. No matter how they lied, they told what ought to be, and what ought to be became what was. Sometimes these travelers appear to stand out from their narratives through an elaborate prose style, but (and Sir Thomas Herbert illustrates the case) they wrote as they assumed their audience would expect, and their style does not push its creator in all his private experiences to the fore. These accounts are something like those given by the tribesmen of Luristan to Sir Henry Layard, who found he had to discount most of them with his characteristic gruffness. "Such accounts are not to be relied on when coming from ignorant Orientals, who are at all times disposed to exaggerate very greatly what they may have seen, in order to excite the wonder and curiosity of Europeans, and are, moreover, incapable of accurately describing such things, even when desirous of doing so in good faith."[41] The last phrase is important, for his respondents also assumed a kind of transparency and thought they were telling something as anyone else would tell it, and that the world of reality resided in the objects of the world—even when those objects would look to us like myth.

Then, and quite suddenly, the narrator's transparency becomes clouded with the concern in the process of perception, his own feelings, his private ruminations, and chills and fevers. It is not that the narrator felt that he was telling us something less true, but rather that his tale was more true because truth had moved from the generality of the world of phenomena to the specificity of uniquely personal experience. There grew in the West a universal assumption that truth lay in the breast, so although a writer like Wordsworth might give us just a few glimpses of his outer world—like a few select frames from a movie film that pass by in an eye-blink—his readers sighed in British unison and said, "Ah, yes, that is true." One of the most visually memorable scenes in the *The Prelude* is the episode of the stolen boat. In this there are some marvelous touches that give an almost kinesthetic sense of the experience to the reader.

> It was an act of stealth
> And troubled pleasure, nor without the voice
> Of mountain-echoes did my boat move on;
> Leaving behind her still, on either side,
> Small circles glittering idly in the moon,
> Until they melted all into one track
> Of sparkling light.[42]

Yet the whole point of the episode is that through a confusion of the senses the young Wordsworth believes that nature in the form of a looming mountain upbraids him for his stealth, and he is left with "grave / And serious thoughts." It is the poet's and the traveler's tremor that becomes reality, and the narrator feeds his audience on the belief that truth is private, unique, and experiental—all notions which were anathema to an earlier age. Such ideas in that dawn of romance and revolution were thought to be the key to the world's secrets. But just as the abyss between the scholastic's paradigm and the nature to which it referred could never be bridged, so the difference between the Romantic's knowledge of the self and the universe to which it was supposed to be coordinate could never be explained. Now we simply suffer a new illusion.

10

Whores and Rakes in the Gardens of Delight

> . . . true wisdom consists infinitely more in doubling the
> sum of one's pleasures than in increasing the sum of one's
> pains; that, in a word, there was nothing one ought not to
> do in order to deaden in oneself that perfidious sensibility
> from which none but others profit while to us it brings
> naught but troubles.
>
> —Marquis de Sade, *Justine, or*
> *Good Conduct Well Chastised*

When the Romantic traveler places himself before us as the mediator through whom we know his experiences, he excuses his inter-
position by emphasizing the subtlety of his eye and sense. He does
not insist on the truth of what he tells us, as did earlier writers; he
rather demonstrates it through the minuteness and texture of his
description and reflection. He insists on his existence through his experience and the impressions of that experience on his senses. This
sense is more often than not etherealized into a vague feeling of the
passage of time or the romantic strangeness of an alien land. This
heightened emotion is even superior to the facts related, for *they* do
not help to define the traveler's self as does this sense of a pure and
noble mind and heart. There are moments, however, when the
traveler's feeling of self focuses on his physical body. This comes
through in the descriptions of weariness and privation, the actual
threats to his life made by brigands, or the fevers and dysentery on
the road, and the detailed descriptions of the bastinado. In such passages there is an immediate—although often vicarious—feeling that
the self in some way depends on creature comfort, although creature
discomfort resulting from a virus or the whip endears us to our
bodies. "When a man knows he is to be hanged in a fortnight," said
Doctor Johnson, "it concentrates his mind wonderfully."[1]

We are, according to such a view, exceptionally aware of the self
when caressed, tickled, or whipped. This is the hypothesis of porno-

graphic literature—at least that written from the middle of the eighteenth century on, for before then sexual ecstasy was a mere polluting or comic frenzy of the flesh. But with the age of sensibility in the nether world of pornography (Cleland and Casanova serve best as illustrations) sexual encounter is seriously described in religious or sentimental terms, and the intent is to show the self in its fullest form in the flesh. The most dramatic result of this change is that pornography is quite suddenly written in the first person, whereas before it had almost always been written from the viewpoint of an innocent bystander who generalized the sexual hanky-panky into a comic fabliau (as Chaucer), or chose his recreants to both titillate and to make a point of social satire (as Boccaccio), or was mainly interested in the human machinery (as Aretino). Of course, most writers that employ the salacious, including these, combine their intentions, but whatever these intentions are they avoid creating complex characters—indeed, their characters' motives are no more complex than those of dogs or the lascivious sparrow.

There are three types of books that often sink into obscurity: children's books, cookbooks, and pornography. The first get shredded, the second bespattered, and the third hidden under floorboards by adolescents and roués. Because of this, there may well be a much larger literature in these forms than the bibliographers know. This is especially true of pornography, for the obliteration there is often deliberate and not accidental. Peter Fryer, who has studied the pornography in the British Museum, contends that there is very little lascivious literature in England before the middle of the seventeenth century, and also that for some time after the spice was imported from France and Italy.[2] This may be, but it might also be that fire and forgetfulness destroyed the earlier illustrations of the form. For example, Pepys records that he picked up a copy of *L'éscholles des filles* in a bookshop because he was always interested in education. When he saw that the work was devoted to education in boudoir gymnastics, he slammed it shut and replaced it on the shelf. But the next day he returned and bought the book, read it in private and thought it very interesting, but not the sort of thing for the eyes of women, and so burned it.[3] Other copies survived, but had they not, it would have been possible to make sound generalizations about pornography from what remains, for what we have is tediously redundant in subject, form, and position, and nothing that has come to light has opened new vistas for reinterpretation.

Many students of pornography like to take the high moral road and insist that earlier, more primitive cultures, and a kind of subculture within Western Christian society, have an honest and open attitude

toward sex that is superior to ours, and may even be spiritually en-
riching. The argument goes back at least to *Thérèse the Philosopher* by
the Marquis d'Argens in the middle of the eighteenth century, and
finds present expression in the promposities of Hugh Hefner. The earliest primitive pornography is probably not pornography in that there
was little sense of the forbidden about it. Those turnip-shaped fertility
figures of Sumer do not seem intended to raise a humanizing sexual
imagination so much as to suggest desperate supplication to the gods
for fertility. They are often headless, and the resulting focus on the
etched pubic delta hardly encourages the tender emotions that result
from an open and frank acceptance of sex. This dehumanization, especially of the woman or the youth, is pervasive in the ancient world.
Those marvelous ladies with honeyed limbs and bellies like heaps of
wheat in the *Song of Songs* are anonymous, and we are not told the
thoughts of the young thing who was unsuccessfully bedded with the
aged King David to restore his vital juices. Much ancient Greek red-
ware has a border design of figures performing fornication, sodomy,
and fellatio, but the mechanical and geometric complications seem the
major interest, for the faces uniformly wear a fixed and angular grin.[4]
These mannequins on the everyday bowls and plates of the ancient
Greeks suggest a very different view from that of the romantic historians and poets who liked to present Hellenism as an apotheosis of
clarity and restraint.

This brutal dehumanization of men and women through their sexual functions may achieve its most attractive expression in Petronius's
Satyricon, an ur-picaresque written during the reign of Nero. Only
fragments remain, but it has titillated classicists for generations, and
offered them a mine of vulgar Latin available from no other author.
Petronius laments the loss of the dignity, freedom, and rhetoric of the
Republic:

> To turn to the plastic arts, Lysippus was so preoccupied with the lines of
> one statue that he died of starvation, and Myron, who almost captured the
> souls of men and animals in his bronzes, left no heir. But we, besotted with
> drink and whoring, daren't study even arts with a tradition. Attacking the
> past instead, we acquire and pass on only vices. What has happened to dialec-
> tic? Astronomy? Or the beaten road of wisdom? Who has ever gone into a
> temple and prayed to become eloquent—or to approach the fountainhead of
> philosophy? People do not even ask for a sound mind or body, but before they
> touch the threshold one man immediately promises an offering if he can ar-
> range the funeral of a rich relation, another if he can dig up some treasure,
> another if he can come into a safe thirty million. Even the senate, the standard
> of rectitude and goodness, habitually promises the Capitol a thousand pounds

of gold, and to remove anyone's doubts about financial greed, tries to influence even Jove with money.[5]

This is nice mockery, but there seems also to be a weary mockery of
the self-righteous mocker. The difficulty is that Petronius insists on
making his satiric points through the activities of such low rascals that
the point becomes obliterated.

    The work is narrated by Encolpius, a Roman student who is so
indolent that it is hard to imagine him recording his experiences. The
frame of the work concerns his battles with Ascyltus for the sexual
possession of Giton, a handsome and pliant youth. Affection is not
involved, in spite of the occasional amazement at the wickedness of
the world expressed by Encolpius, and certainly love is far from his
thoughts. As soon as he is able to be alone with Giton and enjoy his
kisses ("I held the boy in my arms as though I'd never let him go"),
Ascyltus breaks in and lays on with a strap.[6] The work is not actually
very graphic, and has achieved its naughty reputation through its language and inferences. Petronius seems more interested in the social
satire of the Menippean tradition than with sexual stimulation, so his
interest is highest when he recounts the absurdities of the dinner of
Trimalchio, a *bourgeois gentilhomme,* or the ancient bawdy tale of the
grieving widow and the soldier who guards the crypt. Yet for a satire
the tone wavers, and perhaps Petronius only laments that the quality
of debauchery has declined in his day. The three rogues go to a bawdy
house, and after a great deal of drinking it is proposed by the madam
that Giton be bedded with a seven-year-old girl after a mock marriage
is performed in the "appropriate sacriligious way." Encolpius is
"taken aback" at the suggestion, but not for the sake of the little girl.
His concern is with Giton, who is "a very nice boy."[7] This commend-
able possessiveness passes in a moment and the assembly hides to
watch the proceedings. These, however, are not described, for Petronius appears to think it an adequate jest and debasement of his
characters simply to set up the situation. For him the trick is enough.
He has these rogues buy a cloak for a song, which they had lined with
loot and then had stolen from them.[8] Trimalchio threatens to whip his
chef for not gutting a pig, and his guests plead he be merciful. So he
allows the chef to gut the pig in their presence, and out pours a stuf-
fing of fish and sausages.[9] Such jests were probably thigh-slappers in
ancient Rome, but considering their perpetrators Petronius may be inviting his readers to laugh at them for thinking such pranks funny.
Still, the wit insists on turning upon knavery, sodomy, sadism, drunkenness, and impotence, and its vigor of narration and parodic qual-

ities barely overcome its weary view of the world. Here are those coupling figures of demonic Greek art come to life—or a kind of half-life. Trimalchio's wife complains that he has only two faults. "He's circumcised and he snores"; as if he were not the one and did not do the other he would be a perfect husband.[10]

The *Satyricon* is technically in the first person, yet Encolpius is normally an innocent bystander, and even when he is involved his passions appear barely engaged. The episode in Croton is the one in which he is most involved, and even there he passively permits an old crone to apply unguents and switches to his genitals in a vain attempt to arouse him for performance with a lusty country wench.[11] The scene is fragmentary, and it might as well be told by another, for although he tosses and turns he offers little reflection on his state. Such faceless anonymity characterizes pornographic literature. The bawdy tale and the fabliau are invariably told by an omniscient narrator who rarely offers an explanation for his inside information, and his tale involves characters as stereotypic as the farmer's daughter. Another distancing device is the treatise which coolly reflects on method and motive in the manner of Ovid, Sheik Nafzawi of *The Perfumed Garden*, or Stendhal.[12] But the most usual Renaissance form of pornography is the dialogue in which the old whore instructs the young one in her trade.[13] This is again technically a first-person narrative, but the narrator is so far from her working days that her experience is blurred into a general commentary. The form often suggests a satire on education or the methods of instruction in more proper apprenticeships, so that the ruses of this trade are suggested to be no worse than those employed in other forms of commerce. Shaw belatedly made the same point in *Mrs. Warren's Profession*, to the horror of his Victorian audience. Yet although this intent may have the respectability of social satire, it can only be carried out if the people involved are as uncomplicated in their cupidity as the merchant who lives for buying cheap and selling dear.

The dialogue was used by the ancients to discuss the art of love, as Plato does on one level in the *Symposium*, and Lucian on another in a dialogue in which two gentlemen debate the merits of pederasty and heterosexual love. But the writer who did most to establish the dialogue as a standard form for pornography was Aretino. His work became famous beyond its availability, and the illustrations for his work done by Giulio Romano were praised by the naughty, even though most copies were kept unseen under lock and key. The dialogues are divided into two parts, and those parts (in the manner of Boccaccio's *Decameron*) into three days—which makes a suspiciously irreligious six days of creation. In the first part, Nanna, whose life has run the gamut of nun, wife, and whore, amuses and shocks Antonia, an aged procuress who can no longer even "get a bark from a dog."[14] Nanna's stories are punctuated by Antonia's cackles at lusty tricks and indignant groans at examples of the perfidious hypocrisy of men. Through these tales, she leads the windy Nanna to a decision of what to encourage her daughter, Pippa, to be. Her own experiences shows clerics to be a disgrace to their vows with their congregational sodomy, and wives to prefer anything—especially vile hermits—to their husbands, but that whores live the only honorable lives, because with them the vices to which nature condemns us become virtues. "My opinion is that you should make a whore of your Pippa. The nun betrays her sacred vows and the married woman murders the holy bond of matrimony, but the whore violates neither her monastery nor her husband; indeed she acts like the soldier who is paid to do evil, and when doing it, she does not realize that she is, for her shop sells what it has to sell."[15]

The second part of the *Dialogues* involves two days of conversations between Nanna and her daughter Pippa, in which the lass is willingly instructed in how to be a prostitute. On the third day, a midwife instructs a wet nurse in the art of being a procuress. All of the dialogues are anecdotal or presented in very general terms, as when Nanna instructs her daughter in the various positions. Although Nanna uses anecdotes in the nondirective counseling of Pippa, the bawdy stories do not involve her directly. The only exceptions to this are when she masturbates with a hollow glass dildo, or when she is wholly satisfied in a comparatively normal and wholesome way—and then the coy language draws a discreet curtain over the details. There is a great deal of anticlerical debauchery in the monastary (again in the manner of Boccaccio), but the hypocrisy is so universal that, given the evidence, we must agree with Antonia that the world is a filthy place.[16] If there is a moral observation that can be drawn from the work, it is that those who are most sanctimonious in public (like the monks or the world's mighty) are the vilest in their sexual tastes, and those who accept the sway of nature over reason (as do the whores) are the most normal and even delicate. Nanna tells her daughter that if a girl goes into the trade to satisfy her sexual appetite, she will die a pauper, and that the way a girl keeps meat on the table is to give the illusion of satisfaction through chatter, restrained use of cosmetics, thievery for her by well-trained servants, refined caresses, and ultimately the simulation of ecstasy. The work might be considered an attack on those who do not accept the animal within man, and yet that animal is hardly seen as a glorious beast. The whore has only the moral advantage of honesty. The nuns and priests sing orisons to God while they are coupling, to distract Him from their acts. The whore, in contrast, does not glory in her earthy acts, but rather her merit depends on her insouciance to fornication that permits her to sell it with the indifference of the draper who sells a bolt of goods.

Nanna, like most first-person narrators, insists on the reality of her tale. "I do think," she says, "that [Boccaccio] should at least admit that my things are alive and breathing whereas his are painted."[17] There is a remarkable gusto in the work which suggests a side of Renaissance Italian life that is not perfectly clear in Dante or Petrarch. And yet much is obviously distorted and much left out. No one is described unless he, and more usually she, is either an ugly dog or a paragon of beauty. The women are usually described in a dorsal position and only from the waist to the knees. This is not unusual in pornography, but the attention to the nates in Aretino is remarkable. Nanna tells how an amorous young priest first seduces her with elaborate compliments, and these she presents mockingly, but they result in the only description we have of her. "Inside there was a long, long rodomontade. It began with my hair, which had been shorn in church, and said that he had collected it and made a necklace of it. Next, how my brow was brighter than the heavens, while he compared my eyebrows to the black wood from which combs are made and declared that my cheeks filled milk and cream with envy. My teeth he likened to a row of pearls, my lips to pomegranate blossoms."[18] This is the broad mock-heroic style, and years later Nanna is wily enough to suggest mockery of it, but her own style is just as full of circumlocutions and fancy tropes. Even Antonia becomes impatient with it:

ANTONIA. Oh, I meant to tell you and then I forgot: Speak plainly and say "fuck," "prick," "cunt," and "ass" if you want anyone except the scholars at the university in Rome to understand you. You with your "rope in the ring," your "obelisk in the Colosseum," your "leek in the garden," your "key in the lock," your "bolt in the door," your "pestel in the mortar," your "nightingale in the nest," your "tree in the ditch," your "syringe in the flap-valve," your "sword in the scabbard," not to mention your "stake," your "crozier," your "parsnip," your "little monkey," your "this," your "that," your "him" and your "her," your "apples," "leaves of the missal," "fact," "*verbigratia*," "job," "affair," "big news," "handle," "arrow," "carrot," "root," and all shit there is—why don't you say it straight out and stop going about on tiptoes? Why don't you say yes when you mean yes and no when you mean no—or else keep it to yourself?[19]

To this breathless catalog, Nanna replies that "respectability looks all the more beautiful in the whorehouse."

There is no doubt that the style gives us a clear idea of what happens, but it is nonetheless one that Aretino so obviously enjoys devising that to it he sacrifices his moral satire and sociological realism. This style also suggests that there is an unseemliness about the body which should be cloaked in metaphors. He is much more interested in the tricks of the whore that bring her property than in those that bring delight to the senses. In this world there is no love, only a grotesque lust which the wise manipulate in others for their own material gain. Such hard-boiled attitudes can give the impression of a stark realism, and yet the realism is very selective. People are either beautiful and virile beyond belief, or they are uglier than beggars. And in the depiction of orgy in which ultimate intimacies are supposed to be presented, the whole results in a caricature. In later pornography the reader may have a stronger sense of realism, yet it is still highly selective. In the world described by Cleland or Xaviera Hollander, no one appears to do the dishes or take out the trash. Although Aretino's Antonia is described as having been made ugly by the diseases inherent to the trade, the anecdotes do not suggest fear of the "French pox" or any other venereal maladies. The result is that much of the real business of living is excluded from the pornographer's frank reality, just as are the graduations between the beautiful and the ugly. Because of this selectivity, there is a flaw in the argument implicit in pornography that it is a truer picture of life than that presented by writers who only concern themselves with what W. D. Howells called "the smiling aspects of life."

The form of the dialogue dominates pornographic writing until the middle of the eighteenth century, when memoirs and long epistles become the fashion. Most of these dialogues are written in imitation of Aretino, and the speakers use the same voices and employ the same tropes. There is *L'éscholles des filles*, which Pepys read and burned, and *The Whore's Rhetoric*, in which the old crone gives advice to a novice whore in terms that satirically suggest a mother's advice to her daughter who is to be a bride.[20] Although these are first-person narratives—which overcomes the reader's disbelief that such intimate matters would be known by an omniscient narrator—the colloquy never turns out to be an intimate confession. Indeed, the language of the religious confession is only attributed to others in moments when they are excessively beastial, and such language is particularly ironic. The situation (as in Aretino) is invariably used for anticlerical propaganda, but almost never suggests that the body is the true temple, or that sexual ecstasy is preferable to sincere religious ecstasy. In this there is a cynical materialism that turns the body into marketable but perishable goods, and fornication simply results in a louder snigger than does defecation.

For the Renaissance pornographer the body is a mere machine, and he uses sacred language to describe its generative functions for satiric purposes. The fools in his world are those who overvalue the fleshly delights. But by the middle of the eighteenth century there is a radical change. The satiric dialogue is passé, and instead we have the memoir in which the narrator is himself (and often herself) an enthusiastic participant. Sex is no longer treated as the worst burden of the animality in man, nor is it treated in an off-hand manner. Consistent with the general movement of eighteenth-century thought which makes God beneficient and tends to identify Him with nature, and also believes that man can only know the world through his own experience, the mid-century pornographer has his narrator praise the body of the beloved as he might a holy icon. This new eroticism argues that since a meliorative God created the world for His delectation. He must also have intended man to take delight in his senses. These attitudes are probably most elaborately presented in *Thérèse the Philosopher* by the Marquis d'Argens. Thérèse recounts her education in the reasoned acceptance of her passions, with many touching illustrations, to her beloved Count, with whom she has been living in dalliance for ten years without the encumbrance of children. We are not told why it has taken her ten years to get around to telling him her story. It is reiterated that they have been delightfully distracted during the time, but it may be that like Sheherazade she entertains her master every night with her tale.

The story begins with Thérèse's mother chastising her for abusing herself at a precocious seven years of age. She is troubled that what she does seems so natural to her and so forbidden to her elders. The difference between the two views is increased by the instruction of nuns and priests at a convent. The truth that nature cannot be countervailed by the pious is dramatized for her when another novice invites her to hide in a closet so that she can witness the divine ecstasy she experiences under the ministrations of a Father Dirraq. The priest's method is to whip the kneeling penitent on the nates with a bit of cord from the habit of Saint Francis, and then, when she feels the presence of God, to enter her from behind with his own instrument. Throughout the narrative Thérèse is often found to be a voyeur (later from behind a hedge, still later it is a couch) viewing such goings on. And each time she must relieve herself in the handiest manner. Her memoir for the Count is punctuated with little essays on what she has learned from all this. Passion, she learns, cannot be mastered by reason, but since it is reasonable that everything comes from God, those who accept the sensual do so in homage to the Author of all things. Those like Father Dirraq, who are hypocrites about their sexual impulses, are made beasts by their passions, whereas those who accept them are made more human. Her beloved Count, who can accept passion, is a regular Adonis, but Father Dirraq is a beast. "Imagine a satyr, his lips foaming, jaw hanging half open, teeth grinding now and then, snorting like a bull about to bellow, nostrils flaring. His palms, opened, were near touching the delicate curved flesh of Eradice, but he dared not find a resting place for them. So they stayed there, his fingers convulsing and curling like the toes of a roasting capon."[21]

Such a description might suggest that the Marquis d'Argens is working in the same anticlerical vein as Boccaccio and Aretino. This is not the case, for he has Thérèse argue with the zeal of the reformer, and implies that if the worship of Venus were added to the Church calendar things would be much more wholesome. There is even an urbane priest whom Thérèse encounters among the household of a wealthy widow. He is a philosopher of nature, which leads him to practice *coitus interruptus* with the widow, and although he thinks that inconsistency is demeaning to man or woman, he argues that infidelity is perfectly natural.[22] This may sound like a too nice distinction, but it is one which permits the priest to suggest to the worldly widow that he should introduce Thérèse to the delights of his ministrations, and the widow can only agree that it would be vain of her to be jealous—that out of love she would be pleased to know that he is pleased. The first step is for the widow to advise Thérèse to go to the friendly abbé and confess her confusions. He soothes her fears and suggests that she use a dildo.[23] His argument is that it is unreasonable to ruffle the surface of good manners and the social calm, but that anything that is done in private between consenting adults (as the view is presently stated) is acceptable in the light of reason, and so how much more pleasing to nature would be indulgence in the solitary sexual pleasures.

There was a common eighteenth-century view that saw the body as an assembly of levers, hinges, and plumbing. The Renaissance tended to see it as a metaphorical house of the soul—an idea that is carried to delightful limits in Spenser's "House of Alma." But the logicians of the eighteenth century thought they were freed of such analogical fallacies, and tended to believe literally in their mechanical schemas. So the view is often expressed in pornographic literature of the period that the monkish celibate was an odd sort because he could not accept his need for periodic flushing. This is why he must be hypocritical about his lusts, and why they take such violent and unnatural turns. Such a view lies behind the scabrous anticlerical and antibourgeois scenes in a great deal of pornography which pretends to moral purpose by its attack on hypocrisy. But in *Thérèse the Philosopher* it is not a simple matter of the necessity of recognizing the calls of nature. The tender nurturing of the sexual passions becomes an occupation that is both humanizing and religious. Although the reader is told little about the high plane on which Thérèse and her Count conduct their nocturnal lives, it is suggested that they have developed and refined sensual pleasure with the fervor of saints. Just any partner in this quest will not suffice, as is so often the case in Aretino. At one time Thérèse is destined to couple with an ugly old man, but she is able to repulse him at the right moment by breaking wind. She already has her eye on the Count as her perfect partner in searching out love's secrets. When she surrenders herself to him (and this is what appealed to the Marquis de Sade), it is with the completeness of the nun's acceptance of her discipline. "I am yours. Be kind, be kind to the tender love given freely by one who cherishes you! Your sentiments assure me that you would never abuse mine. I give you my fears, my weakness, my habits, with myself. Only let time—and your wise counsel—act upon them. You know the human heart, the power of the sensations over the will. Please use the advantages you have over me in these areas to create in me what sensations, what ideas, what feelings you believe will best lead me to contribute unreservedly to your pleasure."[24] Poor Thérèse is such a tender morsel that for over two months she and the Count indulge only in foreplay. He objects that this is mere self-love, and slowly educates her with the help of his extensive collection of pornographic art. She is finally able to perceive that God could not have meant man to be denied the pleasure He allowed Mars and Venus, and with a little further tender training is completely converted. "I will repeat it, then, you peevish critics: we do not think as we would like to. The soul has no will, is determined only by the senses, by matter, finally. Reason makes all clear to us—but it determines nothing. Self-love, the pleasure that we long for, the pain that we hope to avoid, these are the motives that determine all our actions. Happiness is the result of the conformation of our organs, of education, and of the external sensations we receive."[25]

In the pornography of the Renaissance there is a contempt for the flesh that is consonant with the theology of the time, even though the participants may act like secret freethinkers. Those cloistered orgies and the lust of decent wives for hunchbacked beggars in Aretino tend to confirm the dark view that the Church took of the bodily functions.

But when freethinking became the fashion among a certain class in the eighteenth century, one response to the vacuum left on the now empty altar was to fill it with the human form. That form was not the antique Grecian one, although it often looked like it. The ancient Greeks, for all the astonishing three-dimensional quality of their art, tended to idealize the human form and consider it in its abstract proportions. The eighteenth-century worshipers of the human form divine saw it as an instrument of ecstasy, an ecstasy that gave definition to the participants through the heightening of their passions. They existed, as it were, because through heightened sensation they experienced a sense of otherness. In one of her final exclamations, Thérèse says that "No religion has any meaning. Only God will do, and He suffices alone."[26] On one level the thought is anticlerical in the tedious tradition of pornographic writing, but Aretino and his brethren would never have contemplated turning copulation into praise of God. This is what Thérèse is, essentially, doing here. For her "only God" is the natural drives that make us satisfy the natural physical appetites, and even her nightly onanism with her beloved Count is conducted for the greater glory of the deity.

The redundancy of pornographic literature is very deceptive. Even during its flowering in the eighteenth century there is a surface repetitiveness that after some exposure makes the reader long for the sprightly variety of a Graveyard Poet. The early pornographers, such as Nicolas Chorier in his *Satyra Sotadica*, attempt to hold the reader's interest with the clever ruses that precede the beddings, while d'Argens and his Thérèse attempt to do it more with philosophy than sex.[27] The work which focused most narrowly on the sexual details is undoubtedly John Cleland's *Memoirs of a Woman of Pleasure*, more commonly known as *Fanny Hill*. And here Fanny admits and apologizes for the redundancy at the opening of the second of the two long letters to a noble lady which tell her history.

I imagined, indeed, that you would have been cloy'd and tired with uniformity of adventures and expressions, inseparable from a subject of this sort, whose bottom, or groundwork being, in the nature of things, eternally one and the same, whatever variety of forms and modes the situations are susceptible of, there is no escaping a repetition of near the same images, the same figures, the same expressions, with this further inconvenience added to the disgust it creates, that the words JOYS, ARDOURS, TRANSPORTS, EXTASIES, and the rest of those pathetic terms so congenial to, so received in the PRACTICE OF PLEASURE, flatten and lose much of their due spirit and energy by the frequency they indispensibly recur with, in a narrative of which that PRACTICE professedly composes the whole basis. I must therefore trust to the candour of your judgment, for you allowing for the disadvantage I am necessarily under in that respect, and to your imagination and sensibility, the pleasing task of repairing it, by their supplements, where my descriptions flag or fail: the one will readily place the pictures I present before your eyes; the other give life to the colours where they are dull, or worn with too frequent handling.[28]

She is quite right, there *is* a redundancy. But she tries to enliven her account with the variety of faces and parts of her gentlemen, or the variety of their tastes, for one needs whips, another is an old gentleman who likes to comb her hair, another is a cunnilingus, and so forth. But her apology also suggests something else. Whereas Aretino tends to treat sex as though it were just one of the many natural functions, although one that is curious because it reflects on morality and the marketplace, and whereas d'Argens throws the mantle of a deified nature and reason over copulation, Cleland writes about sex as though it were not an end in itself, but a means to the heightening of passion. This is one result of that eighteenth-century secularized philosophy which believed (as did Hobbes) that sensory experience was the only philosophical reality. However, there is a problem that lies in the nature of this sensory experience. For Thomas Gilpin it might be the intellectualization of a gentle rural view. But even though he attempts to make his reader aware of the moment of his impression, his theories about the picturesque attempt to plumb universal laws of beauty that lie without him. Fanny Hill's sensations are just as specifically described, but for her there is also a sense of otherness through the transport and delirium that takes her out of herself. If sensory experience is the basis of philosophy, and physical sensation is at the root of that, then the victim of anonymous torture might be the wisest philosopher. But it doesn't ultimately work that way. That might be a step toward truth, but even Fanny Hill is aware of the distinction between sensation and ecstacy, or lust and love. The first is pleasurable, but it really doesn't touch her, and her true fulfillment must come with her beloved Charles, her first seducer and eventual husband.

Cleland's novel serves many purposes besides titillation. It is a mine of information about London lowlife during the mid-eighteenth century, for it gives a convincing portrait of the plight of a poor country girl adrift in London. There is an attention to clothes, food, and money that is rare in the pornographic novel, even though this realism is a limited one, for Fanny's experience is of necessity closeted. The work is also one of several (Fielding's *Shamela* and *Joseph Andrews* are others) that mocked the morality of Samuel Richardson's *Pamela*, for Cleland uses the genteel diction of the novel of sentiment while discussing matters that would horrify Pamela.[29] Cleland also has his heroine marry her heart's delight, although it is hardly a case of virtue rewarded. Yet the main concern of the novel is to defend a delight in "pleasure" while lamenting the nefarious London trade in buxom and innocent country girls. Fanny is aware that her experience during two and a half years as a whore has been a lucky one, for she is not only rescued by Charles but she is unmarred and has saved a goodly sum. So her case is not quite the exemplum that Hogarth's "The Harlot's Progress" is. The most convincing intent of the work is the defense it makes of the distinction between lust and love.

In other ways Fanny's experience was probably quite normal. She goes to London from Liverpool upon the death of her parents from smallpox (which leaves her only a handsome dimple), and is there befriended by a procuress who hires her as a servant. Her true duties are introduced to her covertly by a lady of the house who is her bed-mate. A little caressing of her budding fifteen-year-old's body leads to demonstrations seen through the handy chink with which such establishments are always furnished. She soon discovers that her clitoris is the "center of all my senses," but that when she manipulates it there is a confused feeling of guilt: "I lay transported, though asham'd at what I felt."[30] Through unbelievably happy chance her virginity is saved for the lucky Charles, and her experience with him suggests the idea that there is mere sensation without love, but that sensation and love produce a supernal state. Even as a novice, Fanny is aware of the value of her favors, but when she falls in love with Charles she is not only free with her affections, but rashly risks discovery and destruction.[31] She is put to the test upon the pain of her deflowering, but "I return'd his strenuous embraces and kisses with a fervour and gust only known to true love, and which mere lust could never rise to."[32] The point is even more impressively put when she is finally reunited with her love and, in spite of her hard use, is bedded as though she were a virginal bride.

But now the true refining passion had regain'd thorough possession of me, with all its train of symptoms: a sweet sensibility, a tender timidity, love-sick yearnings temper'd with diffidence and modesty, all held me in a subjection of soul, incomparably dearer to me than the liberty of heart which I had been long, too long! the mistress of, in the course of those grosser gallantries, the consciousness of which now made me sigh with a virtuous confusion and regret. No real virgin, in view of the nuptial bed, could give more bashful blushes to unblemish'd innocence, than I did to a sense of guilt; and indeed I lov'd Charles too truly not to feel severely that I did not deserve him.[33]

This distinction between the "pleasure purely animal . . . struck out of the collision of the sexes" and true love is made in many other ways.[34] After Charles first absconds with her, they live together for eleven months while he gives her the genteel education that explains her circumlocutory prose, and the heady curriculum endears him to her all the more. When his wicked uncle sends Charles off to the colonies to save him from London, Fanny is so benumbed that when she is seduced by another it makes no difference to her. Indeed, her whole life as a woman of pleasure can be supported because she now knows true love, and can keep the other indulgences safely in a corner of her experience. And yet the relation between love and lust still forms her attitudes toward her trade. She sometimes finds herself at the mercy of patrons with sexual quirks, but she sees her business as the simulation of love's act, and so normally sells her favors in the missionary position. Even the orgies have the discrete pattern of a minuet. She is saddened by whips, disapproves of fellatio, and is horrified by homosexuality. There is also the suggestion that true love comes when the partners are of the same class, and best when the class is closest to nature and the more impulsive feelings. Charles is educated, but we hear that his family is neither old nor wealthy. Conversely, her aristocratic patrons are apt to have fancy sexual tastes, but Fanny's beauty satisfies them with the rudimentary means. Her encounters with lower-class lovers (a footman, a sailor, "Good-natured Dick," the moronic flower seller) suggest that honest innocence is rewarded with impressive physical endowments, and perhaps that family, position, and wealth shrink the male generative member.[35] True worth, it would seem, begins with sensation, but it ends in the selfless mutuality of true love.

Cleland's *Fanny Hill* may be seen as one of many attempts to respond to the feeling of his age that the individual should express his personal and unique knowledge of himself, for this was ultimately the only form of knowledge. This is the drive that resulted in the outpouring of personal narratives which pretended no acknowledgment of the long tradition of formulaic religious confession. The new attention to the specific details of time and place might have created a new convention, but it was a convention within which the author could convey a sense of a unique and ideosyncratic life. In pornography, this fashion for intimacies revealed in the first person became so firmly established that it could be lampooned, as in the understandably anonymous *Autobiography of a Flea*, published in London in 1789. But the work that best illustrates the tendency to turn accounts of amorous encounters into an assertion of personal worth is Jacques Casanova's *Memoirs*. Casanova does not use the clanking philosophical machinery that is found in *Thérèse*, nor does his work use the sly satiric play between creator and fictional confessor that we find in *Fanny Hill*. Yet Casanova's work is in most respects more interesting. This is not simply because it involves the memories of the most famous boudoir gymnast of all time, for he spends most of his effort telling his reader of the stratagems of the conquest, and discreetly draws the curtain on the details of the consummation. He often tells us that he had very intellectual conversations with men—and women—but he never gives us their substance, and if we didn't know that he was found to be charming by a great many people, we would think him a bore. Yet even when Casanova tells us once again that he has given some lady an undying token of his love while in her bed, there is a certain naïve force that makes him live for us.

Casanova is sometimes compared with Rousseau because they were almost exact contemporaries, and because they were alike in their romantic egoism. But the differences are more striking. Rousseau saw society streaked with sin and sought natural scenes, whereas Casanova was most at home in the houses of the great, and nature was only interesting to him in the form of a garden where he had an assignation. Rousseau made feeling and morality synonymous; Casanova is concerned with a Latin sense of dignity which has little to do with morality, and feeling is only an instrument used for the conquest. He never invites the reader to appreciate a view, unless it is of a pretty woman, and although he claims that his love of food is almost as great as his love of woman (and prefers a woman who is a hearty eater), he rarely gives us a menu. Yet for all the vacancies in his observation, and even though he is a moral and philosophical nitwit, his work is pleasant company. Few have lived more ready to see a pretty face, and although he turns quarrelsome as he grows older and the pretty faces don't return his smiles, he is still more than willing to find beauty. Although Casanova leans on standard allusions to Eve and Venus to describe his charmers, he describes them more fully than does the mere pornographer who confines his gaze to the pubic region. This is even ignored by Casanova, for it is, in his mind, a higher beauty that he adores.

Casanova's *Memoirs*, in much the same manner as Rousseau's *Confessions*, begins with a recitation of very early and choice traumatic experiences. The assumption behind this commencement is that men are an accumulation of their experiences, and passions that they pursue in later life find their impetus in these early searing exposures to the world. Rousseau clearly explains the relationship between his schoolroom beatings and his later desire to be subject to an imperious woman, but Casanova is not so psychoanalytical. He simply recounts two early traumatic experiences. The first involves a nosebleed which was cured by an old sorceress who locked him in a chest. Casanova's comment is that even at a tender age he knew that such superstitions

were nonsense, although he will later play the sorcerer himself for profit. A Freudian might dare the opinion that he ever after sought darkness and blood in the bed of seduction, but the cure couldn't have
subjected all who experienced it to this psychological reaction, and
Casanova's light dismissal of the event may be the proper attitude.
The second experience concerns his theft of a crystal from his father's
workbench, which he slips into his brother's pocket when his father
misses it. The brother is beaten when he doesn't confess to the theft,
and Casanova tries to pass it all off as a joke. This scene is almost
exactly duplicated by Rousseau's story of the stolen riband, but here
the unjust accusation of the innocent servant girl haunts him for the
rest of his life. Casanova seems to be haunted by nothing, and his
memories are invariably delightful. Perhaps these two early memories,
which involve imprisonment and dexterity, come together later in his
famous escape from the Leads in Venice where he was imprisoned by
the Inquisition. This would make them predictive, not motivational,
but Casanova offers no such relationships—that is up to the reader.
And this is the delight of the work, for few have lived so wholly in
their own skins and from day to day as Casanova.

Not that he doesn't have ideals. The first is himself. He says that
he was "born for the fair sex," and given his life he may have been
right.[36] So although he is a devotee of feminine beauty, and says that
when he is in love he needs but one woman, he considers himself a
kind of high priest of the worship of love, who must exercise his office
by extending his congregation. Twice he almost marries, but a fortunate impediment comes up. First there is Catarina, a desirable
fourteen-year-old of good family.

During this time my charming Catarina had lain down on the bed fully dressed.
I told her that veils were displeasing to love, and in less than a minute I had
transformed her into a modern Eve, beautiful and naked as though she had just
left the hands of the Supreme Artist. Her skin, soft as satin, was dazzling white,
which enhanced the beauty of her superb jet-black hair. Her slender waist, her
well-rounded hips, her perfectly molded breasts, her pink lips, her large eyes in
which both gentleness and the spark of desire were visible—everything about
her presented to my avid gaze the perfection of a Venus enhanced by the added
attractiveness which modesty gives to the charms of a beautiful woman.[37]

The description here is complete and full-length, but with the allusions (even to the "Supreme Artist") there is an idealization that does
not even admit an interesting mole. She is the product of "my gaze," a
new secular Virgin for a freethinker who longs to worship, and
Catarina is a handy and willing idol. But one does not marry his idol,

who in any case will age and cease to represent that idealized Love that Casanova seeks. So he introduces her to a hardened courtesan, a lecherous lord, the works of Aretino, and the pleasure of a *ménage à trois*. He laments that he debauches Catarina, but has no notion that he might have wished to so that he wouldn't have to marry her. The second time that he almost marries is when he comes across the equally beautiful Leonilda, the mistress of the impotent Duke of Naples. The Duke is delighted to assist in the arrangements, and sends for the bride's mother. But when Casanova sees Lucrezia, the happy bride's mother, he recognizes her as an old love. He does some hasty calculations and realizes that Leonilda is his own daughter. The Duke attempts to arrange permission from the Pope for them to marry, for Casanova and Leonilda are still eager to be man and wife-daughter, but there are delays and the plan falls through. Casanova is heartbroken, and yet he allows the reader to sense a feeling of relief. The episode ends with an ecstatic and sentimental romp with both mother and daughter in the same bed. Later Casanova is to come across Leonilda in Barcelona married to still another impotent wealthy man. There he begets a son-grandson on her to the delight of the husband, who longs for an heir. But he doesn't have to marry the girl.

The ego of Rousseau was a trembling thing. It was often affronted by real or imagined wrongs, and Rousseau usually ran away on such occasions. Not so Casanova. His ego was rooted in a hard Italian *machismo* much like Cellini's. He stabbed a suspected thief in Paris, shot a Polish general in a duel in Warsaw, and ran through an assassin in a dark alley in Barcelona. He always acts in defense of dignity and his good name. Yet he is terribly afraid of being laughed at, even though his service of love gets him into some very comical situations. Once in a crowded carriage in Paris he kissed the hand of the pretty young thing who must sit on his lap. But it is the hand of the gentleman sitting beside him, and Casanova retires from society for several days to avoid the rollicking laughter at his expense in the salons. The world should not give offense to the high priest of love. He was a novice, a soldier, a secretary, a freebooter—but these roles were all disguises for his true mission, which was "Cultivating the pleasure of the senses."[38] This pleasure is not so much carnal as it is simply amorous. Also, Casanova usually describes his experiences in religious terms. "As soon as a natural movement informed me that love was ready to receive the offering, I set about performing the sacrifice."[39] The attitude is very like that expressed by Thérèse, but Casanova doesn't bother with the load of natural theology that might cool ardor. For Casanova, love is the true miracle, and he is evidently able to convey this notion to his friends, as after two hours of abandonment with one of them he writes: "we looked at each other and cried out spontaneously together, 'Love, we thank you!' "[40] It is only at such moments as these that Casanova's ego appears obliterated and his true self finds expression in this service of Love or Nature, which subsumes it. This experience is a miracle and a mystery, and like all such experiences is not and cannot be described. Casanova was so able to communicate his sense of religious fervor that one of his ladies cries at the proper moment, " 'Thy will be done.' "[41] At such moments the ego, so essential to the conquest, seems buried, and the true self speaks wordlessly through the "Supreme Artist."

This is an odd piety, but Casanova had certain standards that, to his mind, kept his form of worship pure. When he first goes to Paris, he is shocked at the freedom with which the actresses and dancers offer their favors. In London he is troubled when someone offers to sell him a mechanical chair which swiftly locks a lady into a position for easy ravishing. And when he is importuned by a licentious but wealthy old hag in Paris, he pleads the pox and escapes with her thanks for the warning. He was often infected himself, but thought that gonorrhea was simply one of the risks of his form of devotion, and cured himself with Spartan living so that he could return to the lists. But he disapproves of women who carelessly spread the vile disease. He is shocked by a lesbian performance in a bath in Zurich, and although he is reticent in describing such matters, he appears vigorous in his entirely heterosexual encounters. He frequents brothels, but it is as though it were for his health, and not in the service of Love, for there the delight in the strategems and honied words is missing, and that is what intrigues Casanova. "I have always found," he writes, "that if one is not able to communicate in words, the pleasures of love hardly deserve the name of pleasure."[42] He elaborates on this thought on the occasion of going to the bath in Zurich, where he was accompanied in the tub by a pliant attendant. "She had everything a man could want to find in a woman: a pretty face, a healthy complexion, shapely breasts and well-rounded hips, with everything else to match. Furthermore, she was only eighteen. And yet I remained cold to her. I wondered why. Perhaps it was because she was too close to nature, because she did not have the coquettish graces by which women make themselves attractive to us. We like only artifice and falseness! Perhaps, also, we need to discern a woman's charms through a veil of modesty in order to arouse our senses."[43]

It is the drama of secret glances and pressures, waiting in dark hallways until the husband snores, detours by a certain shop window, and tenderly phrased notes that make the game worthwhile. Yet even though he charms his companions, he does not tell us what he says.

They were no doubt always the same sweet nothings, but this mindless and phatic communication prevented Casanova from getting involved with a woman to the extent that he would be distracted from his service to an abstract vision of love. The circumstance which is curiously repeated in his life is that in which he is involved with two ladies at once. It is never with another man and a woman, but always two women, for this fulfills his priestly role. And there is never, according to his account, any jealousy or acrimony or invidious comparisons. Indeed, all three love each other—or Love—all the more intensely as a result of the experience. We may doubt his version, as we doubt Rousseau's idyllic version of the love he shared with Madame de Warens and Claude Anet, or the belief of the adulterer that his mistress would get along famously with his wife if they just gave it a try. Casanova's initial sexual experience is with two lusty sisters who seduce him when he is fourteen, and regularly share his caresses for two months. There is Catarina (whom he thought he would marry) and Lucrezia (who becomes the mother of Leonilda whom he later wants to marry) who get a chance to share his bed. Still later, it is Catarina and the charming nun, Maria Maddalena. Then it is Madame Dubois and Sara, her maid, who worship at the same temple. Most memorably there is the romp with Lucrezia and their daughter, Leonilda.[44] In such situations permanent commitments are obviated, and the participants can glory in their animal spirits and worship an abstract Love.

Casanova sees himself as a materialist, and thoroughly liberated from superstition. There is an occasional anticlerical aside, and one of the first things he does when he meets Pope Benedict XIV is to ask permission to read the forbidden books in the Vatican—and clearly has the pornographic ones in mind.[45] He cynically uses his knowledge of necromancy and Rosicrucian lore to get money from the crazy Madame d'Urfe, who thinks he can make her the mother of the new Messiah and then be reborn as a man.[46] Yet with all this liberation, he believes that his birthdays have a special significance, and on a couple of occasions thinks that he should go into a monastery. He understandably feels that love and passion are superior to reason, and yet that we are responsible for our acts, and pities fools who ascribe their miseries to fate.[47] Philosophy was hardly Casanova's main concern, and when we put his various speculations side by side the result is a mishmash. Yet for all his calculation in the conduct of his affairs, there is a dominant sense that he is putty in the hands of a power greater than himself. He felt that his life had a pattern—he once speaks of it in terms of a three-act drama—which might be revealed through his experience, but was not those experiences themselves.[48] Once when he thinks that he will go into a monastery, he first confesses everything to the abbot. "This was how, without any premediated intention and without knowing very well what I was saying, I committed myself to making a confession to the abbot. It was a peculiar quirk of my character: whenever I acted on a spontaneous impulse, an idea which I had not reflected on in advance, it seemed to me that I was following my destiny, that I was yielding to a supreme will."[49] That destiny was to be an acolyte and then a high priest of love. Carnality was not enough. Toward the end of his career, he rescues a girl in Poland from poverty and she accompanies him to Dresden. "I was sure that my new companion had decided to accompany me with the intention of becoming my mistress, but that was not enough for me. The reader knows by now that my folly was to want to be loved. Since leaving Zai're, I had had nothing but fleeting sensual pleasures, so my imagination now began to fabricate a full-scale love affair."[50] "Cultivating the pleasures of the senses," as Casanova states his purpose in life, does not then mean a simple coital pinching to make sure he exists. It is service rendered to an abstract Love. The vision of love here is certainly somewhat lower than that of Blake or Shelley. But it is also certainly nobler and more humanizing than that of Petronius or Aretino. It is a vision of love that allows the worshiper a more active role in his service to an abstract Beauty than that permitted in the doctrine of d'Argens's Thérèse. That, too, is prone to use the analogy between the devotion to God and the devotion to Love, but in d'Argens the shrine is aloft and the worship humbling. By comparison, Casanova is a Protestant reformer of the worship of Love, for he insists on personal testament. Thérèse tends to equate orgasm with the Divine presence, but Casanova makes the service of Love determine the very texture of his life. In this respect, his vision is also more mystical than Cleland's Fanny Hill. Her account insists on the separation between love and lust, and although she must come to recognize and accept the power of natural sexual urges, she ultimately praises these, as they reenforce— in a decent British fashion—chaste married love. In each case the narrator of these erotic adventures ends with a vision of the body as an instrument of a higher service. They begin with unthinking acceptance of the traditional view that the body, and especially its sexuality, is a shameful dross that must be kept pure through the control of its urges. Then the materialism and natural philosophy of the age teaches them that their bodies must be accepted, even gloried in. Through them the passions which ennoble us and make us more human find expression. But it is *through* the bodies, and in the end they are but instruments in the service of a higher and universal reality.

11

The Circumference of the Self

> The individual is imprisoned within a destiny in which
> he himself has little hand, fixed in a landscape in which
> the infinite perspectives of the long term stretch into the
> distance both behind him and before.
> —Fernand Braudel, *The Mediterranean and the*
> *Mediterranean World*

The more that we know about our past the less we are certain about our future. In earlier ages, when men were ignorant for lack of records about what went before them, they could with impunity substitute symbols and myths that often gave them significance and dignified their place in the larger, if imagined, scheme of things. The ironmonger could be the heir of Vulcan, who might be crippled and blackened, but he was also chosen by the goddess of Love for a mate. If the past could be known through such faith, the future was not immune from like certainties. Such assurance bound men to a chain of events, but they were free to be what they were within such certainties. Then the forbidden knowledge of a self was presented for our delectation, and it appeared to offer a new freedom two centuries ago. But like that original fruit, this one has brought more woe than weal.

The difficulty is that this new self has been as intangible as the soul it replaced. It is all very well to tell a person that he must discover his innermost being and cultivate his private capabilities so that his true self can be manifest, but the implication is that such a self can only exist in difference and opposition to the world. This in turn means that the self, a self, only exists as a force counter to what is—society, education, the past, indeed, all of nature. What *is*, then, if the self exists, must be wrong, and revolutionary visions must be right. This is why the acceleration of knowledge during the eighteenth century has two aspects. In its accumulation of facts about the past or natural laws it tended to confine men to an ever more minute and insignificant present. But this knowledge (and sometimes it was the same knowledge) also encouraged visions of a future of unimagined freedom and power over the world. History, in the hands of some, could suggest the possibility of utopia based on lost primitive models, and natural laws could be bent to serve a technology that conquered space and eased drudgery.

Men changed because they thought they could change. They deserted a faith that drew its power from an insistence on continuity, and took solace in their connection to a static world and past. Nothing was more mad than change and originality. This is why the heretics, although they themselves always thought they were proposing the reestablishment of older truths, were considered with such horror and treated so severely by the establishment. Under the new faith in the self, the doctrine of originality and uniqueness seemed the only way that a person might attest to his existence. This was a quiet revolution, for this self which seemed so new was treated as though it had always been sleeping in the breasts of men. It was innate, and only had to be revealed through the passions and cultivated by a spontaneous relation to nature. This self might have been a fiction, and the original thoughts might have been old dogmas in new dress, yet the faith in the self and its originality touched everything men did, and so it was as significant as that earlier faith that raised cathedrals.

Until the middle of the eighteenth century there was an assumption that all thought ran in channels which were inevitable and worn by the practices of the past. "Even Shakespeare's sonnets owe more to literary convention than to the singular experience of the poet."[1] So in spite of industrious literary detectives we are still left with the enigmas of Dark Ladies and Mr. W. H.'s. Comparable enigmas simply do not exist in the Romantic poets, for their sense of the original depends on specificity.[2] At the opening of the fourth book of *Paradise Lost* the poet asks for the warning voice of Saint John, so that he might alert Adam and Eve to the dangers ahead and prevent the catastrophe of Original Sin. What an original turn of events it would have been if Milton had written the poem without the Fall. Yet from the very opening and several times thereafter he tells us that the Fall will be. The biblical and epical traditions insist that it will happen as it does, and we know that Milton knows that it can only turn out for the best because the Fall does take place. The plea that the Fall not happen undoubtedly heightens the drama, for we pretend with half our minds that God and history might be wrong. But with the other and saner half we discern a comedy in the belief, no matter how momentary, that originality is possible. Even the earliest novelists did not claim that they were being original. This was a notion that was slow to develop within the tradition of the novel, for the early novelists (and Defoe is the best example) simply pretended to copy nature. Pope, who was more conservative in these matters, cautions the poet to copy Homer, and thereby copy nature, but the novelist bypassed the Classics and went directly to the source. The result was a tale that would draw old men from the fireside and children in from play, and yet invention and originality was not pretended and certainly not paraded. Even Fielding, in the middle of the century, does not emphasize originality when he discusses the qualifications necessary for the writer of such a history as his. In insisting on the term "history" for *Tom Jones*, instead of "romance" or "novel," he casts aspersions on such works for their immoral originality. His own plot devices amuse us for their unoriginality. From his genial tone and bucolic setting, we know that all will turn out well in the end, so the original turns of event along the way both use and mock originality, as does the hoary foundling theme with its inevitable recognition scene that allows the handsome hero to marry the buxom heroine, as well as gain a name to be proud of. But later writers turned their mockery only on unoriginality, and the reader came to expect only the unexpected. This is why the novel dominates the attention of a reading public committed to a hunger for the original, for of all literary forms the novel most holds its conventions at arms' length, and each novel pretends to invent its own form.

Three basic elements of the novel derive from eighteenth-century attempts to define and explore an emerging sense of self. These explorations all assume its uniqueness and originality. One is the attempt to describe the passionate relationship between a viewer and the natural scene. Another is the attempt to form a private and personal past into a narrative that suggests the uniqueness of the rememberer. The third is the attempt to find a defining and yet supernal passion through sexual experience. All of these attempts were pursued contemporaneously with the growth of the novel, and they shared methods and language and strategies. All of these searches finally failed to find the self, for no matter how the finger searched its pulse lay dead under the touch. The quest was, however, such a committed one that its success had often to be suggested. Yet the passionate collector of the picturesque ultimately is more moved by schemes of eternal beauty than by what he sees. The memoirists may give an account of a life which is dense with particularities, yet these seem a burden and (as with Rousseau) turn into a seamless dream. Or if the eye and the mind failed to reveal the self, others thought it could be materialized in a moment of passionate love. And yet the flesh failed too, for the language of coition (even in Casanova and Cleland) stops short of the ultimate defining ecstasy and hides in pale metaphors. It even scurries away from the notion that the self is dependent on the solitary material being, and seeks wholeness in the "ultimate marital fornication," or sees seduction as mere homage to a higher and more abstract Love.[3]

Setting, memory, and love come together more convincingly in the eighteenth-century novel than in any other form, for it is the least encumbered with convention. It is the novelists of the last third of the century who through indirection and from behind disguises drew themselves most clearly. To our eyes now, Sterne is clearer than Pitt, Goethe than Karl August, and even Stendhal than Napoleon. By hiding in their tales, such writers most revealed themselves. A climate had been created that made their audience assume the narrative they told involved a thin disguise over real facts, and although prudence and civility often determined that these facts could not be told, the play between the real unspoken biography and the fable which was spun from it created a sense of truth that was more convincing than outright confession. Such novelists—and they were the first to do so—accepted and manipulated the assumption of their audience that there was an ever-narrowing gap between their real lives and their fictions. It is a gap that is bridged, but never closed. In the end, the author's "self" is most clearly seen in a refracted light, and the feeling of truth is strongest when the reader is faced with a fiction.

The balance which Fielding strikes between invention and imitation is exceedingly delicate. It is a balance which had to be maintained during his age if the novelists to come were to make any sense at all. In the pillaging of his own experience he, as much as Defoe before him, robbed nature's pocket, but unlike Defoe he comically displays himself in the act. In the interlarded comments on his method in *Joseph Andrews* and *Tom Jones* (chapters which he says were the hardest for him to write), he archly pretends to allow the reader to watch him transform what seems to be real experience into art. *Joseph Andrews* begins as an entry in the lists of the literary battles of his age, for it is openly presented as mockery and clarification of Colly Cibber's *Apology* for his life and Richardson's *Pamela*. Fielding proposes to balance such literary pretensions with the truth of nature, yet he repeatedly sacrifices verisimilitude (as we now understand it to be presented in the novel) to a moral point or a comic jest. The typologies of the theater, in matters both of character and plot, are repeatedly employed, and these entertain us. But they also contradict our sense of the reality of the world which Fielding describes.

In the introductory chapter of book 3 of *Joseph Andrews*, Fielding explains and defends his method. He says that fiction creates a greater reality than do histories and biographies of great men because the fact in historical writing is always given the lie by the original event, whereas the fact in a fiction stands by itself, outside of time and space. For this reason, "the renowned Don Quixote [is] more worthy the name of history."[4] Yet Fielding insists that his fiction is based on experience and a true observation of nature. He famously goes on:

I describe not men, but manners; not an individual, but a species. Perhaps it will be answered, Are not the characters then taken from life? To which I answer in the affirmative; nay, I believe I might aver, that I have writ little more than I have seen. The lawyer is not only alive, but hath been so these four thousand years; and I hope G— will indulge his life as many yet to come. He hath not indeed confined himself to one profession, one religion, or one country; but when the first mean selfish creature appeared on the human stage, who made self the centre of the whole creation, would give himself no pain, incur no danger, advance no money, to assist or preserve his fellow creatures; then was our lawyer born; and whilst such a person as I have described exists on earth, so long shall he remain upon it.[5]

So in spite of Fielding's insistence on the necessity for a sense of reality in his work, and even though he distributes real dates and place names and events (especially in *Tom Jones*), his reality is a timeless and overarching one. He means, as he puts it, "not to lash individuals, but all of the like sort."

Here Fielding places himself in the long tradition of satire which uses incident and the specific only to illustrate the general moral point. And yet his work plants the seed of rebellion against the restrictions of form and convention that he inherited. He often opens his chapters with mock "fine writing," in which he makes sport of the language and allusions of the epic. When he describes the dawn as Aurora opening her casements, or the bloody mock-epic battle in the churchyard, or even the beauties of Sophia, he also makes it clear that plain language better serves truth. This is the opposite use to which the mock-epic style was put by Pope in the beginning of the century. He mocks not the epic style, but its inappropriate use to describe the piddling events he records in *The Rape of the Lock*. Fielding rather dismissed the epic style as dishonest when contrasted to either the burning concerns of his characters or even the real beauties of a sunrise. At the significant middle of *Tom Jones*, in the introductory chapter of book 9, Fielding lists the qualities needed by those who "lawfully may" write such histories as his.[6] These qualities straddle knowledge about the world and knowledge from books. These include genius (by which he means invention), learning, conversation, knowledge of "all ranks and degrees of men," and a good heart. Four of these five qualities weight the requirements toward experience, and even in the case of "learning" he appears to include learning in the ways of the world. Without such attributes, the writer is doomed to produce "foolish novels and monstrous romances."

So when he uses the traditional devices, it is invariably in mockery of them. In this respect *Tom Jones* displays a movement toward the real world when compared with *Joseph Andrews*. There Fielding indulges in such characternyms as Tom Whipwell, Tom Suckbribe, and Mrs. Graveairs—names which plaster their owners with a comic flatness out of the theater. But in *Tom Jones*, the portrait of Squire Allworthy (in spite of the characternymic) may be a tribute to his friend Ralph Allen, and the beauty of Sophia (again, in spite of the wisdom implied by her name) may be a tribute to Fielding's wife. Both novels employ the traditional machinery of plot in order to mock such machinery. The metamorphosis of *Shamela* into *Joseph Andrews*, however, suggests that Fielding was feeling his way in those two works toward the accomplishment of *Tom Jones*, and that the use of the foundling plot at the end of *Joseph Andrews* is as much a crutch as a joke on such artificial devices.

In *Tom Jones*, the creaking mechanism of the plot is suggested in the very title, and the eighteen books proceed from country to highway to city with the formal complexity and elegance of the Mozartian sonata. Yet there are liberating jests along the way that mock the reader's expectations. Tom's father is neither Allworthy nor Partridge, but a worthy young student named Summer who never appears in the novel. How very different this is from Mr. Wilson's role in *Joseph Andrews*. And what an ultimate mockery of the devices of plot is the resolution of Tom's fear that he has committed the Oedipal sin, and the eventual discovery of his true paternity.[7] All of this frees the novel from its inherited conventions by making light of them. Yet Fielding still secrets himself in the novel so thoroughly that we find him nowhere and everywhere. In this he remains very conservative, for although he insists on the need for the artist to depend on his own "good heart" and experience, he refuses to make the novel the secret history of himself. Indeed, those who are most contemptible are those who make "self the centre of the whole creation."

At the end of *Tom Jones*, when the plot knits together its revelations and reconciliations, there are many occasions for tears, embraces, and falling to the knees. Such scenes are described with a moist eye by Richardson and he creates many occasions for such descriptions, but of course Fielding avoids such direct descriptions as much as he can— even though he wishes to praise the goodness of heart that leads to such emotional excess. So his method tends to mock such scenes, while at the same time it insists on their validity. "The first agonies of joy which were felt on both sides are indeed beyond my power to describe: I shall not therefore attempt it."[8] Such indirection, with its ambiguous use of "agonies," holds the scene away from us and from the author, as though Fielding wished to put distance between the head and heart, his Stoic learning and his heartfelt experience. The very style tends to preach against the self-indulgence of wallowing in sentiment, yet the moral of the whole suggests that only the *good* (the most recurrent conceptual word in the whole work) can truly feel these emotions.

It is just such a device and confusion that forms the style and wit of Sterne's *Tristram Shandy*. Yet Sterne comes precariously closer to the sentimental scene before he, at the last moment, backs away. One reason for this is that Sterne narrows the compass of his subject. Fielding diffused himself through the whole of his many-peopled work so that in their very numbers the characters must dangle like puppets. The very name of Tom Jones, who might most tempt the reader to empathy and identification with Fielding, suggests in its commonness anonymity and universality. But the life and opinions of Tristram Shandy, or what we have of it and them, invite the reader to suspect that the hero is the author's ghost. In many ways he is, and what we know of Sterne's life can be seen fragmented in the novel. Walter Shandy, in his character and obsessions is very like Sterne's father, and Mrs. Shandy like his wife.[9]

If Fielding may be thought to have written a mock history in *Tom Jones*, Sterne's *Tristram Shandy* could be considered a mock biography. Fielding dismisses the historians' mere fact, as when he complains about their penchant for filling up the dull stretches of time with as much matter as the eventful ones.[10] Sterne has Tristram say that he is not only going to present his own life, but his opinions, and that even though the latter are slippery, they are necessary for the understanding (he says "relish") of the facts.[11] But the style is so antic and skittering that the mind reflected in this style is often the only thing that suggests the relationship between the two, and eventually the reader ceases to be amazed at the discontinuities. In earlier first-person fictions, such as those by Defoe, speculation is so slight that the main character seems to be no more than a mere vessel of disconnected events. But in Sterne it is the events that are slight, and they are so oddly presented and arranged that we are not always certain they have taken place. Much of this is due to the untrustworthiness of the narrator, for Tristram begins with his conception and ends when he is not yet a year old, so although the work is in the first person there is a false intimacy between the narrator and the event.

In one sense, Sterne does just the opposite of what Fielding does, for he proposes that there are *no* dull reaches in a personal history, and sets about to fill in every niche of Tristram's life. Fielding mocks the idea of the bald mechanism of the history of a man by exclusion; Sterne does it by inclusion. The basis for his scheme is presented in the fourth chapter of the first volume, where he joshes those readers who want to know everything there is to know about a character. "I know there are readers in the world, as well as many other good people in it, who are no readers at all—who find themselves ill at ease, unless they are let into the whole secret from first to last, of every thing which concerns you."[12] The arrangement of the clauses here suggests, but politely does not state, that readers who want to know everything about a character may not be as "good" as honest illiterates who commonsensically know that a man is not the mere sum of events and opinions. For such fools, Sterne proposes to supply an overflowing cup of Tristram. The project is marvelously adapted to his wit, but the general implication could be the conservative one that a person does not equal his life and opinions, that he must be something more than this. Further, if a person *is* the totaling of the facts about him, as Sterne suggests in his deadpan fashion, he still cannot be known, for it is impossible to plumb all of his secrets. The whole project is a false one and doomed to be incomplete. The later Romantics often didn't complete their grand projects (*The Prelude, Childe Harold, Don Juan,* and virtually everything Coleridge attempted) out of despair; Sterne aborts his task as a jest. So there is mockery when he continues this passage: "It is in pure compliance with this humour of theirs, and from a backwardness in my nature to disappoint any one soul living, that I have been so very particular already."

When he began *Tristram Shandy* in 1759, Sterne's life was more provincial and circumscribed than was Fielding's a decade earlier, and as all novelists must be confined by the limits of their experience, the result is that *Tristram Shandy* has a more intense focus than *Tom Jones.* This is not to say that Sterne wears his life on his sleeve. What is significant is that he pretends to, while he actually hides behind his style as adroitly as any writer ever has. He traveled much in books, and his allusions result in a regular Catherine wheel whirling out from the presumed center. Fielding's allusions are rarer, and used to pin down an idea through contrast or likeness, but Sterne's are deliberately used to create a sense of teetering over uncertainties. *Tristram Shandy* allows us a firm sense of what *is* only within the digressions—the sermonettes and tales—but these are patently fictions, and arch away from the facts of the life we are told. The very last lines of the work suggest that what is left is fare for the credulous. "L——d! said my mother, what is all this story about?—A COCK and a BULL, said *Yorick*—And one of the best of its kind, I ever heard."

Sterne claims that his work will be absolutely original and that he will follow the rules of no other man—even Horace.[13] But then in the following paragraph he confesses that much of his method might be explained by Locke's description of the way in which the mind works.

As with everything else in the work, the dependence on Locke could be comic, for he certainly carries the Lockean system to a silly extreme. In the *Essay Concerning Human Understanding*, Locke rejects the notion of the existence of innate ideas or principles.[14] In this, he throws out a basic Platonic concept which was often used to support Christian theology, and one which persisted in the philosophies of such of Locke's contemporaries as Descartes, Spinoza, and Leibniz. The belief in innate ideas could be used to support the belief in an innate soul or an abstract and immutable Reason, and Locke wished to see man freed from such ironbound priorities. Instead he describes the mind at birth as a blank sheet, or *tabula rasa*, on which our sensations are scrawled as we experience them. Our beliefs or opinions are the harmonies that we draw from these accumulated sensations, and our personal identity, as opposed to our mere physical existence, depends on our memory and the arrangement of these sensations. Such a view places great emphasis on perception, experience, and nature—all concerns which in the following century are linked with the emerging sense of self. Locke, and the empirical associationists who followed him, such as Bishop Berkeley and David Hartley, tended to think of the process of the association of ideas in highly mechanistic and even mathematical terms. They replaced the mystical analogical thought of the Renaissance with what they thought were truer and more scientific analogies. Hartley, for example, talked about the sensations that men receive as being conveyed by longitudinal vibrations in the bloodstream, which conveyed these to the mind, where they apparently piled up like silt and eventually resulted in moral precepts in the higher mind.[15] Such notions, which treated the mind more as a file cabinet than a muscle, were widely popular in eighteenth-century salons, and the romantic absolutism of these systems often created a reaction which burst through to the other side of certainty, and the result was pietism, Mesmerism, and Gothic horrors. What Sterne does is to show how his characters absurdly associate one thing with another. The result is not a moral precept springing from the purer mind, but an obsessive hobbyhorse and tragicomic domestic confusion.

Tristram's very conception is famously star-crossed because at exactly the wrong moment his mother asks his father if he has wound the clock. In her mind, the two monthly duties of winding the clock and performing her wifely function are connected, and the exasperation that Walter Shandy experiences results in the diminution of Tristram's animal spirits. "From an unhappy association of ideas, which have no connection in nature, it so fell out at length, that my poor mother could never hear the clock wound up,—but the thoughts of some other things unavoidably popp'd into her head,—& *vice versa:*— which strange combination of ideas, the sagacious Locke, who certainly understood the nature of these things better than most men, affirms to have produced more wry actions than all other sources of prejudice whatsoever."[16] What Sterne refers to here is a correlative of Locke's general description of the way in which the mind works. The mind should associate things "in nature," but Locke must honestly recognize that the mind is often wayward, and its associations can be haphazard, if not immoral. In the *Essay*, Locke warns against absurd associations, because they can cause "antipathies" and hinder the proper education of children. "This wrong connexion in our minds of ideas in themselves loose and independent of one another, has such an influence, and is of so great force to set us awry in our actions, as well moral as natural, passions, reasonings, and notions themselves, that perhaps there is not any one thing that deserves more to be looked after."[17] It is just such a way-wardness of the mind that Sterne looks after, and at length. But Locke's attitude is a very dour one. Sterne depends on the mind's waywardness for his wit. As funny as his work is, the implication is the sad one that man is less perfectible than Locke would have him.

Yet in the teeth of their own eccentricities, Sterne shows his characters to be as sure of their own ground as they can be—indeed, that is invariably the source of their eccentricity. Walter Shandy holds dear very odd opinions about names and noses, and claims these views as wholly his own. "My father set out upon the strength of these two following axioms: First, That an ounce of a man's own wit, was worth a tun of other people's; and, Secondly, (Which, by the bye, was the ground-work of the first axiom,—tho' it comes last)—That every man's wit must come from every man's own soul,—and no other body's."[18] Such a notion argues for a dogged integrity and freedom of the will in the believer, but the nature of Walter Shandy's convictions and the intellectual quests in which he is engaged—such as the exact location of the soul—are consistently treated with levity. Still, such opinions have merit in Sterne's view of the world, for they make his characters touchingly fallible. Sterne's fools are not treated with a heartless pummeling, as were earlier ones like Malvolio or Sir Epicure Mammon. For Sterne, the sentiment that makes us human may allow us to laugh at absurdity, but it also makes us fond of it. He says that he loves Don Quixote: "with all his follies, I love him more, and would actually have gone further to have paid a visit to, than the greatest hero of antiquity."[19] There are many illustrations of the quixotic in the Shandy family that endear them to us, but it is always an affection that includes a wry smile. Perhaps the best illustration is the scene that follows Walter Shandy's discovery that the newfangled forceps of Dr. Slop has crushed the nose of the newborn Tristram. Walter is convinced that his son's merit would be commensurate with the grandeur of his nose, and he is prostrated by this ruin. For an hour he lies as still as death across his bed. As absurd as his conviction is, the reader is touched by his grief, but then when Walter's senses return he and we discover that his hand is dangling in the chamberpot.[20]

In *Tristram Shandy* the human condition, which Sterne proposes to pin down once and for all through the life of his narrator, turns out to be a wild oscillation between the sentimental and the grotesque. The picture that he offers of a household is marvelously convincing, but an account of a "life and opinions" it is not. Sterne's point would seem to be that man is both more and less than what Tristram conceives. He is more in that Tristram is led into blind alleys in his mind where memory's doors are closed, and he can only assume that there might be more to tell. But man is also less than this detailed tale of every moment, for his essence would be crushed by such baggage. Tristram claims originality in his undertaking, and that claim is as much a jest as the very title of the work, for although the work is original the announcement makes fun of those (like Rousseau whose *Confessions* were not published until 1781) who claim originality with absolute seriousness. Sterne's is an odd book which will last long, but not because it gives the portrait of a man with candor and completeness. Sterne himself is everywhere in the style of the work, but he never allows us to see him plain. He is not Tristram, whose life, in any case, has barely begun when the book ends. Most often Sterne, on title pages, in letters, and in his conversation, identified himself with Yorick. And he is dead.

Perhaps the first novel to tell the whole truth—or as much of it as can be told—about its author is Goethe's *Wilhelm Meister's Apprenticeship*. It is one thing for Defoe to speak of *Robinson Crusoe* as his spiritual biography, for Fielding to insist that all of his characters have their originals "in nature," or for Rousseau to use an idealized version of himself to propound his educational philosophy in *La Nouvelle Héloïse* and *Émile*. Such are modest and almost accidental uses of the author's own character and experience, and the statements these writers make which relate reality with fiction seem forced and after the fact. But with his first tremendous success in 1774 with *The Sufferings of Young Werther*, Goethe invited his readers to see the connections between his life and his art. Surely later writers (Lord Byron and Benjamin Constant come to mind) might have been just as artistically autobiographical as they were without Goethe's example, but he led the way. In this he is different from his immediate predecessors. Fielding drew a generality from nature and his experience. Even though he mocked the neoclassical conventions of narration, the mockery was intended to arrive at a truer general moral statement. In some respects Fielding was a man of feeling who made his point through a mock neoclassical form. Sterne was a neoclassical satirist who made his point through a mock romantic form. In his case, there is only a pretense of revealing a life, and *Tristram Shandy* results in a dissertation on the impossibility of the task, for the particularity of his characters is always comic. Goethe, however, strives for a serious particularity, and his major characters are all fragments of himself.

Werther is based on Goethe's unrequited love for Lotte Buff in Wetzlar (and a later attachment to Maximiliane La Roche in Frankfurt). The problem was how to resolve the tale of a sensitive young man who is rebuffed by a sensible young lady who excels in the domestic virtues and esteems a stable young man. It was not enough to have the hero walk off into the Hartz Mountains—there must be something more dramatic. The drama was suggested to Goethe in a letter from the man Lotte married, which gave an account of the suicide of a young man because of unrequited love. Goethe claims that this suicide crystallized the story for him, although he waited two more years to write it. The suicide could not be just a convenient importation to get the story of Werther over. Goethe had to identify with the suicidal impulse to make it convincing to himself.

Amongst a considerable collection of weapons I had a costly and well-polished dagger. I always put this by my bed, and before I extinguished the light I tried if I could succeed in forcing the sharp point a couple of inches into my heart. But since I could never succeed in this, I at last laughed myself out of it, flung away all hypochondriacal silliness and decided to live. But to be able to do this with cheerfulness I had to bring to execution a poetic task, in which all that I had felt, thought, and fancied on this weighty point should be put into words. I gathered together for this purpose the elements which had been moving about around me for a couple of years; I brought to mind the things which had most oppressed and vexed me, but nothing would take shape; I wanted an incident, a story, in which all could be embodied.

All at once I hear the news of the death of Jerusalem, and immediately after the general report, the most minute and circumstantial description of the event. At this moment the plan of "Werther" was found, the whole shot together from all sides and became a solid mass, like water in a vessel which is on the point of freezing is transformed into solid ice by the slightest agitation. To hold fast this strange prize, to keep before me, and carry out in all its parts a work of such varied and significant contents was for me so much the more pressing, as I had already again fallen into a painful situation which permitted me less hope than those which had gone before, and foreboded nothing but depression if not disgust.[21]

There are several remarkable things in this passage. Most important is the assumption that a fictional narrative does not begin in the conventions of fictional narration, but in the author's own personal experience. The result is a work which tells a truth about the author-hero's life rather than a general truth about men through an elaborated parable. Such a notion would have been repugnant before Goethe's time. Fielding is very careful about introducing bits and pieces of real experience into his novel, and goes out of his way to insist on the general truth of his work in spite of its apparent specificity. Sterne takes another step, and toys with his readers' expectations that he will present personal revelations, and then makes fun of those expectations. Goethe simply assumes that his readers assume that his personal revelations are the only proper subject for his art, and in his account of the inspiration of the work he satisfies as well as toys with these assumptions. In *Poetry and Truth*, he looks back fifty years to the Werther-Goethe he was, but in a sense is more removed from him than his readers are. He had the experience of an unrequited love, and turned it into the first serious roman à clef, not even bothering to change Lotte's Christian name in the novel. But without the story of Jerusalem, the whole, he claims, would not have crystallized, as though he needed that same experience of "standing aside" which allows Boswell to see himself more clearly in the *Journals*. Yet to hear of the suicide was not enough, for Goethe had to attempt to plunge the dagger a few inches into his own breast—although both suicides used pistols. Inspiration, which traditionally came from the stars, or God breathing life into the art of the poet, or from a visitation from one of the sacred sisters of the well, here comes from the deliberately sought pain that unites the artist's body and mind in a personal and solitary frenzy. Art is then not what was always thought, but a public form of autoanalysis.

Yet in Goethe's case art is both a way to understand himself in public and a way to escape from public view. Each step in the conception of *Werther* removes Goethe further from the facts of the original experience.[22] He became smitten by Lotte Buff in June of 1772, and morosely left Wetzlar in September. Jerusalem's suicide took place at the end of October and was reported to Goethe by Kestner, who married Lotte the following April. Some of the qualities of Lotte are mixed with those of Maximiliane La Roche, to whom Goethe paid court the winter of 1772–73. Then in early 1774, Goethe wrote *Werther*, and his reputation was made. Goethe sent a manuscript copy of the novel to Lotte and her new husband, and they had reservations about some of the details of event and character, which Goethe remedied in 1787, making the whole more "objective." So although the work began with the kind of mixture of events and persons that since has been the standard method of novelists, Goethe continued to step out from under the "real" facts in which the novel had its origin. But the die for the autobiographical method was cast with *Werther*, and no matter how much he manipulated the materials of his life in his fictions, the idea of fiction as personal revelation remained. He even encouraged the thought, as in *Poetry and Truth*, where he speaks of writing his works in his own person, and claims that all of his work is confession.[23]

Goethe allows little room in *Werther* for mockery of the hero; perhaps he was too close to the youth he was. Even in making the work more objective and less offensive in the 1787 version, there is the same deadly serious tone. This is partly because the epistolary style, for which Richardson's *Pamela* was the main model, allows the reader to hear only from Werther and his grief-stricken editor. Such wallowing in wrist-to-brow emotions does not characterize *Wilhelm Meister's Apprenticeship*, in which the objectifying process went further. It too went through two versions, for the work was probably begun shortly after Goethe had gone to Weimar and gained the kind of intimate knowledge of the theater to which he exposes Wilhelm. The result was *Wilhelm Meisters Theatralische sendung*, which was probably written between 1777 and 1785.[24] The plot of the work follows the first two thirds of the later *Apprenticeship*, but, as the title suggests, the emphasis is on Wilhelm's desire to create a model for a revived German culture through a German national theater. This was a project dear to Goethe's heart, one that had stirred him as much as it had Lessing before him. Yet his Wilhelm seems a benighted sort to carry such a mission to completion, and as Goethe meditated on the matter he seems to have seen the idea of a theatrical mission for Wilhelm evolve into a concern with his whole education. He must have begun, to state it another way, with the idea of showing Wilhelm guide Germany toward her cultural destiny (as Goethe himself was doing), and ended with the idea of experience guiding Wilhelm. Life is repeatedly more complicated than Wilhelm thinks it is, and the gap between his assumptions and reality is a subject for sad raillery.

Wilhelm is a character out of the tradition of naïve heroes, and so has a kinship with Candide, and, in the German tradition, Wieland's Agathon and Grimmelshausen's Simplicius Simplicissimus. But in those earlier works the hero is used as an instrument by which the author displays examples of the difference between appearance and reality. The author's main concern is the ironic comedy or tragedy that results from this difference, and the plight of the hero is simply an illustration of the confusions that can result. But in *Wilhelm Meister* the vantage from which the actions are observed is less secure, and we are invited to laugh or cry both at and with the hero. The abandonment of the epistolary form is one indication of this change, for in *Wilhelm Meister* Goethe employs a style which hovers ambiguously between the mind of the hero and that of an ironic omniscient narrator. It is a style called *erlebte rede*, in which objective assertion and subjective consciousness become strangely mixed. In it the narrator does not withdraw behind his characters (as does Fielding), but rather is a present ironic commentator who still exhibits and manipulates his characters (more in the manner of Sterne). By presenting subjectivity as subjective, the narrator creates an ironic objectivity.

In the first book of *Wilhelm Meister*, the callow hero keeps company with Mariana, an actress with more charm than talent, of whom his burgher family does not approve. In idealistic spite, he feels his own destiny is in the theater, and sees himself (shades of the earlier *sendung*) as a founder of a national theater, or as he says, "The theatre has often been at variance with the pulpit; they ought not, I think, to quarrel."[25] This first book also allows Goethe to have Wilhelm tell his life story to Mariana, who falls asleep while he drones on for pages. He is a self-important and pompous young man, and the reader is invited to laugh at him. When he is sent away from Mariana on business for his father, he hires musicians to serenade his beloved while, unknown to him, she entertains another and richer admirer. Wilhelm sits on a bench across the way and admires the beautiful evening. "The music ceased, and he felt as if fallen from the element in which his thoughts had hitherto been soaring. His restlessness increased, as his feelings were no longer nourished and assuaged by the melody. He sat down upon the threshold, and felt more peace. He kissed the brass-knocker of her door; he kissed the threshold over which her feet went out and in, and warmed it by the fire of his breast."[26] Such romantic excesses were common among young men of feeling during this period, but there is too much evidence—culminating with the departing shadow of Mariana's other nocturnal visitor—to suggest that we share Wilhelm's emotion uncritically, and the ironic hovering becomes operative.

In his conversations with Eckermann, Goethe confessed that he was never sure just what Wilhelm added up to, and I think the reader senses that he is being honest here, for in the novel he seems to be reaching for a truth which is just beyond his fingertips. Thirty years after its publication Goethe says:

but this work is one of the most incalculable productions; I myself scarcely have the key to it. People seek a central point; that is hard, and not even right. I should think a rich manifold life, brought close to our eyes, would be enough without any express tendency; which, after all, is only for the intellect. But if anything of the sort is insisted upon, it will perhaps be found in the words Frederic at the end addresses the hero: "Thou seem'st to me like Saul,

the son of Kish, who went out to seek his father's asses, and found a kingdom." Keep to this; for, in fact, the whole book seems to say nothing more
than that man, despite all his follies and errors, being led by a higher hand,
reaches some happy goal at last.[27]

The comment seems perfectly just, for the novel tends to stumble on
truths and meanings that are very different from those that Wilhelm
assumes or seeks. Also, Goethe maintains a much greater distance between himself and Wilhelm than he does between himself and
Werther. Wilhelm may be Goethe without the genius, yet the details
also lead us into an imagined world. The novel takes place in the decade of Goethe's birth, a time when the ramshackle Holy Roman Empire offered a chaotic stage for the novel's action. Goethe's main concern is hardly political, but in this society there are still the signs of
social bankruptcy that resulted in revolution just three years after the
publication of *Wilhelm Meister*.[28] The novel offers him an opportunity
to describe characters on all social levels. More than half of the work,
left over from the earlier *sendung*, is an account of Wilhelm's drifting
in search of a life in the theater. This itinerant design involves a rejection of his middle-class upbringing, but it also takes him to the castles
of aristocratic patrons. In the end, he may find a kingdom instead of
asses, as did Saul, but the tone of hovering irony may even leave this
happy resolution of the novel in doubt.

The work is in eight books, and each is dominated by a woman
who has great influence on Wilhelm's life. This offers an indirect way
to comment on his views on art, business, class, and the theater, as
well as on love and woman. The first is of course Mariana, the actress
who is beneath him, and who offers occasion for him to express his
passionate sensibilities. The second is Philina, a lively, flippant actress who shares a *ménage à trois* with Wilhelm, and thinks babies
should be shaken from trees. Third is a Countess, a patron whose
affection for Wilhelm he mistakes for love. Fourth, there is the mysterious boy-girl waif, Mignon, whose protector Wilhelm becomes.
Fifth, there is Aurelia, the sister of the tyrannical and talented Serlo,
who has a sad tale of being jilted by a noble lover. In the sixth book,
Wilhelm and we read the history of the *Schöne Seele*, or Fair Saint, a
tale of pious rejection of the world based on that of a real pietist who
was close to Goethe's mother. The seventh book concerns Theresa, a
model of German efficiency and industriousness, whom Wilhelm almost talks himself into loving. But in the last book it is revealed to
him (as life so often comes to him rather than he to it) that he really
loves Natalia, a paragon of feminine virtues, whom Wilhelm marries.

Such an account of *Wilhelm Meister* might suggest that the work was made up by Goethe as he went along, following every whim. The work is strangely episodic on this level, as though Goethe were following the episodic tradition of the picaresque, and perhaps of Grimmelshausen in particular. The result may be a "rich manifold life," but it is not seen from the inside. The idea of a gallery of eight women lends the work an incremental design, but in terms of the understanding of Wilhelm's character, it is a design that works indirectly. Wilhelm is often not a participant in the actions and passions that swirl about him, and in many instances he simply sits and listens to the tales of others—even joining the reader in reading passively the story of the *Schöne Seele* in book 6. We understand him through the women, not them through him, and this is a radical change from the method used in *Werther*.

Such indirection extends to Goethe's use of more formal eighteenth-century plot devices. His fellow novelists invariably used plot to make that which had been dark clear, and although the unravelings of mysteries in the closing scenes (as in *Tom Jones*) might be comic, the reader is given a sense of release and clarity. Sterne stands this tradition, as well as others, on its head, and suggests an alternate clarity in the world that has nothing to do with his deliberate avoidance of normal narrative sequence on which plot depends. Goethe's approach is still different. The major plot elements do not involve the hero, and they are often so mysterious and haphazard that the final unraveling of events leaves us more with a sense of uneasiness than of clarity. As the novel progresses, we slowly discover that four of the major characters (Lothario, the Countess, Natalia, and Friedrich) are siblings, but since Wilhelm does not discover that he is related to them too, except that he marries Natalia, our response is no more than a "Well, well!" Goethe also uses the traditional foundling plot, but hardly in the traditional fashion. Wilhelm knows very well who his father is, and the novel is an account of his escape from his world, rather than a conscious or unconscious search for his true father. Halfway through the work, he is informed by letter that his father has died. That evening he performs the role of Hamlet, and has the impression that the actor playing King Hamlet is his father—but it is a fancy that slowly passes. It is others, and repeatedly, who must discover their true paternity. Theresa believes that Lothario and Mme. St. Albans are her parents, but discovers that they are M. St. Albans and his housekeeper, so she is able to marry Lothario. In one of the tales within the novel there is the account of Sperata, who thinks that her parents are an old soldier and his wife, but it turns out that she is the daughter of a count. In this manner, the question of the hero's paternity is deflected to other characters, and the whole larger question of

who the hero is becomes one of who we all are. The most curious twist
to this convention is that in book 6 Wilhelm sets off with the boy Felix
to take him to his true father. He believes that Felix is the son of the
deserted and now dead Aurelia and the rich Lothario who jilted her.
In this, Wilhelm feels he is righting a wrong and is pleased at his own
moral indignation. But after some recognitions and reversals he discovers that Felix is actually his own son by Mariana. The switch is a
comic one, but Goethe is obviously also serious about the idea of
Wilhelm setting off to find the father of another, and actually discovering a son.

Many of the traditional plot devices used in *Wilhelm Meister* seem
to be more accidental than deliberate. They certainly do not form the
trellis on which the work hangs, as is the case with other eighteenth-
century novels. Goethe is more concerned with holding the whole together with repeated motifs, but again Wilhelm is not always directly
involved in these. Of course he *is* involved in his own dreams. There
are three of these, and each is predictive. In the first, he dreams that
he is separated from Mariana, and he shortly is. In the second, he has
an erotic dream about Philina, and shortly afterward she seduces him.
In the last, at Lothario's castle, he dreams of Mariana, his father, of
Aurelia (all of whom are dead), and then of Natalia, the "Fair Amazon," who saves Felix from drowning, and afterward walks off with
Wilhelm. These dreams are almost simplistic in their function, but the
last also suggests the significant thematic movement from an un-
wholesome brooding about death to an acceptance of life.

Another motif uses transvestism. It grows naturally out of the
twists of plot that characterize the eighteenth-century novel and belongs in a novel that is so concerned with playacting. Goethe does not
use disguise simply to create suspense or amusing scenes. The transvestism suggests a concern with sexual identity, and yet it also goes
beyond that to the larger questions of identity. Disguise in literature is
usually used to suggest the difficulty of discerning the reality behind
the appearance, but in terms of the plot a disguised character invariably puts on false garb to avoid discovery or to gain some material
end. This is the way it is used in Shakespeare's Forest of Arden, or in
the screen scenes (another form of disguise) from Molière to Fielding.
In *Wilhelm Meister* the disguise is often worn by a character to test an
alternative role on himself, and the deception of others is not involved. Wilhelm is first seen falling in love with Mariana as he stands
in the wings of the theater, and she dances on stage in the uniform of
a soldier. Then after he has lost her he thinks he sees her dressed in
the same soldier's uniform run off with Philina. It is not she (it is
Friedrich), but the vision suggests a wobble in his passion between

the very feminine Philina and the male-attired first love. There is also Mignon, who dresses as a boy, and only slowly Wilhelm discovers her to be a child-woman toward whom he can feel a pure love. In the third book, Wilhelm agrees to a prank in which he dresses as the absent Count and sits where the Countess will come upon him and be amusingly astonished. Instead the Count comes home unexpectedly, comes upon this vision of himself, and is cruelly aged on the spot. Wilhelm's agreement to the prank suggests that there are complicated reasons for his willingness to perform temporarily in the office of the Count, for the Countess is an attractive woman. In this case, there is deception through disguise (which goes awry), but there is also a kind of willing self-deception on Wilhelm's part. There are other instances in which his costume deceives no one but himself. After he rejects the humdrum life of a businessman, he sets off with a squabbling, tacky theatrical troupe with absurd visions dancing in his head. To complete his rejection of a life of getting and spending, he dresses to fit some ancient and dashing role.

He now began to think about his dress. It struck him that a waistcoat, over which, in case of need, one could throw a little short mantle, was a very fit thing for a traveller. Long knit pantaloons, and a pair of lacing boots, seemed the true garb of a pedestrian. He next procured a fine silk sash, which he tied about him, under the pretence at first of securing warmth for his person. On the other hand, he freed his neck from the tyranny of stocks; and got a few stripes of muslin sewed upon his shirt; making the pieces of considerable breadth, so that they presented the complete appearance of an ancient ruff. The beautiful silk neckerchief, the memorial of Mariana, which had once been saved from burning, now lay slackly tied beneath this muslin collar. A round hat, with a particolored band, and a large feather, perfected the mask.[29]

In the original, the final word is *Maskerade,* which may suggest more levity at the scene than Carlyle's somber choice of "mask." The passage continues to suggest that his fellow troupers are amused at his appearance, for "The women all asserted that this garb became him very well. Philina in particular appeared enchanted with it." Yet there is an ambiguous seriousness behind this playacting too, for the garments are Wilhelm's pangs of maturation made visible. This is a different matter from those earlier scenes of fools that play cock of the walk: the foolish lovers like Malvolio, or the strutting Miles Gloriosi of the Renaissance stage. Those characters are ripe for ridicule and we are expected to show them no sympathy. This is not the case with Wilhelm, for he is shown, even here, as a representative as well as a specific child of his age. He is also different from those provincial youths in later novels who rise by their wiles and wits in the big city.

The first thing they do in the Paris or London of Stendhal, Balzac, Flaubert, Thackeray, or Dickens is to be outfitted by a tailor, and then head for their chambers where they can admire themselves in their private mirrors. These fops—Julian Sorel, Rastignac, Frederic Moreau, George Osborne, Pip—may be extensions of their creators, but they are also players in a simpler, more social satire. In them, the point is the hollowness behind the gaudy clothes they wear; but in Wilhelm's case, there are unexplored vistas just beyond his "mask."

Another motif in the work is that which uses love triangles, often with the added spice of a desire that bridges the generations, and may even be incestuous. The image that recurs and brings all of these together is that of the painting in Wilhelm's grandfather's collection of Renaissance Italian works. It is a painting of the king's son dying of a secret love of his father's bride. Wilhelm's father is a practical man and sells the collection, including the painting of the king's son, and Wilhelm vaguely feels this as a rejection. The painting also is remembered when Wilhelm becomes enthusiastic about *Hamlet,* and the connection suggests a psychological interpretation of the tragedy that was not elaborated until a century and a half later. The painting appears again at the end of the novel when Wilhelm has completed his apprenticeship and is led into the Hall of the Past, where the mysterious Brotherhood, which has secretly been overseeing his education, has hung the painting. But the motif is suggested from the very beginning, for Mariana has her secret love, Norbert. Later Wilhelm must share the charms of Philina with the morose Laertes, and still later with Friedrich. At the end of the novel, there is a more aristocratic triangle involving Lothario, Lydia, and Theresa. Such simple triangles, however, barely touch the surface of the flux of life and love. When he first leaves home, Wilhelm meets an eloped couple who have been captured and are being taken before a magistrate. Wilhelm is enchanted by the thought of lovers in flight, and especially by this couple because they have been on the stage. He accompanies them before the magistrate and takes their part, but the relationships are much more complicated than he would ever suspect. "The father would gladly have kept his daughter near him, but he hated the young man, because his wife herself had cast an eye upon him; while the latter could not bear to have in her stepdaughter, a happy rival constantly before her eyes."[30]

Here there is raw material for a fabliau or bedroom farce, but the reoccurrence of such situations and their complications suggest that Goethe has something more in mind than a simple guffaw. At one point, Philina lightly suggests a round robin of love. "She earnestly requested Wilhelm to fall in love with Aurelia, for then the chase would be worth the beholding. 'She pursues her faithless swain

[Lothario], thou her, I thee, her brother [Serlo] me. If that will not divert us for a quarter of a year, I engage to die at the first episode which occurs in this four times complicated tale.' "[31] The diversion does not come off, but the proposal of an imaginary "tale" is one way in which Goethe constantly pushes the "reality" in this novel into the world of art. At the beginning of the novel, Wilhelm dedicates himself to the theater (although he wonders at one point if he loved Mariana or the theater first), yet still feels that there is a nice division between life and art. Increasingly, he senses that the line between them is not easily drawn. One of his earliest memories (and one which Goethe recounts as his own in *Poetry and Truth*) is of playing with marionettes in the family attic. After he gets his stage all arranged, the strings untangled, and the puppets in place, he discovers that he has no lines for them and no audience. He discovers that he must spin tales out of his own imagination and life. "I wished at once to be among the enchanters and the enchanted, at once to have a secret hand in the play, and to enjoy, as a looker-on, the pleasure of illusion."[32] Poetry and Truth, *Dichtung und Wahrheit*, must merge in artful illumination. Yet this is not easily accomplished, the strings of the marionettes become hopelessly entangled, and Wilhelm must give up art and understanding for the present. It is a mutuality, however, that is repeated again and again in the novel. Wilhelm is introduced to the plays of Shakespeare, and in his enthusiasm feels a kinship, for his name is also William. Then he plays the role of Hamlet, and sees his father in the ghost. This sliding into roles is often comic, as when the eccentric Count demands that the players continue wearing their costumes after the play is over, and they humor him by doing so. Such playacting comes naturally to Wilhelm, and when still pretending to be a businessman he invents roles for himself in private.

Brought up in a substantial burgher's house, cleanliness and order were the element in which he breathed; and inheriting as he did a portion of his father's taste for finery, it had always been his care, in boyhood, to furbish up his chamber, which he regarded as his little kingdom, in the stateliest fashion. His bed-curtains were drawn together in massy folds, and fastened with tassels, as they are usually seen in thrones: he had got himself a carpet for the middle of his chamber, and a finer one for his table; his books and apparatus he had, almost instinctively, arranged in such a manner, that a Dutch painter might have imitated them for groups in his still-life scenes. He had a white cap, which he wore straight up like a turban; and the sleeves of his nightgown he had caused to be cut short, in the mode of the Orientals. By way of reason for this, he pretended that long wide sleeves encumbered him in writing. When, at night, the boy was quite alone, and no longer dreaded any interruption, he usually wore a silk sash tied round his body, and often, it is said, he would fix in his girdle a sword, which he had appropriated from an old armory, and thus repeat and declaim his tragic parts; nay, in the same trim he would kneel down and say his evening prayer.[33]

In such a passage there is a marvelous lightness of touch which results in an irony—since Wilhelm is admittedly a fragment of Goethe himself—that is as much psychological protection as satire. The turban, short sleeves, and ("it is said"!) sword become implements with which Wilhelm hopes to discover his true nature. But as he proceeds, he discovers that such understanding through art is impossible. Playacting turns out to be merely playacting, and besides the actors themselves are revealed as hollow and vain. So he imagines himself a creator of dramas, but is humbled by Shakespeare. Finally, his apprenticeship is completed when he discovers that he has not been the master of his destiny, but that it has been chosen for him by the Brotherhood into which he is inducted. Self-creation and self-knowledge are impossible. This is so even for the masters of the Brotherhood, like the Abbe and Lothario, for Goethe makes it clear they have their own absurd delusions. Life is then not understood through art; it *is* art, and we are all vain and hollow players in a dark and comic plot. "What is destiny," Wilhelm asks himself, "but Chance": "The theatre, the world had appeared before him, only as a multitude of thrown dice, every one of which upon its upper surface indicates a greater or a smaller value; and which, when reckoned up together, make a sum."[34] And so he sees himself and is shown to us only through reflected lights, and his final knowledge is that he is nothing, except in relation to the world about him. Through love of the boy Felix and the serene Natalia, he is content to accept the day before him and the task it brings. The lesson is that the self is an unknown and invisible cause seen only in its effects. The torment of most Romantics was the result of their desperate plunges into the secrets of the self, and they were shaken when they came up with nothing. So they had to be content (and yet were not) with its mirrored image, and were frightened by the insubstantial in the shadow. The quest was so noble it was assumed that there had to be a treasure. Goethe was not so sure.

It has been said and repeated, that man should strive to know himself: a singular requisition, with which nobody complies, or ever will comply. Man is by all his senses and efforts directed to externals—to the world around him; and he has to know this so far, and to make it so far serviceable, as he requires for his own ends. It is only when he feels joy or sorrow that he knows anything about himself, and only by joy or sorrow is he instructed what to seek and what to shun. Altogether, man is a darkened being; he knows not whence he comes, nor whither he goes; he knows little of the world and least of himself. I do not know myself, and God forbid that I should.[35]

12

Into Our Age

I have moved the typewriter into the next room where I
can see myself in the mirror as I write.
                    —Henry Miller, *The Tropic of Cancer*

The heroism and comedy of the modern age may best be seen in our
stalking of the self, with everything from pen to microscope, in the
coverts of experience. It has turned out to be a snark. This does not
mean that the results have not been impressive, even grand. Most of
mankind's achievements have been based on illusions; in this case an
Orient of the self was sought, and a New World of bumptious
egalitarianism and technological materialism was found. The reason for
this is that the modern scientific "conquest" of nature is rooted in our
faith in a unique self. To see, so as to describe and test the material fact,
requires a belief in the truth of private investigation, and that in turn is
based on the belief in a self from which experience *can* be observed.
This faith was coincident with the beginning of the technological
revolution at the end of the eighteenth century. Without such a faith
men would not have been able to see nature with eyes that they felt
were entirely their own. Before the eighteenth century (Galileo, Har-
vey, Boyle, and Descartes predict the attitude) they assumed that their
senses were like any others, and since the world was still tinged with
animism their eyes could only see a universal truth, not *in* the fact, but
through the fact. Science slowly became a cooperative venture with
one's contemporaries rather than with the ancients. John Dalton, for
example, assumed that he saw the world as everyone else did, but by
comparing his observed fact and that of others he discovered his own
red-green color blindness. It was necessary for the scientist to see
himself solitary and beginning, as it were, at the start of time if he was
to see the isolatable fact in a manner that made it fit in a new way into
the cosmos. His life took on importance in that it was a reenactment of
the life of Man, and yet his experience was only verified by its
congruence with the experience of his contemporaries, and ontogeny
recapitulated phylogeny. So Alexander von Humboldt went to the top
of Mount Chimborazo, Darwin explored the Great Barrier Reef, and

Wallace tramped the fields of Wales instead of staying in their studies with Aristotle and Pliny. Science and technology piled up with the motes of experience based upon individual observation.

A similar relation to the fact characterizes the Romantic poets, for in their verse the leap to the universal is not facilitated by dependence on the received doctrines of the past, but from the sensations of the heart rooted in their own experience. For them to see and to feel was to be. Yet, unlike their scientific brethern, the truth of their seeing and feeling was not validated by its ultimate universality, but rather by its originality and uniqueness. This is perhaps the origin of what T. S. Eliot has famously termed "the dissociation of sensibility"—although he finds the origins further back in time.[1] It was in the Romantic period, certainly, that writers became aware of this dissociation, for Milton or even Gray do not appear to feel themselves cut off from the world of science. When the Romantics did employ the discoveries of the laboratory they did so in strange ways, as Wordsworth used Hartley, or Byron mocked all forms of mechanical progress.

A stunning illustration of the turn during this age is given by M. H. Abrams in *The Mirror and the Lamp*. The very title of this work suggests the difference between that view of art which sees it as the truthful reflector of a fixed and enameled nature, and that which demands of the artist that he allow his unique inner illumination to shine forth. Abrams quotes Doctor Johnson's judgment that "Shakespeare is above all writers, at least all modern writers, the poet of nature; the poet that holds up to his readers a faithful mirrour of manners and of life." Shakespeare, for all his genius, is in such a view but the incidental accessory to our understanding of the world, and what we understand (the "at least all modern writers" tends to confirm this) is fixed and immutable. Carlyle, however, has the mirror turn into a window, and a window that looks out not on the world or nature, but into the artist himself. He says that Shakespeare's works "are so many windows through which we see a glimpse of the world that was in him."[2] What Carlyle says here was undoubtedly true for Carlyle, but it was probably not true for Shakespeare, and this would be just another case of one age imposing its expectations and assumptions on another.

That lamp of the expressive artist's self has given a persistent glow in the past two centuries, even though in a philosophical sense it might have been an *ignis fatuus*. It is usually thought that the Romantic poets covered their tracks in their autobiographical creations out of coyness or tradition. But it might also be that Wordsworth quibbled over the autobiographical elements in *The Prelude* and that Byron altered "Childe Byron" to *Childe Harold* because of the felt failure to find the true self they sought through poetry. It is notable how evasive the poets of the Romantic age are in the light of their protestations of personal revelation. Patricia Ball presents the standard view of "creativity as an aspect of self-discovery" in both "Romantic theory and poetic practice."[3] But then her poets turn out to be very uncomfortable with the notion, and they appear to write not to reveal themselves but to hide themselves. She quotes Shelley: "Poetry and the principle of Self . . . are the God and Mammon of this World."[4] And Keats: "A poet is the most unpoetical of any thing in existence; because he has no Identity—he is continually [informing] and filling some other Body."[5] Or Byron: "To withdraw *myself* from *myself* (oh that cursed selfishness!) has been my sole, my entire, my sincere motive in scribbling at all."[6] Poetry is then seen not so much as the instrument of personal revelation as it is God, or another identity, or a humbling exercise. The Romantics painted themselves not to show themselves in the flesh, but to cover themselves. The process is acutely described by Coleridge, the scion of the age. His approach is based on conservative political and theological attitudes, but his articulation is consistent with a wide spectrum of Romantic poetic practice. "In human life," Coleridge says, "the seat of individuality, now become self-conscious personality is . . . to be sought for not in any centre of isolated and isolating feeling, but in the degree to which a man passes beyond the limits of temporal and spiritual within which mere feeling confines him, and identifies himself, in thought, feeling, and action, with the larger life about him while remaining a self-integrating member of it."[7] Here there is a dismissal of that "mere feeling" through which the early Romantics attempted to define themselves. The analysis of the passions by Burke or Diderot is here seen as a dead end; as dead as the analysis of the picturesque scene as it was dissected by William Gilpin. We only take on meaning within a context, and our value may be greatest when the will has annihilated the illusion of the self.

From the Romantic period to our own day literature has largely been concerned with the methods by which men disguise from themselves the gap in their beings where the soul once resided. The question of what a man is was formerly phrased "What am I?"—and the answer could be found in terms of trade, the humors, or class. When the foundling at the end of the twists of plot discovered his true father he then knew his name, and this satisfied him. But this is not enough for the Romantic hero. In the first place his victory is measured in terms of the success of his escape from the father, for his question is "Who am I?" and a mere name does not serve as answer. The answers offered have been evasive or distressing, yet the question remains and the great energy expended on it continues to suggest that it is a valid question and worth answering. An important way in which writers have attempted to suggest an answer to the question is to create a character who is seen in terms of his public role while his private and "true" self is illustrated through a subsidiary character, a doppelgänger or double. If we think of the self as a concept that grew up in the last two centuries as a substitute for the earlier soul, this is a revealing development. The soul in myth and tradition is not duplicated in a person. The soul may hold a dialogue with the body which imprisons it, or sacred and profane forces might battle to possess it, but two souls in one body, or a soul doubled in another body, appears to be theologically untenable. In ancient literature there are many instances of good and evil brothers contesting for their father's approval. Yet Cain and Abel, Jacob and Esau, Horus and Set, Castor and Pollux, and so forth, are used as illlustrative moral opposites, and in spite of their literal relationship are not seen to be two halves of the same person.[8] Within the Christian tradition the doubling often creates a figure who serves as a guardian angel or moral exemplum. Grimmelshausen's Simplicius Simplicissimus, for example, adopts many disguises, but he does so sequentially so that there is no question of souls coexisting within him. He also encounters at several points in the narrative the saintly Hertsbruder, who serves as a model of constancy and goodness. At one point Hertsbruder convinces Simplicius that they should go on a pilgrimage, and to make the trip worthwhile they put pebbles in their shoes. Simplicius agrees, but after a few miles has covertly removed his pebbles, yet must still feign a limp. These two are more contrasts than they are two sides of the same principle. The same might be said of Don Quixote and Sancho Panza, for although a real person might combine the idealism and appetite illustrated by Cervantes's characters they function comically as diagrammatic opposites.

A man's fear before the Romantic age was that his soul would be corrupted, or worse that some golem or devil would abscond with it. The modern fear is very different. It is that this private and precious self might be duplicated in another, and so our unique individuality would be denied. Freud recounts several examples of this fear. "One cannot suppress a slight feeling of unpleasantness on discovering his own name in a stranger. I had recently felt it very plainly when I was consulted during my office hours by a man named S. Freud. However, I am assured by one of my own critics that in this respect, he behaves in quite the opposite manner."[9] The rare stroke of levity in the comment on the situation is one that Freud himself might admit was a defense mechanism covering the deeper fear that his mirror image had come to life and that his self was not wholly his own. Such shadows in our age are more often a threat than a friendly guide, and so the mask of the personality is used not so much to make the wearer fit into the world but to protect him from it. The mask is also a protection from the void within, the void which would be too painful to acknowledge.[10] In such a situation the heart is never truly bared, and yet we persist in the Romantic assumption that the great man of letters is the one who is able to reveal himself through an account of his real experience in thinly disguised form—that this way lies truth—and that the disguise is a conventional convenience. What the writer displays is simply another protective mask, or he may even distribute his several invented masks among his fictional characters. The Romantic age began in a full flush of revelation in which the writer assumed, like Boswell, that he could stand aside from himself and see himself plain, or that the accretion of minute details could paint the life of such a man as Doctor Johnson. It didn't quite work out that way, and the self was soon to be coated with a gloze that suggested rather than proved its existence. As Masao Miyoshi puts the case, "It was a legacy of heartbreak that the Romantics left the Victorians; on its flight to the Absolute the alone had met only the alone, the self only the self."[11] The result was prolixity and evasiveness.

The novels of Charles Dickens well illustrate the ways in which an author's own life can uncomfortably haunt as well as profitably feed his narratives. By his own account Dickens was much impressed with Fielding, and the relationship between *Tom Jones* and *David Copperfield* particularly has often been noted. Yet the difference that the intervening century makes—especially because the span between 1749 and 1850 witnessed the growth of the phenomenon of authors placing themselves at the front of their stage—results in very different attitudes toward the heroes. Both novels have roots in the tradition of the picaresque, the *bildungsroman,* and the comic and melodramatic devices of the English stage. The heroes, however, are significantly different. Sophia Warren's beauty may be modeled on that of Fielding's wife, but the source of Tom Jones in life and his individuality struggles against his only begetter's abstract notion of natural goodness. The plot illustrates the point, and the eventual victory of natural goodness over the various forms of affectation, illustrated by Blifil, Lady Bellaston, Lord Fellamar, and others of their ilk, never involves the suggestion that Tom is tempted to employ their affectation. Fielding creates his characters with the confidence of his age and the facility of a comic playwright who deals with known stereotypes. Dickens works in a different fashion. He returns again and again to the figure of the angelic youth who is chosen by evil and who is an idealized memory of Dickens's own youthful martyrdom in a brutal age. David Copperfield's initials invert the initials of his creator, and his life involves other slight inversions of Dickens's, yet the details of his experience are clearly rooted in Dickens's memory, whereas Tom Jones's experience is only dimly indebted to the atmosphere of Fielding's.

A more important difference is the nature of the complicity between the hero and the evil in his society. In Fielding such complicity doesn't exist. Tom must learn certain virtues, such as prudence, but it is not suggested that his character overlaps with those who choose to side with evil. This in part is what makes him stereotypic. It is a very different matter with Dickens. His heroes are innocents who are exposed to the temptations of the world, and even hunger after its baubles. Suffering always makes them finally reject the world's false values, whether these involve a self-indulgent opulence or priggish austerity, and end with a sadder-and-wiser bourgeois idyll—modest fare, loving wife, prattling children, warm fireside, and so on.[12] These heroes strive to divest themselves of their humble origins just as Dickens did, and although their success is not as spectacular as was Dickens's, they appear to carry his guilt for deserting the humbler virtues as well as privations. None of Dickens's characters have any of the unseemlier penchants of their author. They do not have a morbid curiosity about penal practices and capital punishment, they do not have a wall built in the bedroom between their beds and their wives', and they certainly do not maintain separate establishments for very youthful and pretty actresses. Dickens himself did, and he surrounds his heroes with the evils in which he participated. But he did not wish to display a contaminated hero to his Victorian readers, and perhaps he wished to sequester his own vices from his heroes in the recesses of his own mind. The result is that he shows the complicity of his heroes in the vices of the age through indirection and symbolic action.

In *Great Expectations* Pip is guilty of ingratitude and snobbery, but his reaction to his own sins suggests that he has committed all of the seven deadly. His folly harms few, and those not very much, but he feels himself doubled in others who are as vicious as villains can be in a Victorian novel. This use of the evil doppelgänger who acts out our blackest thoughts and desires is used as early as *Oliver Twist* in a rudimentary fashion. Oliver is one of the most Christly of Dickens's waifs, and yet Dickens must supply him with Monk, his evil half-brother, who plots his destruction. The relationship, in schematic terms, is not unlike that between Tom Jones and Blifil, yet Blifil's evil is a mere affectation and comic lechery, and Tom's moral relationship to him depends on contrast. The case is not quite the same where Oliver and Monk are concerned. Monk's evil suggests a larger continent of diabolism in the world, and the half-brotherhood is more than a convenience of plot. The technique is both clearer and more complicated in *Great Expectations*. Orlick, the lumbering journeyman blacksmith who is Pip's contemporary in the forge, kills Pip's sister, toward whom Pip himself might have more reason for enmity. After this Orlick dogs his career, an avenging angel who shows up as a dark heap in his entryway. Orlick acts out a lumpen version of evil, and Pip dimly realizes that but for his mysterious and undeserved good fortune he might have gone Orlick's way. In chapter 53 he is captured by a drunken Orlick who addresses him as "wolf" (as he was earlier called a pig by Pumblechook and a young dog by Magwitch). Orlick tells him that "It was you as did for your shrew sister," and his reason is that "You was favoured, and he was bullied and beat. Old Orlick bullied and beat, eh? Now you pays for it. You done it; now you pays for it." Except for a rescue in the nick of time Pip would indeed have paid for his sister's death. The gentleman that Pip aspires to be is mocked in the character of Bentley Drummle, who is his brutal bourgeois doppel-gänger. It is he who successfully courts the cruel and beautiful Estella who has been trained to break the hearts of fops. In chapter 43 Pip returns to his village to visit Estella, and at the inn finds Drummle, his heart's abhorrence, warming his backside by the fire. Pip goes to the fireplace, takes the poker, pokes the fire, and only recognizes Drummle when he is contemptuously addressed by him. They then stand shoulder to shoulder, vying for the fire's warmth, and exchange sneers that echo each other. "I felt here, through a tingling in my blood, that if Mr. Drummle's shoulder had claimed another hair's breadth of room, I should have jerked him into the window; equally, that if my shoulder had urged a similar claim, Mr. Drummle would have jerked me into the nearest box. He whistled a little. So did I."

Pip's sins, then, are vicarious, and borne by Orlick and Drummle, both dark and brutal sons of Cain or Grendel. They in turn are linked in the evil machinations of Compeyson, the gentleman ruffian who is so completely foul that Dickens generally keeps him out of sight. But Pip, through the geneaology of the plot, is linked to both, and so ultimately with the thoroughly corrupt Compeyson. This link grows weaker as the chain of shadows recedes, but the essential guilt is also suggested by a shadow within. As Dickens contains within himself the character of the Pip who narrates his story and the Pip who experiences it, so Pip the narrator contains within his memory and breast the boy that he was. The idea of an outer social self and an inner true self is introduced in the first chapter when Pip encounters the convict Magwitch in the churchyard. Magwitch frightens Pip into bringing him a file and food by saying, "Now, I ain't alone, as you may think I am. There's a young man hid with me, in comparison with which young man I am a Angel." *With* here has the mysterious weight of *within* for Pip, and when he returns to the churchyard with the file he encounters Compeyson and thinks he is the young man—which in a way he is. Pip's complicity with this pervasive evil is later underscored in chapter 32 in London when Wemmick invites him to visit Newgate prison where Wemmick must talk to a client.

"Did your client commit the robbery?" I asked.

"Bless your soul and body, no," answered Wemmick very drily. "But he is accused of it. So might you or I be. Either of us might be accused of it, you know."

"Only neither of us is," I remarked.

"Yah!" said Wemmick, touching me on the breast with his forefinger; "you're a deep one, Mr. Pip!"

And so he is, but Dickens can only represent those depths through shadowy figures that haunt him, or images of puppets that dance in the private theater of the mind. The nature of language itself may stand in the way of the ultimate revelation of a character, for as language must describe through symbol and analogy, so fiction can only suggest the nature of a self through metaphor. In the case of Dickens, his last work, *The Mystery of Edwin Drood*, suggests a final form of desperation in the attempt to pin down the nature of a man. There John Jasper (the alliterated name looks back to his own Nicholas Nickleby, Poe's William Wilson, and ahead to Vladimir Nabokov's whole gallery of characters with alliterated names) publicly wears a pious face and directs the church choir, but privately is a worshiper at the shrine of the bloody cult of Kali. His is a doubled soul, which comes to full flower in the character of Stevenson's Dr. Jekyll and Mr. Hyde.

The history of narrative art since the Romantic period has been in one sense the history of the devices by which writers give the illusion of a real character. The necessity of such an illusion did not occur to earlier ages, and their use of puppets and masks and mirror images suggested an aspect of the character's artistic existence. The twins in Shakespeare's comedies have nothing to do with doubles, doppelgängers, and secret sharers.[13] We now tend to assume that those earlier ages neglected the self out of oversight or ignorance, although our success at pinning it down has been less than satisfactory. In fact the search for a definition in our age has often been sadly ridiculed, as by Samuel Beckett, or been made material for high comedy, as by Nabokov. In his *King, Queen, Knave* there are two chess players who actually turn out to be named Weiss and Schwartz, and in *Pale Fire* there are good and evil twins named Odon and Nodo (who cheats at cards). Robert Langbaum points out that our best writers recognize "that the self is not, as the nineteenth-century romanticists tended to think, opposed to culture, but that the self is a cultural achievement, that it is as much outside us as inside, and that the self exists outside us in the form of cultural symbols."[14] This self, which is a social creation, is something against which the private romantic self rebels.[15] Through the invention of this self the modern age has created a gap between the general and the particular. The makers of earlier literature do not intend to discover—or hide—themselves in their works. For them the particular is merely a convenience from which they can leap to the general. Modern writers do normally intend both to discover and hide themselves in their works, and readers have come to assume this is the case. Because of the resistence of the romantic self to considering itself as a creature of its time and place, it is often removed artificially through art from that which created it. But in a world without gods, that removal results in torment instead of serenity. There are exceptional moments when this is not the case. The early work of Walt Whitman may be one, for there Whitman appears to sense no division between himself and an outer reality, and reality becomes a "realized dream."[16] But such an incorporation of the world into the self more often results in the chilly aestheticism of a Wallace Stevens. As Frederick Hoffman puts it, "The most significant characteristic of twentieth-century thought is that of the self's improvising and experimenting with ways of maintaining self-confidence. We move away from metaphysics and toward forms of epistemology; self-definition becomes a series of improvisational gestures; there is a profound and poignant distrust of traditional schemes of definition. In his most confident moments of self-assertion, modern man is still in the act of willing his wholeness, his prospects of enduring time, his dignity and his worth."[17]

In the realm of art, which may cut closest to the bone of the self, the confident moments are frequent, but the results are hardly more successful than Dickens's as self-realization. Modern writers (one thinks of those working the confessional vein such as Doris Lessing, Robert Lowell, Saul Bellow, Norman Mailer, Philip Roth, etc.), aided by the jargon of popular psychology and expertise in the uses of narrative technique, are always placing rough hands on the material from their own lives. Yet there is a compensatory movement in modern literature away from confessional and toward the universal. The progress of the works of James Joyce depict this contrary arc. These begin with the searingly painful stories in *Dubliners*, especially the early ones in which there is a romantically innocent little boy who is more convincingly the young Joyce than Dickens's youths are the young Dickens.[18] With Stephen, in both *A Portrait of the Artist as a Young Man* and *Ulysses*, he creates a character whose name seems to be changed only to appropriate the myth of Icarus, for Joyce is elsewhere careless about changing names solely to protect the innocent. Yet Stephen is a partial Joyce, more effete and humorless, and by the time we see him in the Proteus section of *Ulysses* he is given a meditation that would have been precocious even for the young Joyce. Reality is done violence to for the sake of art, and Stephen is as much an archetypal artist as he is a fleshed and accurate memory of his creator's day on June 16, 1904. Bloom is another matter. His domesticity and harassing cocnerns are undoubtedly rooted in those of Joyce during the years of composition, yet he is also the archetypal victim and wanderer. There is not an open word in the work beyond the title that links Bloom to Odysseus, yet he is linked, and most readers delight in the manipulation of the analogies. These links allow Bloom to escape (mostly unknown to him) the burdens of the fact and the present, and his self finds solace and meaning only when mysteriously diffused through the epic tradition that has made him. Humphrey Crimpden Earwicker in *Finnegans Wake* is even more thoroughly diffused into the past. Bloom gains his curious stature by shadowing an epical narrative tradition, but Earwicker comes to incorporate everything through the magic of language. This process begins with "the influence of collective tradition on the individual," but Earwicker's very initials reverberate in such a way throughout the work that this "influence" inundates the world in which he exists.[19] "The great fact emerges that after that historic date all holographs so far exhumed initialled by Haromphrey bear the sigla H.C.E. and while he was only and long and always good Dook Umphrey for the hungerlean spalpeens of Lucalizod and Chimbers to his cronies it was equally certainly a pleasant turn of the populace which gave him as sense of those normative letters the nickname Here Comes Everybody. An Imposing everybody he always indeed looked, constantly the same as and equal to himself and magnificently well worthy of any and all such universalization."[20] This is written in high humor, but Joyce's comedy always has its grave underside. The significance of the initials H.C.E. becomes a running jest throughout the whole work, yet beyond the joke the radius of the circle of their implication becomes ever longer. In the first sentence of the work it is "Howth Castle and Environs," then it is "Hush! Caution! Echoland!" When he slips backward it is "Et Cur Heli!", and later it is drawn from the Table of Elements with "H_2CE_3." The initials also conjure up "Elberfeld's Calculatig Horses," "H.C. Enderson," "Huges Caput Earlyfouler," and "Hircus Civis Eblanensis." Finally it is not only a matter of his name assimilating all that is in the memory of the past and the knowledge of the present, but he is the progenitor of the future, and "Haveth Childers Everywhere."[21] Earwicker is then everything simultaneously, and the work is a record of his discovery of the world that is his mind. This is not like those many masks that are worn by a Simplicius Simplicissimus sequentially.

Those are like plaster casts and not intended to reveal that which cannot be there. When this idea is used by a modern writer the result is a feeling of horror when the ultimate mask is removed. Rainer Maria Rilke speculates on the masks that people wear, and as spendthrifts toss away—their children and dogs picking them up and wearing them. Then he writes: "Other people put their faces on, one after the other, with uncanny rapidity and wear them out. At first it seems to them they are provided for always; but they scarcely reach forty—and they have come to the last. This naturally has something tragic. They are not accustomed to taking care of faces, their last is worn through in a week, has holes, and in many places is thin as paper; and then little by little the under layer, the no-face, comes through, and they go about with that."[22]

The treatment of the idea here seems sportive enough, but it is a whistling in the dark, for in the next paragraph Rilke expresses his deep fear of seeing the "naked flayed head without a face." In *Finnegans Wake* this fear is held at bay, for where Earwicker is concerned the more we know of him the more he slips gracefully into the universe. Most writers work from the outer details inward, and find they must allow circumstances to suggest the character. Joyce reverses the process and works from the centerless center outward, past detail, past circumstances, and reconstitutes the frail self in the farthest reaches of the universe. This may be a sad resolution to the Romantic assertion of a self, but it has the advantage of crowding an abyss without, instead of anguishing over an abyss within.

Notes
Bibliography
Index

Notes

Chapter 1: Out of the Void

1. In this, Milton followed the drift of Renaissance learning, which examined every-thing from rocks to language in its attempt to confirm the truths of the Pentateuch. In the next generation the attempt foundered on the shoals of empiricism. Even in Milton there is often a surprising evenhandedness in his placing together of disparate mythological allusions. Satan is described as

> in bulk as huge
> As whom the Fables name of monstrous size,
> *Titanian*, or *Earth-born*, that warr'd on Jove,
> *Briareos* or *Typhon*, whom the Den
> By ancient *Tarsus* held, or that Sea-beast
> *Leviathan*, which God of all his works
> Created hugest that swim th' Ocean stream.   (*PL* 1. 196–202)

Here he mixes Greek, Roman, and Hebrew myth with insouciance, as though they were mutually confirming, although the Fundamentalist could see Leviathan substantiated by confused pagan "Fables." The history of Noah as an example of Renaissance attitudes is interestingly traced by Don Cameron Allen in *The Legend of Noah*.

2. Sir James G. Frazer, *The Golden Bough*, Jessie Weston, *From Ritual to Romance*, C. G. Jung, *The Integration of the Personality*, tr. Stanley M. Dell, and *Psychological Reflections*, ed. J. Jacobi and R. F. C. Hull. The literature on the subject is now enormous, but almost all of it is unitary in its implications, even though the links between cultures are more often assumed than demonstrated. This tendency is evident even in Thomas Bulfinch's *The Age of Fable*. Joseph Campbell presents a recent example of this unitary concept of man's myths. Even though he is greatly influenced by Jung's concept of a universal mythic consciousness, he is a disseminationist. See *The Hero with a Thousand Faces*, *The Masks of God*, and *The Mythic Image*. The point is that a man is denied originality in his myth-making whether his myths come from a buried unconscious or are borrowed from some other culture.

3. Sir Herbert Read, *Education Through Art*. See especially chapter 6 (pp. 183–95) which discusses the mandala phenomenon in children's art, and the Gestalt hypothesis that "a parallelism (or 'isomorphism') exists between individual human experiences and the physical structure of the cortex" (p. 188).

4. Aristotle says that "Reason is but choosing" (*Ethics* 3. 2. 6), which defines by operation or effect, but the idea is central to all liberal eighteenth-century thought. An excellent illustration is offered by James Madison's defense of a Republican as opposed to a Democratic form of government in number ten of the *The Federalist* (1787). His concern is that the choice which is the guide in government be the result of reason rather than "self-love."

5. John Milton, *Complete Poems and Major Prose*, p. 746.

6. C. S. Lewis, *The Abolition of Man*. See especially the final chapter.

7. J. H. Plumb, *The Death of the Past*. The thesis has merit, but at times it seems simply

to serve as a club with which to beat the major nineteenth-century historians for their special pleading. My point is that it was not until the eighteenth century that historians seriously attempted to separate hearsay and myth from documented facts. They still might have had axes to grind, but their professed skepticism forced them to grind slowly. Gibbon, *Decline and Fall*, p. 105, was himself aware of the danger. "The voice of history . . . is often little more than the organ of hatred or flattery."

8. Had Shakespeare left us letters, a journal, or a proper autobiography, as would have a decent eighteenth-century man of letters, much ink might have been saved in the long run. But he and his contemporaries evidently thought such scribblings vanities—if they thought of them at all. The history of the anti-Stratfordians has been told many times, but with most verve by William F. and Elizabeth S. Friedman in *The Shakespearean Ciphers Examined*. Not only did a J. T. Looney propose Oxford, but George M. Battey proposed Defoe. As curious as these capers are, the Stratfordians include a parcel of eccentrics. Louis C. Alexander "edited" an *Autobiography of Shakespeare* in 1911, which is a pasting together of the relics. Even the academic Shakespeareans indulge in odd exercises. Edward Wagenknecht has shown the Bard to be a splendid fellow in *The Personality of Shakespeare*, and Alfred Harbage, by tabulating the good, bad, and indifferent characters in the plays, has proved that Shakespeare's view of life was generally "kindly." See Wagenknecht, p. 60. It is always sad to see humanists seduced by the methods of the social scientists. The basic materials of the life of Shakespeare have been brought together by E. K. Chambers, Tucker Brooke, and most recently by Samuel Schoenbaum, *William Shakespeare*.

9. Johnson was aware—how could he not be?—of Boswell's intent to write his biography, and even poured advice on how it was to be done into his ear. Boswell showed Johnson his journal during their tour to the Hebrides. On September 19, 1774, he recorded Johnson's reaction. " 'Sir,' said he, 'it is not written in a slovenly manner. It might be printed, were the subject fit for printing.' " Then Boswell appends the note, "As I have faithfully recorded so many minute particulars, I hope I shall be pardoned for inserting so flattering an encomium on what is now offered to the publick." Boswell is pleased that his prose is not judged to be sloven, but he is silent on the implied criticism of the fitness of the subject. A tour of the Hebrides is itself a fit subject for Johnson, as he published his own *Baedeker* to that little-known land the next year. What he objects to is the very minutia which gives the *Life of Samuel Johnson* its charm and immortality. Boswell probably knew this, for his account of their tour of the Hebrides was not published until after Johnson was dead. No doubt he didn't wish to compete, and no doubt he wished to stake out his claim to being the Great Cam's biographer, but he surely also knew that he was not writing another *Life of Mr. Richard Savage*.

10. Jacques Casanova, *The Memoirs of Casanova*, p. 2. "I have not written these memoirs for young people who, in order to avoid going astray, need to spend their youth in ignorance, but rather for those who have had enough experience in life to make them impervious to seduction. Since the true virtues are only habits, I hazard the opinion that truly virtuous people are those who practice them without effort. These people have no idea of intolerance, and it is for them that I have written."

11. In book 1 of *The Prelude* Wordsworth contemplates various topics for his epic: "some British theme, some Old / Romantic tale by Milton left unsung;" or perhaps a Spenserian tale of "Christian meekness hallowing faithful loves," or the story of Mithridates, Gustavus, or Wallace, but puts these off for when he has a "riper mind." He settles on "A Tale from my own heart, more near akin / To my own passions and habitual thoughts;" even though this lays him open to charges of a lack of humility and even selfishness (11. 166–269).

12. Ambiguously there follows the sub-sub-title, *An Autobiographical Poem*.

13. Cited by Peter Gay in *The Party of Humanity*, p. 46.

14. Northrop Frye, "Towards Defining an Age of Sensibility," in *Eighteenth-Century English Literature*, pp. 311–18. Peter Gay has characterized these nomenclative battles as "definition by larceny" in *The Party of Humanity*, pp. 253–54. Yet the exercises will go on. What is important is that the major battles over labels have concerned the eighteenth century. I think that it is a question of the self-consciousness of the age which could not be content with an historical-political tag, like "The Age of Anne," or a definition dependent on analogy, like "The Augustan Age." By implication the question came down to "What am I to call me (or us) in my uniqueness?" In such a situation labels are not easy. To put it another way, when poets went to the coffee house, you knew where to find them; when they went for walks for their inspiration, they could be anywhere.

Two other essays of interest on the subject are M. H. Abrams, "English Romanticism: The Spirit of the Age," in *Romanticism Reconsidered*, pp. 26–72, and Roland Mortier, " 'Sensibility,' 'Neoclassicism,' or 'Preromanticism'?" in *Eighteenth Century Studies Presented to Arthur M. Wilson*, p. 153–64.

15. Donald Frame, "Introduction" to *Montaigne's Essays and Selected Writings*, p. vi.

16. It is the thesis of Marjorie Hope Nicolson in *The Breaking of the Circle* that the character of Hamlet announces the collapse of Shakespeare's assurance in the old morality and cosmology—a trouble that built and caused his retirement in 1610. She is certainly not alone in seeing Hamlet as the first modern.

17. George Psalmanazar was a Provençal who came to London in 1703 and passed himself off as a Formosan. He published his description of Formosa in 1704, invented a native language for himself, and to the delight of his fashionable patrons was converted to Christianity. Society was agog, but the imposture was discovered, and Psalmanazar went on to become a Hebraist. Johnson knew and respected him. He died in 1763. He is simply the best known of a number of waggish fakes who preyed upon the hunger for news of exotic and faraway places.

18. Percy G. Adams, in *Travelers and Travel Liars*, presents a history of the cunning and ignorant eighteenth-century rogues who contributed to tales of Patagonian giants, a Northwest Passage, a Mississippi which flowed to the Pacific, and so forth.

19. And thries hadde she been at Jerusalem;
    She hadde passed many a straunge strem;
    At Rome she hadde been, and at Boloigne,
    In Galice at Seint-Jame, and at Coloigne.
    She Kould muchel of wandrynge by the weye.   (11. 463–67)

"Prologue" to *The Poems of Chaucer*, ed. F. N. Robinson. Even some of the place names appear to be introduced for the sake of the rime, although there were many holy ones from which to choose.

20. These narratives (which date from the fourth century) are important because they describe a Byzantine Jerusalem much altered in the seventh century. One of the most interesting is *The Pilgrimage of S. Silvia of Aquitania to the Holy Places*. Coming and going was a bore, and the text offers little more than directions: "Starting from Tarsus, I arrived at a certain city above the sea, but still in Cilicia, called Pompeiopolis. Thence I entered the borders of Hisauria, and halted in a city called Coricus" (p. 43). Valleys, trees and rocks are mentioned only when they have some biblical association, but even then are shapeless and monochrome. There is much account of religious ceremony and practice, but the celebrants are voiceless and faceless.

21. Howard Mumford Jones, *O Strange New World*.

22. The question of Johnson's insularity was raised by Macaulay and countered by G. B. Hill in his edition of *Boswell's Life of Johnson*. Hill presents a list of Johnson's actual and

proposed trips (3:449). But the point is that Johnson only traveled or wished to travel in order to get somewhere. In Boswell's *Journal of a Tour to the Hebrides* he records Johnson as saying "No sir; there are none of the French literati now alive, to visit whom I would cross a sea. I can find in Buffon's book all that he can say" (September 19). The next day he writes, "Dr. Johnson said this morning, when talking of our setting out, that he was in a state in which Lord Bacon represents kings. He desired the end, but did not like the means." Or this from the *Life* in 1779: "*Boxwell.* 'Should you not like to see Dublin, Sir?' *Johnson.* 'No, Sir; Dublin is only a worse capital.' *Boswell.* 'Is not the Giant's-Causeway worth seeing?' *Johnson.* 'Worth seeing, yes; but not worth going to see' " (3:466). It is a pun, but Johnson was not the sort to sacrifice his meaning for a pun.

23. A. Gordon Laing, *Travels in Western Africa.* Many of the British explorers of the period were slightly mad and very hardy Scots, and Laing is an example. Mungo Park is another. Laing's major accomplishment was to cross the Sahara from north to south in 1826, but he was killed near Timbuctoo. He was one of the first to disguise himself (first as a Turk, later as a Kaffir), to the discomfort of his father-in-law, the British Consul at Tripoli, and the Colonial Office which supported the expedition. This practice was not as obvious as it was later to be to Henry Layard, Richard Burton, or T. E. Lawrence. A sprightly account of Laing's career is given by Brian Gardner in *The Quest for Timbuctoo*, pp. 51–108.

24. The passage may be an illustration of Johnsonian bowwow, but there are enough others like it that we must assume the position to be strongly held. What is important is the implied contrary attitude held by Boswell.

> Talking of our feeling for the distresses of others;—*Johnson.* 'Why, Sir, there is much noise made about it, but it is greatly exaggerated. No, Sir, we have a certain degree of feeling to prompt us to do good: more than that, Providence does not intend. It would be misery to no purpose.' *Boswell.* 'But suppose now, Sir, that one of your intimate friends were apprehended for an offence for which he might be hanged.' *Johnson.* 'I should do what I could to bail him, and give him any other assistance; but if he were once fairly hanged, I should not suffer.' *Boswell.* 'Would you eat your dinner that day, Sir?' *Johnson.* 'Yes, Sir; and eat it as if he were eating it with me. Why, there's Baretti, who is to be tried for his life to-morrow, friends have risen up for him on every side; yet if he should be hanged, none of them will eat a slice of plumb-pudding the less. Sir, that sympathetic feeling goes a very little way in depressing the mind.' (*Boswell's Life of Johnson*, 2:108).

25. There is a level-headed praticality to the reformers of the middle of the century. They were projectors (as Defoe termed it) who were as much concerned with eliminating inefficiency as discomfort in their social proposals. Hogarth and the Fielding serve as illustrations. Later in the century such a reformer as William Cowper is made queasy at the thought of human suffering. But it probably required such poetic trembling as his to cause the elimination of the grosser abuses in the next century: the slave trade in 1806, the pillory in 1816, flogging of women in 1820, bullbaiting and cockfighting in 1822, and man-traps for poachers in 1827. The case of Cowper is examined by Lodwick Hartley in *William Cowper*.

26. Herbert James Paton, *The Good Will*, pp. 58–63.

Chapter 2: Dancing on the Head of a Pin

1. *The New York Review of Books*, May 5, 1974, pp. 5, 10. Recent lists of dissertations on modern literature, sociology, and education are clotted with such terms.

2. John Locke, *Essay Concerning Human Understanding*, 1:458–59.

3. Locke, 1:462.

4. *The Philosophy of David Hume*, p. 23.

5. Hume, p. 173.

6. Hume, p. 174.

7. Hume, p. 176.

8. Hume, p. 195.

9. Hume, p. 176.

10. Terence Penelhum, "Hume on Personal Identity," pp. 571–89. In many ways, this essay is an attack on Hume based on a quibble about Hume's quibble, and motivated by ethical pragmatism. Also see A. J. Ayer, *The Concept of a Person*. Ayer's main concern is legal and social, and so he sees the experiences of *a* self as discrete and unlike comparable experiences of another (p. 115). To this we must say of course, but the philosophical question of the self remains. Patricia Meyer Spacks, *Imagining a Self*, p. 3, says that the search for the self became desperate after Hume. Roy Pascal, *Design and Truth in Autobiography*, writes, "Hume's *Life* (1776) is the most extended account of a writer till that time" (p. 34).

11. Quoted by Sydney Shoemaker, *Self-Knowledge and Self-Identity*, p. 10.

12. Bertrand Russell, *The Analysis of Mind*, pp. 17–18.

13. Herbert James Paton, *The Good Will*, pp. 58–63. Also see P. F. Strawson, *Individuals;* in which the argument is linguistic. Bernard Williams attacks Strawson's view that persons need not be bodies, contending that personal identity depends on body, in *Problems of the Self*, p. 19. Much of this debate takes us down a very impressive garden path.

14. Bernard Mayo, *The Logic of Personality*, p. 93. This grammatical approach to the self goes back at least to Samuel Alexander. See his "Self as Subject and as Person," p. 3.

15. Mayo, p. 58. The same point is made by Herbert J. Muller in *Freedom in the Ancient World*, p. 21: "[In the Neolithic village] there were no self-conscious individuals. The village did not deliberately suppress the individual—he had simply not emerged yet. The villager who knew his world so thoroughly knew everything but his self. He was not idealistically surrendering himself to the community, because he had not yet found himself. Hence he could not even have a full, vivid consciousness of community, for to realize oneness it is necessary to realize difference." Mircea Eliade, *The Myth of the Eternal Return*, p. 5, makes the same point in religious rather than social terms. "In the particulars of his conscious behavior, the 'primitive,' the archaic man, acknowledges no act which has not been previously posited and lived by someone else, some other being who was not a man. What he does has been done before. His life is the ceaseless repetition of gestures initiated by others."

16. Mayo, p. 93.

17. Hume, p. 260.

18. Quoted by Garrett L. VanderVeer in *Bradley's Metaphysics and the Self*, p. 237.

19. Alburey Castell, *The Self in Philosophy*, p. 39. In taking this position Castell acknowledges that he is following in the footsteps of Leibnitz rather than those of Locke (p. 46). There is still a sense of the arbitrariness of this position.

20. Henry W. Johnstone, *The Problem of the Self*, p. 15.

21. Quoted by Johnstone, p. 25.

22. *The Portable Jung*, p. 139.

23. *The Portable Jung*, p. 142.

24. June Singer, *Boundries of the Soul*, p. 240.

25. C. G. Jung, *Psychological Reflections*, p. 209.

26. Jean-Paul Sartre, *The Transcendence of the Ego*, pp. 98–99. The statement might be considered the ultimate illustration of solipsism.

27. J. Milton Yinger, *Toward a Field Theory of Behavior*, p. 145. To balance such

thick-tongued phrases as "significant reference group" one might refer to Thomas Mann's meditation on the derivative nature of most individualistic and eccentric behavior. In *The Story of a Novel* (p. 155) he comments on how John of Patmos borrowed from other visionaries: "I was struck, as the text puts it, by the fact 'that a raving man should rave in the same pattern as another who came before him; that one is ecstatic not independently, so to speak, but by rote.' This psychological item seemed to me extremely interesting and worth stressing, and I thought I knew why. It coincided in a way with my own growing inclination, which as I discovered was not mine alone, to look upon all life as a cultural product taking the form of mythic clichés, and to prefer quotation to independent invention. *Faustus* shows many a trace of this leaning."

28. Johnstone, p. 149.

Chapter 3: Once Upon a Time

1. See Peter Ucko and Andreé Rosenfeld, *Palaeolithic Cave Art*, and Lucien Levy-Bruhl, *The "Soul" of the Primitive*. Levy-Bruhl focuses on the totemism and animism implicit in cave art.

2. Anselm L. Strauss, *Mirrors and Masks*, p. 20.

3. Booker T. Washington, *Up From Slavery*, p. 91.

4. Alexander Marshack in *The Roots of Civilization* discusses the recurrent hand symbol in cave art. Marshack has applied much modern technology to the interpretation of cave art.

5. Bruno Snell, *The Discovery of the Mind*, pp. 6–7.

6. Snell, p. 6.

7. On the occasion of a review of Robin Lane Fox's *Alexander the Great* in the *New York Review of Books*, E. Badian surveys the difficulty of getting the facts about Alexander: "After his death, articulate Greeks began to collect the legend, and in Greek Egypt it ultimately became the Alexander Romance, the fiction best seller of all time, translated into a dozen languages at least, and favorite reading right through the Middle Ages and beyond. Penetrating into Jewish, Christian, and Muslim myth, it was carried by the Arab armies back to the centuries that had seen Alexander, and reinforced what was already there, until authentic local legend became inextricably intertwined with literary and even religious inspiration" (p. 8).

8. Snell, pp. 17–19.

9. Stephen Toulmin and June Goodfield, *The Discovery of Time*, p. 31.

10. Chester G. Starr, *The Awakening of the Greek Historical Spirit*, p. 65, and Eric R. Dodds, *The Ancient Concept of Progress*, p. 3.

11. Michael Grant, *The Ancient Historians*, p. 48.

12. Aubrey De Sélincourt, *The World of Herodotus*, p. 25.

13. Herodotus, *The Histories*, p. 13.

14. Herodotus, p. 14.

15. Herodotus, p. 15.

16. Robin George Collingwood, *The Idea of History*, p. 42.

17. De Sélincourt, p. 25.

18. De Sélincourt, p. 33.

19. Toulmin and Goodfield, p. 60.

20. Toulmin and Goodfield, p. 76.

21. E. Bréhier, *Philosophy and History*; p. 160.

22. Peter Burke, *The Renaissance Sense of the Past*, p. 1.

23. Burke, p. 21.

24. Burke, pp. 25, 39, 41, 42, 60.

25. Don Cameron Allen, *The Legend of Noah.*

26. Toulmin and Goodfield, p. 151.

27. Mario Praz, *On Neoclassicism*, p. 71. Also see Robert M. Adams, *The Roman Stamp.*

28. Quoted by Toulmin and Goodfield, p. 130.

29. Toulmin and Goodfield, p. 143.

30. Jan Hendrick van den Berg, *The Changing Nature of Man*, p. 36.

31. Collingwood, p. 209, and J. H. Plumb, *The Death of the Past.*

Chapter 4: Biography

1. André Parrot, *Sumer*, pp. 106–9. Here there is a discussion as well as excellent photographs of the Tell Asmar discoveries. In a gushy introduction, André Malraux writes: "The God Abu is far from being a clumsy imitation of an imaginary figure; it does not imitate anything. Such statues made the sacred beings present in the spectator's emotion, as their ideograms made them present in his mind" (p. xxv). This may well be, but the supposition requires quite a leap across the centuries.

2. James D. Breckenridge, *Likeness*, p. 39.

3. Breckenridge, p. 7.

4. John Alber Wilson, *The Culture of Ancient Egypt*, p. 132.

5. Breckenridge, p. 5.

6. Breckenridge, p. 145.

7. E. H. Gombrich, in *Art and Illusion*, comments on the other side of this deception committed to glorification and spiritualization. He asserts that pictorial caricature did not appear until the Renaissance because "Caricature presupposes the theoretical discovery of the difference between likeness and equivalence" (p. 343).

8. Gombrich, p. 36.

9. Edwin Panofsky, *The Life and Art of Albrecht Dürer*, p. 237. Panofsky's general comment on this is that "Northern artists had no wish to eternalize the individual by isolating him from any empirical context and reducing his physiognomy to a diagram as self-contained and unchangeable as a Platonic idea."

10. John Pope-Hennessy, *Portrait in the Renaissance*, p. 72.

11. Pope-Hennessy, p. 28.

12. Gombrich, p. 200.

13. Xenophon, *The Persian Expedition*, p. 52.

14. Herodotus, pp. 58–60.

15. Marcus Aurelius, *Meditations*, pp. 39–40.

16. Marcus Aurelius, p. 45. This is one of the neatest presentations of the Stoic war against the flesh. The battle is one that seems to lend itself to epigrammatic statement, whether the material body is denigrated by Reason (as here), by Christian Grace (as in Augustine), or by mystic Transcendence (as in Emerson).

17. Anna Comnena, *The Alexiad*, pp. 109–10.

18. Anna Comnena, pp. 110–11.

19. Anna Comnena, p. 54. There is a remarkable contemporary description of Charlemagne by Einhard, the emperor's scribe. But Suetonius was Einhard's model, and for his description he lifts whole passages from the *Lives of the Twelve Caesars*. See C. Warren Hollister, *Medieval Europe*, p. 80.

20. Donald A. Stauffer, *English Biography Before 1700*, p. 5.

21. Stauffer, p. 88.

22. Stauffer, p. 42.

23. Stauffer, p. 117. Harold Nicolson, in *The Development of English Biography*, says that

Walton failed as a biographer and that the art of biography was only liberated by realism in the 1780s (p. 65).

24. The accounts in the *Newgate Calendar* are in prose and always conclude with heavy moralizing. A selection of these have been edited by Sir Norman Birkett, *The Newgate Calendar.*

25. See William Robert Irwin, *The Making of "Jonathan Wild."*

26. Richard Altick, *Lives and Letters;* p. 46. Nicolson describes North's work as racy, inaccurate, vivid, and slangy (p. 74).

27. Samuel Johnson, *Essays from the "Rambler," "Adventurer," and "Idler",* pp. 111–12. This is from the *Rambler,* no. 60; a similar view is held in the *Idler,* no. 84 (pp. 346–49).

28. *Boswell's Life of Johnson,* 2:510. Also see 2:191, where the same sentiment is expressed.

29. The fact that nearly everyone rushed in to recount his memories of Johnson is significant. Of course Johnson's character gave cause, but articulate eccentrics had lived before his time and an anecdotal deluge had not followed their deaths. See, for example, William Shaw, *Memoirs of the Life and Writings of the Late Dr. Samuel Johnson,* and *Anecdotes of the Late Samuel Johnson, L.L.D., During the Last Twenty Years of his Life,* by Hester Lynch Piozzi. There were also memories from Richard Cumberland, Bishop Percy, Dr. Campbell, and others.

Chapter 5: Autobiography

1. *OED.*

2. Paul Delany, *British Autobiography in the Seventeenth Century,* p. 1. Also *OED.*

3. Snell, *The Discovery of the Mind,* p. 48.

4. Sir Thomas Browne, *Religio Medici and Other Works,* p. 64.

5. *Boswell's Life of Johnson,* 3:195.

6. Sir Herbert Read, *Icon and Idea,* p. 75.

7. Georg Misch, *A History of Autiobiography in Antiquity,* p. 355. The modification in the sentence permits Misch to pursue the project he sets himself. Read states more bluntly that the Greeks wrote no autobiography (p. 112). Roy Pascal, *Design and Truth in Autobiography,* p. 2, says that autobiography "belongs to Europe, in its essentials to the post-classical world of Europe."

8. Acts. 9:1–21.

9. Marcus Aurelius, *Meditations,* p. 45.

10. Misch, p. 453.

11. Marcus Aurelius, p. 35.

12. Misch, p. 591.

13. Misch, p. 635.

14. William Barrett, *Irrational Man,* p. 96.

15. Misch, p. 635. Robert J. O'Connell, *St. Augustine's Confessions,* says that Augustine is a dualist in the tradition of Plato and Plotinus, and that he treats his life as a shadow of the hexameral so that a person only has meaning in the light of God's act of creation. For Augustine, then, the real "I" is the soul (p. 25).

16. Saint Augustine, *Confessions,* p. 253.

17. Augustine, p. 22. The passage alludes to Romans 11:36.

18. Augustine, p. 136.

19. Augustine, p. 170.

20. Augustine, p. 171.

21. Augustine, p. 181.

22. Augustine, p. 25.

23. Augustine, p. 47.

24. Augustine, p. 83.

25. Augustine, p. 122.

26. Benvenuto Cellini, *The Autobiography,* p. 84. Such confidence during the Italian Renaissance was based on a sense of individuality or what we might now call ego, but this is not the same thing as the later concept of self. Jacob Burckhardt, over a century ago, attributed the emergence of this individuality to the changed political climate. He wrote that in the Middle Ages man " . . . was conscious of himself only as member of a race, people, party, family, or corporation—only through some general category. In Italy this veil first melted into air; an *objective* treatment and consideration of the State and of all things of this world became possible. The *subjective* side at the same time asserted itself with corresponding emphasis; man became a spiritual *individual,* and recognized himself as such" (1:143). The opening sentence is almost exactly that of my epigraph from Saul Bellow to the first chapter of this work.

27. Cellini, p. 19.

28. Cellini, p. 75.

29. Cellini, p. 51.

30. Cellini, p. 56.

31. Cellini, p. 184.

32. Girolamo Cardano, *The Book of My Life,* p. xviii.

33. Cardano, *p.* 94.

34. Michel de Montaigne, *Essays and Selected Writings,* p. 3.

35. Marvin Lowenthal, *The Autobiography of Michel de Montaigne.*

36. Sir Francis Bacon, *Essays,* p. 7.

37. Montaigne, p. 9.

38. Erich Auerbach, *Mimesis,* p. 290.

39. Georges Gusdorf, "Conditions et limites de l'autobiographie," pp. 108–9.

40. Montaigne, p. 75.

41. Montaigne, pp. 77, 79.

42. Montaigne, p. 89.

43. Montaigne, p. 51.

44. Montaigne, p. 315. Donald Frame, in *Montaigne's Discovery of Man,* writes that at the end of his life Montaigne "sees the resemblance between men that makes knowledge of a self mean knowledge of mankind. Now he sees man as a social being, not merely as an individual" (p. 140). Montaigne insists on being the harbringer, or at least the rule-proving exception. He also writes, "there is no one who, if he listens to himself, does not discover in himself a pattern all his own, a ruling pattern which struggles against education and against the tempest of the passions that oppose it" (Frame, p. 142).

45. Edward Herbert, *The Life of Edward, Lord Herbert of Cherbury,* p. 2.

46. Herbert, p. 22.

47. Herbert, p. 95.

48. Herbert, p. 102.

49. Delany, p. 174. Joan Webber, in *The Eloquent "I",* makes the same point; "in showing himself [the seventeenth-century writer] shows his time. More typically in the seventeenth century is his habit of generalizing his 'I' into a representative of all Englishmen, or a comic personality symbolic of all men" (p. 4).

50. Joseph Spence, *Anecdotes, Observations, and Characters of Books and Men.*

51. Laetitia Pilkington, *Memoirs,* p. 25. She uses almost the same language as Colly Cibber in defending the project of telling her life. She proposes to tell a cautionary tale, and yet is quick to show how she has been wronged. She probably was, for her husband was a cad who arranged at least the appearance of infidelity so that he could divorce her and pursue his own pleasures.

Chapter 6: Rogues and Adventurers

1. See William Robert Irwin, *The Making of "Jonathan Wild."* Defoe also wrote a life of Wild and there is another account in the *Newgate Calendar*, but these appear to have no political overtones.

2. Richard Head, *The English Rogue*, p. 3.

3. Head, p. 5.

4. Head, pp. 54–60. George Lillo's *The London Merchant* (1731) presents the situation most memorably.

5. Head, p. 112.

6. Head, p. 157.

7. Head, p. 264.

8. J. J. C. von Grimmelshausen, *Simplicius Simplicissimus*, p. 10.

9. Daniel Defoe, *Roxana*, pp. 47–48.

10. Head, pp. 153–54.

11. Defoe wrote lives of Mary Read and Anne Bonny.

12. The bibliographic problems are suggested by the entry in the British Museum catalogue. The text used here is in *The Novels of . . . Defoe*, ed. Walter Scott [?], 7 vols. (London, 1856–75), vol. 4.

13. Davies, pp. 361–62.

14. Davies, p. 364.

15. Davies, pp. 415–16.

16. Wayne Shumaker, *English Autobiography*, p. 21.

17. Shumaker, p. 1.

18. Shumaker, p. 28.

Chapter 7: Confessional High Tide

1. James Boswell, *London Journal: 1762–1763*, p. 39. My examination of Boswell is illustrated solely by this first volume of the *Journals* because in it Boswell is most candid and open.

2. *London Journal*, p. 47.

3. *London Journal*, p. 62.

4. *London Journal*, p. 54.

5. *London Journal*, p. 71. Martin Price, in "The Other Self," p. 280, says that this situation in which a narrator is both the subject and the observer begins with Boswell.

6. *London Journal*, p. 126.

7. *London Journal*, p. 127.

8. *London Journal*, p. 203. The idea of the "furniture of the mind" can be seen in Fielding and Sterne.

9. *London Journal*, p. 87.

10. *London Journal*, p. 182.

11. *London Journal*, p. 84.

12. *London Journal*, p. 138.

13. *London Journal*, pp. 158–60.

14. The history of the Boswell papers is given by F. A. Pottle in his introduction to the *London Journal*.

15. *London Journal*, p. 137.

16. Jean-Jacques Rousseau, *The Confessions*, p. 55.

17. Rousseau, p. 17.

18. See William H. Blanchard, *Rousseau and the Spirit of Revolt*, and F. C. Green, *J.-J. Rousseau*.

19. Rousseau, p. 19.

20. Jan Hendrik van den Berg, *The Changing Nature of Man*, p. 30.

21. Rousseau, pp. 38–39.

22. Rousseau, pp. 40–41.

23. Rousseau, p. 67.

24. Rousseau, p. 26.

25. Rousseau, p. 30.

26. Rousseau, p. 33.

27. Rousseau, p. 89.

28. Rousseau, p. 128.

29. Rousseau, p. 365.

30. Rousseau, p. 144.

31. Irving Babbitt, *Rousseau and Romanticism,* and Mario Praz, *The Romantic Agony.* Jacques Barzun, in *Romanticism and the Modern Ego,* p. 27, makes the case in opposition to Babbitt.

32. Barzun, p. 30.

33. Rousseau, p. 56. Blanchard discusses this description of the meeting with Mme. de Warens and makes the same point that Rousseau is attracted to that in her which he sees in himself. But this also leads to speculations about Rousseau's latent homosexuality, and here I think Blanchard is on thin ice.

34. Rousseau, p. 59.

35. Rousseau, p. 172.

36. Rousseau, p. 194. Several critics have speculated that Anet was a suicide.

37. *Boswell's Life of Johnson,* 4:426.

38. Rousseau, pp. 112–13.

39. Rousseau, p. 184.

40. Rousseau, p. 186.

41. Rousseau, p. 190.

42. Rousseau, p. 126.

43. Rousseau, pp. 262. The idea is expressed again on the following page.

44. Rousseau, p. 248.

45. Rousseau, p. 242.

46. Rousseau, p. 243.

47. Rousseau, p. 301.

48. Rousseau, p. 301. Casanova also knew Giulietta, but failed to notice her deformity. To him the world invariably measured up to his expectations for it.

49. Rousseau, p. 108.

50. Rousseau, p. 352.

51. Rousseau, p. 330. Roy Pascal, *Design and Truth in Autobiography,* p. 43, states that Rousseau's purpose is to show that the true self is elusive.

52. See, for example, Gustave Flaubert, *Sentimental Education,* p. 282, where the hero spends one of several afternoons gazing into the street. Here there is even a revolution brewing, but his boredom and passivity are emphasized.

53. Rousseau, p. 225.

54. Northrop Frye, *Romanticism Reconsidered,* p. 10.

55. Louis L. Bredvold, *The Natural History of Sensibility,* p. 24.

56. Johann Wolfgang von Goethe, *Poetry and Truth,* p. xiii. Carl Hammer, Jr., in *Goethe and Rousseau,* p. 86, contends that the letter from the friend is of Goethe's own composition. Roy Pascal, p. 47, implies that the letter really is from one of Goethe's admirers.

57. *Poetry and Truth,* p. 692.

58. *Poetry and Truth,* p. xvi.

59. *Poetry and Truth,* pp. 426, 428.

60. *Poetry and Truth*, p. 37. Rousseau also recounts playing with marionettes as a child (*Confessions*, p. 35).

61. *Poetry and Truth*, p. 244. Goethe also writes that "I spoke in my own person" in the novels (p. 37).

62. Green quotes Rousseau's "la raison rampe, mais l'âme est élevée [reason crawls, but the soul rises aloft]" (p. 215).

63. *Poetry and Truth*, p. 183.

64. Rousseau, p. 237.

65. *Poetry and Truth*, p. 38.

66. *Poetry and Truth*, p. 42.

67. Rousseau, p. 163.

68. *Poetry and Truth*, p. 27.

69. *Poetry and Truth*, p. 190.

70. *Poetry and Truth*, p. 190.

71. Rousseau, p. 55.

72. *Poetry and Truth*, p. 240. Roy Pascal, p. 47, writes that "being is for him [Goethe] becoming; one is never oneself, one becomes oneself."

Chapter 8: Travelers East

1. Quoted by Howard Mumford Jones, *Revolution and Romanticism*, p. 260. Wylie Sypher, in *Loss of Self in Modern Literature and Art*, traces the history of this kind of self in the nineteenth century. He says it is the invention of rebellious heroism, but it has since been pared down to the existential self (p. 34). Paul Zweig, in *The Heresy of Self-Love*, traces this rebellious self back to the late Roman empire, and suggests that Christianity was in part a response to the moral anarchism that resulted (pp. 3–21).

2. Adams, *The Roman Stamp*, p. 1.

3. Adams, *The Roman Stamp*, p. 2.

4. *Boswell's Life of Johnson*, 3:330.

5. There is an excellent study of these fabricators by Percy G. Adams, *Travelers and Travel Liars*. Also see Raymond H. Ramsey, *No Longer on the Map*. This literature then runs off into purer fantasy in such works as Swift's *Gulliver's Travels*. See Philip Babcock Gove, *The Imaginary Voyage in Prose Fiction*, which lists 215 such voyages.

6. Ronald Latham, "Introduction" to *The Travels of Marco Polo*.

7. There are many mysteries about Sir John Mandeville's *Travels* (written about 1356), but the best guess is that the work is mainly a compilation. The narratives of the Elizabethan travelers (of which there will be more later) curiously combine brevity and invention. William Dampier's *A New Voyage Around the World* (made in 1679–91) was published in 1697, and Richard Waters's *Anson's Voyage Round the World* in 1748. Travel literature was tremendously popular in the eighteenth century and several lavish collections were published. For example: Thomas Oborne, *A Collection of Voyages and Travels* [from the library of the Earl of Oxford] (London, 1745); Thomas Astley, *A New General Collection of Voyages and Travels* (London, 1745–47); John Harris, *Navigantium atque Itinerantium Bibliotheca, or A Complete Collection of Voyages and Travels* (London, 1748); J. Carrer, *The New Universal Traveller* (London, 1779). Such literature has been studied as it relates to the work of specific writers (as Wordsworth or Thoreau), but it has been generally neglected otherwise. There is, however, a bibliography of travel to the East by Richard W. Bevis, *Bibliotheca cisorientalia*.

8. A recent and thorough account of Cook's methodical approach is given in J. C. Beaglehole, *The Life of Capitan James Cook*. On the later voyages Cook insisted that every one of the

crew who was literate keep a journal. His intent was to serve accuracy and science, but the request acknowledges the variety in subjective accounts. Two of the more interesting were published by Georg Forster (a Scot raised in Danzig, who became a friend of Alexander von Humboldt), and John Ledyard (an American who later crossed Russia and finally died trying to discover the source of the Nile.)

9. *Marco Polo*, p. 17.

10. *Marco Polo*, p. 68.

11. *Marco Polo*, p. 88.

12. *Marco Polo*, p. 86.

13. *Marco Polo*, p. 77.

14. *Marco Polo*, pp. 329–30.

15. *Marco Polo*, p. 77.

16. *Marco Polo*, p. 84.

17. Anthony Jenkinson, *A compendious and brief declaration of the journey [from] London into the land of Persia* . . . [1561] p. 97.

18. Jenkinson, pp. 100–101.

19. Jenkinson, p. 102.

20. Jenkinson, p. 105.

21. Jenkinson, p. 104.

22. Sir Thomas Herbert, *A relation of some yeares travaile begunne Anno 1626*, p. 102. Herbert (and Chardin) is discussed as a travel writer in Michiel H. Braaksma, *Travel and Literature*. There is much praise of Herbert's style, as on page 47.

23. Herbert, p. 98.

24. Herbert, p. 85.

25. Herbert, p. 96.

26. Herbert, p. 97.

27. Sir John Chardin, *Travels in Persia*, pp. 72–73. The work was originally published in Paris in 1686, then Amsterdam in 1711, and in London in 1724.

28. Chardin, p. 44.

29. Chardin, p. 46.

30. Chardin, p. 93.

31. Chardin, p. 45.

32. Chardin, p. 187.

33. Chardin, p. xxi.

34. Chardin, p. 223.

35. Chardin, p. 97.

36. Chardin, pp. 73–74.

37. Sir [Austen] Henry Layard, *Early Adventures in Persia, Susiana, and Babylonia*, 1:37.

38. Edward Ives, *A Voyage from England to India* . . . [in 1754] p. 283.

39. Ives, p. 288. For all of his freethinking bluster Ives comes at the end of an era. William Francklin, who was in the Indian service, spent eight months living in Shiraz in 1787 to learn Farsi and there wore Persian dress. See his *Observations Made On a Tour from Bengal to Persia, in the Years 1786–7*, p. 61.

40. George Forster, *A Journey from Bengal to England* . . . [in 1782], 1:ix.

41. George Forster, 1:x.

42. George Forster, 2:101.

43. George Forster, 2:107.

44. George Forster, 2:108.

45. George Forster, 2:3.

46. George Forster, 1:68.

47. George Forster, 2:196–97.

48. Herbert, pp. 22–23.

49. Herbert, p. 6.
50. Gombrich, *Art and Illusion*, p. 81.
51. Quoted by Gombrich, p. 174.
52. James Morier, *A Journey through Persia, Armenia, and Asia Minor to Constantinople, in the Years 1808 and 1809*, p. 73.
53. Morier, p. 129. His drawing of the scene is in sharp contrast to that made by Sir Thomas Herbert (p. 58). Henry V. S. and Margaret S. Ogden, in *English Taste in Landscape in the Seventeenth Century*, give Herbert much credit as a drawer of landscapes (p. 23). Francklin *(Tour from Bengal to Persia)*, who visited Persepolis on September 1, 1786, illustrates a way station between the reactions of Herbert and Morier—or Claudius Rich. He records his reaction as though it were his at the moment, but refers to "the mind," and the moral drawn is the conventional *ubi sunt*. " . . . whilst viewing them, the mind becomes impressed with an awful solemnity!—When we consider the celebrity of this vast empire, once the patron of the arts and sciences, and the seat of a wise and flourishing government . . . we must consequently feel the strongest conviction of the mutability of all human events!" (p. 207).
54. Morier, p. 39.
55. Morier, p. 58. His drawing of the great maidan at Isphahan displays this attention to shade and perspective, and once more is in great contrast to Herbert's rendering of the same scene.
56. George Forster, 1:284.
57. Claudius James Rich, *Narrative of a Residence in Koordistan*, 1:169.
58. Rich, 1:339.
59. Layard, 1:52, 125, 177.
60. Morier, p. 86.
61. *Don Juan*, 5:62.
62. Rich, 1:10. The reference is to Byron's poem "Darkness," published in *Domestic Pieces* (1816).
63. Rich, 1:327.
64. Rich, 1:308.
65. We tend to think of these romantic adventurers as all having iron constitutions, like Sir Richard Burton and Layard himself. But many did not. In passing, Layard mentions the demise of Dr. Forbes, Captain Grant, Lieutenant Fotheringham, and M. Outray (1:327, 260, 262).
66. Rich, 1:332.
67. Rich, 1:48.
68. Rich, 1:349, 373.
69. Rich, 1:282.
70. Rich, 1:100.
71. Rich, 2:87.
72. Rich, 1:354.
73. Rich, 1:358.
74. Rich, 1:48.
75. Rich, 1:356.

Chapter 9: The Traveler at Home

1. Celia Fiennes, *The Journeys of Celia Fiennes*, p. 1.
2. Fiennes, p. 2.
3. Fiennes, p. 16.
4. Thomas Pennant, *A Tour in Scotland and Voyage to the Hebrides* [in 1772], p. 3.

5. Pennant, p. 28.

6. Pennant, pp. 39–40.

7. Samuel Johnson, *Journey to the Western Islands* . . . and James Boswell, *Journal of a Tour to the Hebrides* . . . [in 1775], pp. 214, 258.

8. *Hebrides*, p. 14.

9. *Hebrides*, p. 15.

10. *Hebrides*, p. 277.

11. *Hebrides*, p. 287.

12. Thomas Campbell, *Dr. Campbell's Diary of a Visit to England in 1775*, p. 43. A comparable shift in the nature of observation is noted by Patrick Anderson in *Over the Alps*. He begins by describing the tour made by Horace Walpole and Thomas Gray in 1739, and remarks the vagueness of their descriptions. "Quite obviously this Grand Tour has little to do with romantic self-revelation, with the search for a 'country of the heart' or with the shattering experiences so beloved of youth" (p. 20). But in the case of Boswell and those who follow him it is a matter of "an experience lived rather than sights seen" (p. 21.).

13. This work was translated by Henry Vaughan, and is in his *Works*, 1:123–36.

14. William Gilpin, *Observations on the River Wye . . . Relative Chiefly to Picturesque Beauty*, pp. 1–2. The history and influence of the doctrine of the picturesque is traced by Walter J. Hipple, *The Beautiful, the Sublime, and the Picturesque in Eighteenth-Century British Aesthetic Theory*, and in J. R. Watson, *Picturesque Landscape and English Romantic Poetry*, and Christopher Hussey, *The Picturesque*, who gives a history of the term (p. 32 ff.).

15. Gilpin, pp. 65, 70, 115, 145.

16. Gilpin, p. viii.

17. Gilpin, p. 57.

18. Gilpin, p. 60.

19. Gilpin, pp. 30–31. Gilpin says that the one good thing Cromwell did was to create ruins for the admiration of the seeker of the picturesque (p. 89).

20. Gilpin, p. 59.

21. Gilpin, p. 70.

22. Gilpin, p. 94.

23. Gilpin, p. 96.

24. Gilpin, pp. 62–63.

25. For a discussion of Hartley's influence see Arthur Beatty, *William Wordsworth*, pp. 97–127.

26. Gilpin, pp. 45–47.

27. Gilpin, pp. 48–49.

28. Fiennes, p. xx.

29. Pennant, pp. 228–29.

30. Gilpin, p. 80.

31. See Chapter 8, n. 5 above.

32. Rousseau, pp. 167–68.

33. Meriwether Lewis and William Clark, *The Journals of Lewis and Clark*, pp. 175–76.

34. *Lewis and Clark*, pp. 178–79. The entry is for June 13, 1805.

35. Sir Austen Henry Layard, *Early Adventures in Persia, Susiana, and Babylonia*, p. 336.

36. Layard, p. 38.

37. Quoted by Gordon Waterfield, *Layard of Nineveh*, pp. 199–200, from *Nineveh and Its Remains*.

38. Layard, pp. 125, 177, 198, 210, 231, 281, 291, 294.

39. Ralph Waldo Emerson, *Selected Prose and Poetry*, p. 25. Emerson's point is that nature is always inviting us to look beyond it, and this is one of his illustrations: "Turn the eyes

upside down, by looking at the landscape through your legs, and how agreeable is the picture, though you have not seen it anytime these twenty years!" This may be the sole moment of slapstick in all of Emerson.

40. Henry David Thoreau, *Walden*, p. 125.

41. Layard, p. 363.

42. *Prelude*, 1:361–67.

Chapter 10: Whores and Rakes in the Gardens of Delight

1. *Boswell's Life of Johnson*, 3:190.

2. See the introduction to Peter Fryer's *Private Case—Public Scandal*, a history of pornography in the British Museum.

3. David Foxon, *Libertine Literature in England*, p. 5.

4. See the plates in Gaston Vorberg, *Ars Erotica Veterum*.

5. Petronius Arbiter, *The Satyricon*, p. 97.

6. Petronius, p. 34.

7. Petronius, p. 43.

8. Petronius, p. 35.

9. Petronius, p. 63.

10. Petronius, p. 79.

11. Petronius, p. 159.

12. H. Montgomery Hyde, in *A History of Pornography*, p. 50, seems a little disappointed to report that Ovid is mainly concerned with the techniques of courtship, not seduction.

13. This is consistent with the original meaning of *pornography* which in Greek refers to the talk of whores.

14. Pietro Aretino, *The Dialogues*. Some of Romano's illustrations can be seen in Robert Melville, *Erotic Art in the West*, a coffee-table book for liberated families.

15. Aretino, p. 175.

16. Aretino, p. 51.

17. Aretino, pp. 46–47.

18. Aretino, p. 48.

19. Aretino, pp. 39–40.

20. Ferrante Pallavicino, *The Whore's Rhetoric*.

21. Marquis d'Argens, *Thérèse the Philosopher*, p. 23. An account of the original case is given by Jules Michelet in *La Sorcière*, translated as *Satanism and Witchcraft*.

22. d'Argens, p. 51.

23. d'Argens, p. 53.

24. d'Argens, pp. 127–28.

25. d'Argens, pp. 137–38.

26. d'Argens, p. 138.

27. Foxon, p. 38.

28. John Cleland, *The Memoirs of a Woman of Pleasure*, introduction by Peter Quennel pp. 159–60. William H. Epstein, *John Cleland*, p. 106, comments on this passage and Cleland's diction generally.

29. The satires on Richardson are described by Epstein, p. 99, and Bernard Kreissman, *Pamela-Shamela*.

30. Cleland, pp. 65, 77.

31. Cleland, p. 80.

32. Cleland, p. 89.

33. Cleland, pp. 288–89.

34. Cleland, p. 121.

35. Cleland, pp. 260–61. "Good-natured Dick" is always referred to by this phrase. Not only is his given name selected with a smile, but the goodness of his nature may put Fielding's doctrine of good nature in a new and interesting light.

36. Jacques Casanova, *The Memoirs*, p. 1. The work was begun in 1789 and published in 1797.

37. Casanova, p. 103.

38. Casanova, p. 1.

39. Casanova, p. 17.

40. Casanova, p. 31.

41. Casanova, p. 121.

42. Casanova, p. 245.

43. Casanova, p. 272.

44. Casanova, pp. 18, 35, 133, 275. Also see pp. 121, 403, 418, and 421.

45. Casanova, p. 32.

46. Casanova, p. 345.

47. Casanova, pp. 134, 291.

48. Casanova, p. 335.

49. Casanova, p. 235.

50. Casanova, p. 378.

Chapter 11: The Circumference of the Self

1. Paul Zweig, *The Heresy of Self-Love*, p. 143.

2. The revelations of Émile Legouis, *The Early Life of William Wordsworth*, are a case in point, for they are accepted, whereas comparable revelation about Shakespeare must always be based on airy speculations.

3. Malcolm Bradbury, "Fanny Hill and the Comic Novel," p. 275. There is a high-toned reply to Bradbury's article by David Holbrook, "Pornograpy and Death," which argues that pornography is nihilistic because for fulfillment man needs the "significant other" (p. 30).

4. Henry Fielding, *Joseph Andrews*, p. 179. The full title of the work says that it is "Written in Imitation of the Manner of Cervantes, Author of *Don Quixote*."

5. *Joseph Andrews*, p. 180.

6. Henry Fielding, *The History of Tom Jones*, pp. 413–18.

7. The point is amusingly elaborated by William Empson, "Tom Jones."

8. *Tom Jones*, p. 862.

9. Laurence Sterne, *The Life and Opinions of Tristram Shandy, Gentleman*, p. 496. The details are elaborated in Overton P. James, *The Relation of "Tristram Shandy" to the Life of Sterne*.

10. *Tom Jones*, pp. 40–42.

11. Sterne, p. 8.

12. Sterne, p. 5.

13. Sterne, p. 6.

14. John Locke, *Essay Concerning Human Understanding*. The idea is stated in the very headnote to Book 1.

15. See Chapter 9, n. 25 above.

16. Sterne, p. 7.

17. Locke, 1:531.

18. Sterne, p. 111.

19. Sterne, p. 17.

20. Sterne, p. 205.

21. *Poetry and Truth*, p. 516. The translation is that of Hans Reiss, *Goethe's Novels*, pp. 10–11.

22. Reiss, pp. 11–17. Also see Kurt Robert Eissler, *Goethe*, p. 1461, one of the most amusing studies of its kind.

23. *Poetry and Truth*, pp. 37, 244.

24. Reiss, p. 68. A copy of the manuscript of this work was discovered in 1910. The bibliographic history is also given by Eric Blackall in *Goethe and the Novel*, p. 61.

25. Johann Wolfgang von Goethe, *Wilhelm Meister's Apprenticeship*, p. 78. Similar enthusiasms are expressed by Wilhelm on page 50. Carlyle's translation may now seem a little stuffy, but it is available and Goethe himself had kind words for it. See J. P. Eckermann, *Conversations with Goethe*, p. 270.

26. *Wilhelm Meister*, p. 84.

27. Eckermann, p. 84.

28. Georg Lukács, *Goethe and His Age*, presents a fascinating Marxist reading of Goethe's situation. He is critical of him for toadying to the titled, and admiring of his satire of a Germany in the last stages of medievalism.

29. *Wilhelm Meister*, p. 204.

30. *Wilhelm Meister*, p. 69.

31. *Wilhelm Meister*, p. 239.

32. *Wilhelm Meister*, p. 36.

33. *Wilhelm Meister*, pp. 70–71.

34. *Wilhelm Meister*, pp. 445, 452.

35. Eckermann, p. 324.

Chapter 12: Into Our Age

1. The idea is discussed in Eliot's essay on "The Metaphysical Poets" where he says that for a poet of the late sixteenth and early seventeenth centuries, such as Donne, a thought "was an experience; it modified his sensibility," and this resulted in a fusion of intellect and feeling. The "dissociation" began with the rise of rationalism and science, and poets and scientists have gone their separate ways ever since. Possibly, but I tend to place the dissociation in the late eighteenth century, yet even here must find exceptions in Goethe and some others, such as Erasmus Darwin.

2. M. H. Abrams, *The Mirror and the Lamp*, p. 226.

3. Patricia M. Ball, *The Central Self*, p. 5.

4. Ball, p. 14.

5. Ball, p. 9.

6. Ball, p. 20.

7. Quoted by J. H. Muirhead, *Coleridge as Philosopher*, p. 264.

8. Carl F. Keppler, *The Literature of the Second Self*, pp. 16–17. The double in literature is also treated by Albert J. Gerard in his introduction to *Stories of the Double*; Robert Rogers, *The Double in Literature*; and Ralph Tymms, *Doubles in Literary Psychology*.

9. Sigmund Freud, *The Basic Writings*, p. 52.

10. Robert Martin Adams, *Nil*, p. 131. With special reference to Melville, Adams says that the mask, screen, and disguise are ways to avoid the void, and create something out of nothing. A similar thesis is developed by Morse Peckham, *Beyond the Tragic Vision*.

11. Masao Miyoshi, *The Divided Self*, p. xi.

12. Mario Praz, *The Hero in Eclipse in Victorian Fiction*, dates the domestication of the hero in fiction from 1755 and attributes it to the rise of mercantilism and Protestantism (p.

20). The type of sentimental hearthside scene in which Dickens often indulges he contemptuously terms Biedermeier art (p. 117).

13. Keppler, p. 7, elaborates on this point.

14. Robert Langbaum, "The Mysteries of Identity," p. 586. Psychologists often hover about the same observation, but they are hesitant to make it because, one assumes, it would complicate their clinical activities. When the self is denied, uplift is difficult. For example, Clark E. Moustakas, *The Self*, p. 13, writes, "Individual and social interests are synergetic, *not* antagonistic. Creative individual expression, that is, expression of one's own intrinsic nature, results in social creativity and growth which in turn encourage and free the individual to further self-expression and discovery." A more mechanistic view of the self is taken by Erving Goffman, *The Presentation of Self in Everyday Life*. For him the self is identified with the social mask or personality, and the individual is no more than his impact on an "audience." "While this image is entertained *concerning* the individual, so that a self is imputed to him, this self itself does not derive from its possessor, but from the whole scene of his action, being generated by that attribute of local events which renders them interpretable by witnesses. A correctly staged and performed scene leads the audience to impute a self to a performed character, but this imputation—this self—is a *product* of a scene that comes off, and is not a *cause* of it" (p. 252).

15. This is the thesis of Charles I. Glicksberg in *The Self in Modern Literature*.

16. The point is developed by Eugene Goodheart in *The Cult of the Ego*, p. 136.

17. Frederick J. Hoffman, *The Mortal No*, p. 317.

18. See Richard Ellmann, *James Joyce*, for the development of this point. He quotes a letter from Joyce which confesses that the early stories in *Dubliners* are "stories of my childhood," and reproduces the program for the fair on which the story "Araby" is based (p. 216, and the plate facing p. 80).

19. James Joyce, *Finnegans Wake*, p. 268.

20. *Finnegans Wake*, p. 32. Eugene Henderson in Saul Bellow's *Henderson the Rain King* possesses initials that invert Earwicker's, and this passage probably inspired this: "Here comes Henderson of the U.S.A.—Captain Henderson, Purple Heart, veteran of North Africa, Sicily, Monte Cassino, etc., a giant shadow, a man of flesh and blood, a restless seeker, pitiful and rude, a stubborn old lush with broken bridgework, threatening death and suicide" (p. 199). Yet Henderson seems to stand for the typical American of his time rather than the man that embodies all men of all times.

21. *Finnegans Wake*, pp. 3, 13, 73, 95, 108, 138, 197, 215, 535.

22. Rainer Maria Rilke, *The Notebooks of Malte Laurids Brigge*, pp. 15–16.

Bibliography

Abrams, Meyer H. *The Mirror and the Lamp: Romantic Theory and the Critical Tradition.* New York: W. W. Norton, 1958.

———. "English Romanticism: The Spirit of the Age." In *Romanticism Reconsidered,* edited by Northrop Frye. New York: Columbia University Press, 1963.

Adams, Percy G. *Travelers and Travel Liars.* Berkeley and Los Angeles: University of California Press, 1962.

Adams, Robert Martin. *Nil: Episodes and the Literary Conquest of Void During the Nineteenth Century.* New York: Oxford University Press, 1966.

———. *The Roman Stamp: Frame and Facade in Some Forms of Neo-classicism.* Berkeley and Los Angeles: University of California Press, 1974.

Alexander, Louis C. *The Autobiography of Shakespeare.* Port Washington, N.Y.: Kennikat, 1970 [1911].

Alexander, Samuel. "Self as Subject and as Person." *Aristotelian Society Proceedings,* n.s. 10 (1910–11).

Allen, Don Cameron. *The Legend of Noah: Renaissance Rationalism in Art, Science, and Letters.* Urbana: University of Illinois Press, 1949.

Altick, Richard. *Lives and Letters: Biography in England and America.* New York: A. A. Knopf, 1965.

Anderson, Patrick. *Over the Alps: Reflections on Travel and Travel Writing, with Special Reference to the Grand Tours of Boswell, Beckford, and Byron.* London: Hart-Davis, 1969.

Aretino, Pietro. *The Dialogues.* Translated by Raymond Rosenthal. New York: Ballantine Books, 1971.

Argens, Marquis d' [Jean-Baptiste de Boyer]. *Thérèse the Philosopher.* Translated by Herbert F. Smith. New York: Grove Press, 1970.

Aristotle. *Ethics: The Nichomachean Ethics.* Translated by J. A. K. Thompson. London: Allen & Unwin, 1953.

Astley, Thomas, ed. *A New General Collection of Voyages and Travels.* London, 1745–47.

Auerbach, Erich. *Mimesis: The Representation of Reality in Western Literature.* Translated by Willard R. Trask. Princeton: Princeton University Press, 1953.

Augustine, Saint. *The Confessions.* Translated by R. S. Pine-Coffin. Baltimore: Penguin, 1961.

Ayer, Alfred Jules. *The Concept of a Person.* London: Macmillan, 1963.

Babbitt, Irving. *Rousseau and Romanticism.* Boston and New York: Houghton Mifflin, 1919.

Bacon, Francis. *Essays.* Edited by C. S. Northrup. Boston and New York: Houghton Mifflin, 1908.

Badian, E. Review of *Alexander the Great,* by Robin Lane Fox. *New York Review of Books* (September 19, 1974).

Ball, Patricia M. *The Central Self: A Study in Romantic and Victorian Imagination.* London: Athlone, 1968.

Barrett, William. *Irrational Man.* Garden City, N.Y.: Doubleday, 1962.

Barzun, Jacques. *Romanticism and the Modern Ego.* Boston: Little, Brown, 1947.

Beaglehole, J. C. *The Life of Captain James Cook.* Palo Alto: Stanford University Press, 1974.

Beatty, Arthur. *William Wordsworth: His Doctrine and Art in their Historical Relation.* Madison: University of Wisconsin Press, 1962.

Bellow, Saul. *Henderson the Rain King.* New York: Viking, 1959.

———. *Humboldt's Gift.* New York: Viking, 1976.

———. *Mr. Sammler's Planet.* New York: Viking, 1970.

Berg, Jan Hendrik van den. *The Changing Nature of Man: Introduction to a Historical Psychology.* New York: W. W. Norton, 1961.

Bevis, Richard W. *Bibliotheca cisorientalia: An Annotated Checklist of Early English Travel Books on the Near and Middle East.* Boston: G. K. Hall, 1973.

Birkett, Norman, ed. *The Newgate Calendar.* London: Folio Society, 1951.

Blackall, Eric A. *Goethe and the Novel.* Ithaca and London: Cornell University Press, 1976.

Blanchard, William H. *Rousseau and the Spirit of Revolt: A Psychological Study.* Ann Arbor: University of Michigan Press, 1967.

Boswell, James. *Boswell's Life of Johnson.* Edited by G. B. Hill. 6 vols. New York: Harper, 1891.

———. *The London Journal: 1762–1763.* Edited by F. A. Pottle. New York: McGraw-Hill, 1961.

Braaksma, Michiel H. *Travel and Literature.* Groningen: J. B. Wolters, 1938.

Bradbury, Malcolm, "Fanny Hill and the Comic Novel." *Critical Quarterly,* 13 (Autumn, 1971).

Braudel, Fernand. *The Mediterranean and the Mediterranean World in the Age of Philip II.* Translated by Sidu Reynolds. 2 vols. New York: Harper & Row, 1975.

Breckenridge, James D. *Likeness: A Conceptual History of Ancient Portraiture.* Evanston: Northwestern University Press, 1968.

Bredvold, Louis I. *The Natural History of Sensibility.* Detroit: Wayne State University Press, 1962.

Bréhier, Emile, ed. *Philosophy and History: Essays Presented to Ernest Cassirer.* London: Oxford University Press, 1936.

Browne, Sir Thomas. *Religio Medici and Other Works.* Edited by L. C. Martin. London: Oxford University Press, 1964.

Bulfinch, Thomas. *The Age of Fable.* Garden City, N.Y.: Doubleday, 1968.

Burckhardt, Jacob. *The Civilization of the Renaissance in Italy.* Translated by S. G. C. Middlemore. 2 vols. New York: Harper Torchbooks, 1958.

Burke, Peter. *The Renaissance Sense of the Past.* London: Edward Arnold, 1969.

Byron, Lord. *Don Juan.* Edited by Leslie A. Marchand. Boston: Houghton Mifflin, 1958.

Campbell, Joseph. *The Hero With a Thousand Faces*. Princeton: Princeton University Press, 1949.
———. *The Masks of God*. New York: Viking, 1959.
———. *The Mythic Image*. Princeton: Princeton University Press, 1975.
Campbell, Thomas. *Dr. Campbell's Diary of a Visit to England in 1775*. Edited by James L. Clifford. Cambridge: Cambridge University Press, 1947.
Cardano, Girolamo. *The Book of My Life*. Translated by Jean Stoner. New York: Dutton, 1930.
Carrer, J. *The New Universal Traveller*. London, 1779.
Casanova, Jacques. *The Memoirs*. Translated by Lowell Blair. New York: Bantam Book, 1968.
Castell, Alburey, *The Self in Philosophy*. New York: Macmillan, 1965.
Cellini, Benvenuto. *The Autobiography*. Translated by George Bull. Baltimore: Penguin, 1956.
Chardin, Sir John. *Travels in Persia*. 2 vols. London: Argonaut Press, 1927 [1724].
Chaucer, Geoffrey. *The Poems of Chaucer*. Edited by F. N. Robinson. Boston: Houghton Mifflin, 1933.
Cibber, Colley. *An Apology for the Life of Colly Cibber*. Edited by B. R. S. Fone. Ann Arbor: University of Michigan Press, 1968.
Cleland, John. *Memoirs of a Woman of Pleasure*. New York: Random House, 1963.
Clemens, Samuel L. *The Autobiography of Mark Twain*. Edited by Charles Neider. New York: Harper, 1959.
Collingwood, Robin George. *The Idea of History*. New York: Oxford University Press, 1956.
Combe, William. *The Tour of Doctor Syntax in Search of the Picturesque*. London, 1809.
Comnena, Anna. *The Alexiad*. Translated by E. R. A. Sewter. Baltimore: Penguin, 1969.
Dampier, William. *A New Voyage Around the World*. London: Argonaut Press, 1927 [1697].
Davies, Christian ["Mother Ross"]. *The Life and Adventures of Mrs. Christian Davies*. London, 1740. Also in the Novels of Daniel Defoe. Edited by Walter Scott [?], vol. 4. London, 1856–75.
Defoe, Daniel. *Roxana: Or the Fortunate Mistress*. Cleveland and New York: World, 1946.
Delany, Paul. *British Autobiography in the Seventeenth Century*. London: Routledge & Kegan Paul, 1969.
De Sélincourt, Aubrey. *The World of Herodotus*. London: Secker & Warburg, 1962.
Dickens, Charles. *Great Expectations*. Indianapolis and New York: Bobbs-Merrill, 1964.
Dodds, Eric R. *The Ancient Concept of Progress*. Oxford: Clarendon Press, 1973.
Eckermann, J. P. *Conversations with Goethe*. London: Everyman's Library, 1946.
Eissler, Kurt Robert. *Goethe: A Psychoanalytic Study, 1775–1786*. Detroit: Wayne State University Press, 1963.

Eliade, Mircea. *The Myth of the Eternal Return: or, Cosmos and History*. Translated by Willard R. Trask. Princeton: Princeton University Press, 1954.

Ellmann, Richard. *James Joyce*. New York: Oxford University Press, 1959.

Emerson, Ralph Waldo. *Selected Prose and Poetry*. Edited by Reginald L. Cook. New York: Rinehart Editions, 1959.

Empson, William. "Tom Jones." *Kenyon Review*, 20 (Spring, 1958).

Epstein, William H. *John Cleland: Images of a Life*. New York: Columbia University Press, 1974.

Erikson, Erik. *Gandhi's Truth: On the Origins of Militant Nonviolence*. New York: W. W. Norton, 1969.

Fielding, Henry. *Joseph Andrews*. New York: Rinehart Editions, 1948.

———. *The History of Tom Jones*. New York: Modern Library, 1950.

Fiennes, Celia. *The Journeys of Celia Fiennes*. Edited by Christopher Morris. London: Cresset, 1947.

Flaubert, Gustave. *A Sentimental Education*. Translated by Robert Baldick. Baltimore: Penguin, 1964.

Forster, Georg. *A Voyage Around the World*. London, 1777.

Forster, George. *A Journey from Bengal to England*. London, 1798.

Foxon, David. *Libertine Literature in England: 1660–1745*. London: Book Collector, 1964.

Frame, Donald M. *Montaigne's Discovery of Man: The Humanization of a Humanist*. New York: Columbia University Press, 1955.

Francklin, William. *Observations Made on a Tour from Bengal to Persia, in the Years 1786–7*. London, 1790.

Frantz, Ray W. *The English Traveller and the Movement of Ideas: 1660–1732*. Lincoln: University of Nebraska Press, 1967.

Frazer, Sir James G. *The Golden Bough*. 12 vols. London: Macmillan, 1911–15.

Freud, Sigmund. *The Basic Writings*. Translated by A. A. Brill. New York: Modern Library, 1938.

Friedman, William F., and Elizabeth S. Friedman. *The Shakespearean Ciphers Examined*. Cambridge: Cambridge University Press, 1957.

Frye, Northrop, ed. *Romanticism Reconsidered*. New York: Columbia University Press, 1963.

———. "Towards Defining an Age of Sensibility." In *Eighteenth-Century English Literature: Modern Essays in Criticism*, edited by James L. Clifford. New York: Oxford University Press, 1959.

Fryer, Peter. *Private Case—Public Scandal*. London: Secker & Warburg, 1966.

Gardner, Brian. *The Quest for Timbuctoo*. London: Cassell, 1968.

Gay, Peter. *The Party of Humanity: Essays in the French Enlightenment*. New York: A. A. Knopf, 1964.

Gerard, Albert J., ed. *Stories of the Double*. Philadelphia and New York: Lippincott, 1967.

Gibbon, Edward. *The Decline and Fall of the Roman Empire*. Abridged by D. M. Low. New York: Harcourt, Brace, 1960.

Gilpin, William. *Observations on the River Wye*. London, 1792 [1770].

Glicksberg, Charles I. *The Self in Modern Literature*. University Park: Pennsylvania State University Press, 1963.

Goethe, Johann Wolfgang von. *Poetry and Truth* [*Aus meinem Leben: Dichtung und Wahrheit*]. Translated by R. O. Moon. Washington, D.C.: Public Affairs Press, 1949.

————. *Wilhelm Meister's Apprenticeship.* Translated by Thomas Carlyle. New York: Collier, 1962.

Goffman, Erving. *The Presentation of Self in Everyday Life.* Garden City, N.Y.: Doubleday, 1959.

Gombrich, E. H. *Art and Illusion: A Study in the Psychology of Pictorial Representation.* New York: Bollingen, 1960.

Goodheart, Eugene. *The Cult of the Ego: The Self in Modern Literature.* Chicago: University of Chicago Press, 1968.

Gove, Philip Babcock. *The Imaginary Voyage in Prose Fiction.* London: Holland Press, 1961.

Grant, Michael. *The Ancient Historians.* New York: Scribner, 1970.

Green, Frederick Charles. *J. J. Rousseau: A Critical Study of His Life and Writings.* Cambridge: Cambridge University Press, 1955.

Grimmelshausen, J. J. C. von. *Simplicius Simplicissimus.* Translated by George Schulz-Behrend. Indianapolis and New York: Bobbs-Merrill, 1965.

Gusdorf, Georges. "Conditions et limites de l'autobiographie." In *Formender Selbstdarstellung,* edited by Reichenkron and Haase. Berlin, 1956.

Hammer, Carl, Jr. *Goethe and Rousseau: Resonances of the Mind.* Lexington: University of Kentucky Press, 1973.

Harris, John, ed. *Navigantium atque Itinerantium Bibliotheca: Or a Complete Collection of Voyages and Travels.* 2 vols. London, 1744–48 [1705].

Hartley, Lodwick. *William Cowper: Humanitarian.* Chapel Hill: University of North Carolina Press, 1938.

Head, Richard. *The English Rogue: Described in the Life of Meriton Latroon.* Edited by Michael Shinagel. Boston: New Frontiers Press, 1961 [1665].

Herbert, Edward. *The Life of Edward, Lord Herbert of Cherbury.* London, 1792.

Herbert, Sir Thomas. *A relation of some yeares travaile begunne Anno 1626.* London, 1634.

Herodotus. *The Histories.* Translated by Aubrey De Sélincourt. Baltimore: Penguin, 1954.

Hipple, Walter J. *The Beautiful, the Sublime, and the Picturesque in Eighteenth-Century British Aesthetic Theory.* Carbondale: Southern Illinois University Press, 1957.

Hoffman, Frederick J. *The Mortal No: Death and the Modern Imagination.* Princeton: Princeton University Press, 1964.

Holbrook, David. "Pornography and Death." *Critical Quarterly,* 14 (Spring, 1972).

Hollister, C. Warren. *Medieval Europe: A Short History.* New York: John Wiley, 1964.

Hume, David. *The Philosophy of David Hume.* Edited by V. C. Chappell. New York: Modern Library, 1963.

Hussey, Christopher. *The Picturesque.* London and New York: Putnam, 1967.

Hyde, H. Montgomery. *A History of Pornography.* New York: Farrar, Straus & Giroux, 1965.

Irwin, William Robert. *The Making of "Jonathan Wild."* New York: Columbia University Press, 1941.

Ives, Edward. *A Voyage from England to India . . .* [in 1754]. London, 1773.

James, Overton P. *The Relation of "Tristram Shandy" to the Life of Sterne.* The Hague: Mouton, 1966.

Jenkinson, Anthony. *A compendious and brief declaration of the journey* [*from*] *London in to the land of Persia* [*in*] *1561.* In The Portable Hakluyt's Voyages. Edited by Irwin R. Blacker. New York: Viking, 1965.

Johnson, Samuel. *Essays from the "Rambler," "Adventurer" and "Idler."* Edited by W. J. Bate. New Haven: Yale University Press, 1968.

————. and James Boswell. *Journey to the Western Islands* and *Journal of a Tour to the Hebrides.* Edited by Allan Wendt. Boston: Houghton Mifflin, 1965.

Johnstone, Henry W. *The Problem of the Self.* University Park: Pennsylvania University Press, 1970.

Jones, Howard Mumford. *O Strange New World: American Culture, the Formative Years.* New York: Viking, 1964.

————. *Revolution and Romanticism.* Cambridge: Harvard University Press, 1974.

Joyce, James. *Finnegans Wake.* New York: Viking, 1939.

Jung, Carl G. *The Integration of the Personality.* Translated by Stanley M. Dell. New York and Toronto: Farrar & Rinehart, 1939.

————. *The Portable Jung.* Edited by Joseph Campbell. New York: Viking, 1971.

————. *Psychological Reflections.* Edited by J. Jacobi and R. F. C. Hull. Princeton: Princeton University Press, 1973.

Keppler, Carl F. *The Literature of the Second Self.* Tucson: University of Arizona Press, 1972.

Kreissman, Bernard. *Pamela—Shamela.* Lincoln: University of Nebraska Press, 1960.

Laing, Alexander Gordon. *Travels in . . . Western Africa.* London, 1825.

Langbaum, Robert. "The Mysteries of Identity: A Theme in Modern Literature." *American Scholar,* 34 (1965).

Layard, Sir [Austen] Henry. *Early Adventures in Persia, Susiana, and Babylonia.* 2 vols. New York: Longmans Green, 1887.

Ledyard, John. *Journal of Captain Cook's Last Voyage.* Edited by J. K. Munford. Corvallis: Oregon State University Press, 1963.

Legouis, Emile. *The Early Life of William Wordsworth.* Translated by J. W. Matthews. London and Toronto: J. M. Dent, 1932.

Levy-Bruhl, Lucien. *The "Soul" of the Primitive.* New York: Praeger, 1966.

Lewis, C. S. *The Abolition of Man.* London: Macmillan, 1947.

Lewis, Meriwether, and William Clark. *The Journals of Lewis and Clark.* Edited by John Bakeless. New York: Mentor, 1964.

Locke, John. *Essay Concerning Human Understanding.* Edited by A. C. Fraser. 2 vols. New York: Dover, 1959.

Lowenthal, Marvin, ed. *The Autobiography of Michel de Montaigne.* Boston and New York: Houghton Mifflin, 1935.

Lukacs, Georg. *Goethe and His Age.* Translated by Robert Anchor. London: Merlin, 1968.

Madison, James. *The Complete Madison.* Edited by Saul K. Padover. New York, Harper, 1953.

Mandeville, Sir John. *The Travels.* Edited by J. Bramont. London: Everyman's Library, 1928.

Mann, Thomas. *The Story of a Novel: The Genesis of "Doctor Faustus."* Translated by Richard and Clara Winston. New York: A. A. Knopf, 1961.

Marcus Aurelius. *Meditations.* Translated by Maxwell Staniforth. Baltimore: Penguin, 1964.

Marshack, Alexander. *The Roots of Civilization.* New York: McGraw-Hill, 1972.

Mayo, Bernard. *The Logic of Personality.* London: Jonathan Cape, 1952.

Melville, Robert. *Erotic Art in the West.* London: Weidenfeld & Nicolson, 1973.

Michelet, Jules. *Satanism and Witchcraft: A Study in Medieval Superstition.* Translated by A. R. Allinson. New York: Citadel Press, 1939.

Miller, Henry. *The Tropic of Cancer.* New York: Grove Press, 1956.

Milton, John. *The Complete Poems and Major Prose.* Edited by M. Y. Hughes. New York: Odyssey, 1957.

Misch, Georg. *A History of Autobiography in Antiquity.* Translated by E. W. Dickes. 2 vols. London: Routledge & Kegan Paul, 1950.

Miyoshi, Masao. *The Divided Self: A Perspective on the Literature of the Victorians.* New York: New York University Press, 1969.

Montaigne, Michel de. *Essays and Selected Writings.* Translated by Donald Frame. New York: St. Martin's Press, 1963.

Morier, James. *A Journey Through Persia, Armenia and Asia Minor to Constantinople in the Years 1808 and 1809.* London, 1812.

Mortier, Roland. " 'Sensibility,' 'Neoclassicism,' or 'Preromanticism'?" In *Eighteenth Century Studies Presented to Arthur M. Wilson.* Edited by Peter Gay. Hanover, N.H.: University Press of New England, 1972.

Moustakas, Clark E., ed. *The Self: Explorations in Personal Growth.* New York: Harper, 1956.

Muirhead, John Henry. *Coleridge as Philosopher.* London: Allen & Unwin, 1930.

Muller, Herbert J. *Freedom in the Ancient World.* New York: Harper & Row, 1961.

Nicolson, Harold. *The Development of English Biography.* London: Hogarth Press, 1947.

Nicolson, Marjorie Hope. *The Breaking of the Circle.* New York: Columbia University Press, 1960.

O'Connell, Robert J. *St. Augustine's Confessions: The Odyssey of Soul.* Cambridge: Belknap Press, 1968.

Ogden, Henry V. S., and Margaret S. Ogden. *English Taste in Landscape in the Seventeenth Century.* Ann Arbor: University of Michigan Press, 1955.

Osborne, Thomas. *A Collection of Voyages and Travels . . . From the Library of the Earl of Oxford.* London, 1745.

Pallavicino, Ferrante. *The Whore's Rhetoric.* New York: Ivan Oblensky, 1961 [1683].

Panofsky, Edwin. *The Life and Art of Albrecht Dürer.* Princeton: Princeton University Press, 1955.

Parrot, André. *Sumer.* Translated by Stuart Gilbert and James Emmons. London: Thames & Hudson, 1960.

Pascal, Roy. *Design and Truth in Autobiography*. London: Routledge & Kegan Paul, 1960.

Paton, Herbert James. *The Good Will: A Study in the Coherence Theory of Goodness*. New York: Macmillan, 1927.

Peckham, Morse. *Beyond the Tragic Vision: The Quest for Identity in the Nineteenth Century*. New York: G. Braziller, 1962.

Penelhum, Terence. "Hume on Personal Identity." *Philosophical Review*, 64 (1955).

Pennant, Thomas. *A Tour in Scotland and Voyage to the Hebrides*. Chester, 1774.

Petronius Arbiter. *The Satyricon*. Translated by J. P. Sullivan. Baltimore: Penguin, 1965.

Pilkington, Laetitia. *The Memoirs*. New York: Dodd, Mead, 1928.

Plumb, J. H. *The Death of the Past*. London: Macmillan, 1969.

Polo, Marco. *The Travels of Marco Polo*. Translated by Ronald Latham. Baltimore: Penguin, 1958.

Pope-Hennessy, John. *Portrait in the Renaissance*. New York: Bollingen, 1966.

Praz, Mario. *The Romantic Agony*. London: Oxford University Press, 1951.

———. *The Hero in Eclipse in Victorian Fiction*. Translated by Angus Davidson. London and New York: Oxford University Press, 1969.

———. *On Neoclassicism*. Translated by Angus Davidson. London: Thames & Hudson, 1969.

Price, Martin. "The Other Self: Thoughts about Character in the Novel." In *Imagined Worlds*, edited by Maynard Mack and Ian Gregor. London: Methuen, 1968.

Ramsay, Raymond H. *No Longer on the Map: Discovering Places that Never Were*. New York: Viking, 1973.

Read, Sir Herbert. *Education through Art*. New York: Pantheon Books, 1945.

———. *Icon and Idea: The Function of Art in the Development of Human Consciousness*. Cambridge: Harvard University Press, 1955.

Reiss, Hans. *Goethe's Novels*. Coral Gables, Fla.: University of Miami Press, 1969.

Rich, Claudius James. *A Memoir of the Ruins of Babylon*. London: 1815.

———. *Narrative of a Residence in Koordistan*. 2 vols. London, 1836.

Rilke, Rainer Maria. *The Notebooks of Malte Laurids Brigge*. Translated by M. D. Herter Norton. New York: W. W. Norton, 1949.

Rogers, Robert. *The Double in Literature: A Psychoanalytic Study*. Detroit: Wayne State University Press, 1970.

Rousseau, Jean-Jacques. *The Confessions*. Translated by J. H. Cohen. Baltimore: Penguin, 1954.

Russell, Bertrand. *The Analysis of Mind*. London: Allen & Unwin, 1921.

Sade, Marquis de. *The Complete Justine*. Translated by Richard Seaver and Austryn Wainhouse. New York: Grove Press, 1965.

Sartre, Jean-Paul. *The Transcendence of the Ego*. Translated by Forrest Williams and Robert Kirkpatrick. New York: Noonday, 1957.

Schoenbaum, Samuel. *William Shakespeare: A Documentary Life*. Oxford: Clarendon Press, 1975.

Shaw, William. *Memoirs of the Life and Writings of the Late Dr. Samuel Johnson*

. . . *Anecdotes* . . . by Hester Lynch Piozzi. Edited by Arthur Sherbo. London and New York: Oxford University Press, 1974.

Shoemaker, Sydney. *Self-Knowledge and Self-Identity*. Ithaca: Cornell University Press, 1963.

Shumaker, Wayne. *English Autobiography*. Berkeley and Los Angeles: University of California Press, 1954.

Silvia of Aquitania. *The Pilgrimage of S. Silvia of Aquitania to the Holy Places*. London: Palestine Pilgrims' Text Society, 1896.

Singer, June. *Boundries of the Soul: The Practice of Jung's Psychology*. Garden City, N.Y.: Doubleday, 1972.

Snell, Bruno. *The Discovery of the Mind: The Greek Origins of European Thought*. Cambridge: Harvard University Press, 1953.

Spacks, Patricia Meyer. *Imagining a Self: Autobiography and Novel in Eighteenth-Century England*. Cambridge: Harvard University Press, 1976.

Spence, Joseph. *Anecdotes, Observations and Characters of Books and Men*. London: Centaur, 1964.

——. *Letters from the Grand Tour*. Edited by Slava Klima. Montreal and London: McGill-Queens University Press, 1975.

Starr, Chester G. *The Awakening of the Greek Historical Spirit*. New York: A. A. Knopf, 1968.

Stauffer, Donald A. *English Biography Before 1700*. Cambridge: Harvard University Press, 1930.

Sterne, Laurence. *The Life and Opinions of Tristram Shandy, Gentleman*. Edited by Ian Watt. Boston: Houghton Mifflin, 1965.

Strauss, Anselm L. *Mirrors and Masks: The Search for Identity*. Glencoe, Ill. Free Press, 1959.

Strawson, P. F. *Individuals: An Essay in Descriptive Metaphysics*. London: Methuen, 1959.

Sypher, Wylie. *Loss of Self in Modern Literature and Art*. New York: Random House, 1962.

Thomas, Lewis. *The Lives of a Cell*. New York: Viking, 1974.

Thoreau, Henry David. *Walden: Or Life in the Woods*. Edited by Owen Thomas. New York: W. W. Norton, 1966.

Toulmin, Stephen, and June Goodfield. *The Discovery of Time*. New York: Harper & Row, 1966.

Tymms, Ralph. *Doubles in Literary Psychology*. Cambridge, Eng.: Bowes & Bowes, 1949.

Ucko, Peter, and Andreé Rosenfeld. *Palaeolithic Cave Art*. New York: McGraw-Hill, 1967.

VanderVeer, Garrett L. *Bradley's Metaphysics of the Self*. New Haven: Yale University Press, 1970.

Vaughan, Henry. *Works*. Edited by L. C. Martin. 2 vols. Oxford: Oxford University Press, 1914.

Vorberg, Gaston. *Ars Erotica Veterum: das Geschlechtsleben im Altertum*. Hanau: Müller & Kiepenheuer, 1968.

Wagenknecht, Edward. *The Personality of Shakespeare*. Norman: University of Oklahoma Press, 1972.

Washington, Booker T. *Up from Slavery*. In *Three Negro Classics*, edited by John Hope Franklin. New York: Avon, 1965.

Waterfield, Gordon. *Layard of Nineveh*. London: Murray, 1963.

Watson, John Richard. *Picturesque Landscape and English Romantic Poetry*. London: Hutchinson, 1970.

Webber, Joan. *The Eloquent "I": Style and Self in Seventeenth-Century Prose*. Madison: University of Wisconsin Press, 1968.

Weston, Jessie. *From Ritual to Romance*. Garden City, N.Y.: Doubleday, 1957.

Williams, Bernard A. O. *Problems of the Self: Philosophical Papers, 1956–1972*. Cambridge: Cambridge University Press, 1973.

Wilson, John Alber. *The Culture of Ancient Egypt*. Chicago: University of Chicago Press, 1956.

Woolley, Leonard. *Digging Up the Past*. Baltimore: Penguin, 1960.

Wordsworth, William. *The Prelude*. Edited by Ernest de Selincourt. Oxford: Oxford University Press, 1926.

Xenophon. *The Persian Expedition*. Translated by Rex Warner. Baltimore: Penguin, 1949.

Yinger, John Milton. *Toward a Field Theory of Behavior: Personality and Social Structure*. New York: McGraw-Hill, 1965.

Zweig, Paul. *The Heresy of Self-Love: A Study in Subversive Individualism*. New York: Basic Books, 1968.

Index

262